All Is Never Said

All Is

The Narrative of

Never

Odette Harper Hines

Said

JUDITH ROLLINS

TEMPLE UNIVERSITY PRESS

PHILADELPHIA

Temple University Press, Philadelphia 19122
Copyright © 1995 by Temple University. All rights reserved
Published 1995

The paper used in this publication meets the minimum requrements of
the American National Standard for Information Sciences—Permanence
of Paper for Printed Library Materials, ANSI Z39.48-1984
Printed in the United States of America

Text Design by Erin Kirk New

Library of Congress Cataloging-in-Publication Data

Rollins, Judith.
All is never said : the narrative of Odette Harper Hines / Judith Rollins.
p. cm. Includes index.
ISBN 1-56639-307-8 (cloth). —ISBN 1-56639-308-6 (pbk.)
1. Hines, Odette Harper. 2. Afro-Americans—Biography.
3. Civil rights workers—United States—Biography.
4. Civil rights movements—United States—History—20th century.
5. Afro-Americans—Civil rights.
I. Hines, Odette Harper. II. Title.
E185.97.H58R65 1995
323′.092—dc20
[B]   94-44317

For my children,
Gretchen, Jimmy, Terry, and Maggi
O.H.H.

For my cousin Vera
J.R.

Contents

Preface

I FIRST SAW ODETTE HINES in the late summer of 1964 as she walked excitedly from the back of her house in Alexandria, Louisiana, to greet us as we parked our car in her driveway. Clearly happy to see us—four young civil rights workers who had just driven the approximately two hours from the state office of the Congress of Racial Equality (CORE) in Plaquemine—she welcomed us eagerly and invited us in. The only thing I knew about her was that she was the person who had agreed to house three workers so that CORE could finally begin working in central Louisiana. Ronnie Moore, the state director of CORE and our escort that day, had been trying all summer to get CORE a base in the central part of the state, especially in Natchitoches and Rapides Parishes (counties). At one point, an undertaker in Natchitoches had agreed to find housing for CORE workers, but he later changed his mind, apparently for the same reason others refused to help us: it was just too dangerous. In addition to the violence that had received national attention—when the New Orleans schools were desegregated in 1960 and when James Farmer was under attack in Plaquemine in 1963—CORE's activism in the state in the early 1960s had elicited job firings, beatings, tear gas attacks, arrests, shootings into houses, and church burnings. Such incidents had happened in Jonesboro and Monroe (to the north of Alexandria), and Clinton, Hammond, Greensburg, St. Francisville, New Roads, and many other locations south of Alexandria. White and black Louisianians knew about this. It was not surprising that no one in central Louisiana would open their homes to CORE. No one, that is, until Odette Hines.

Ronnie introduced us to "Mrs. Hines." As we walked toward the back door of her house, she and Ronnie slightly ahead of the three of us who would be staying, she was excitedly relating something about an incident in a toilet in Mississippi. Unable to hear everything she was saying, I was intrigued. I can still remember those moments walking across her grass and the feelings I was having: excitement and trepidation about beginning a new project; gratitude and respect for this person who would house CORE workers; delight that this wide, red brick house looked safer and more comfortable than the humble, isolated farmhouse in Greensburg I had lived in most of the summer; surprise at her lack of the Louisiana accent my northerner's ear had become accustomed to; and bewilderment at all this talk about a toilet.

I lived with Odette Hines for the next seven months. I was to find out the connection between the Mississippi toilet and her decision to provide housing for us. (This is explained in the fifth chapter of this narrative.) And I was to hear other captivating stories, usually shared late at night when I had come home from my organizing work and she had bedded down the two foster babies she was caring for and her own eight-year-old Maggi and eleven-year-old Terry. There were stories about her pleasant childhood in the Bronx of the 1920s, her activist teen group at Abyssinian Baptist Church, weird and wonderful Uncle Durock, her political awakening in the 1930s, the fascinating people she knew on the WPA's New York Writers Project and on her job in the national NAACP office, her adventures in Europe during World War II, Louisiana in the 1950s, and much, much more. I discovered that not only was Odette Hines politically conscious and personally engaging, she was a great storyteller.

After I left Louisiana, our friendship continued. And so did her anecdotes. Over the years, I'd often tell her that she should write all of this down. But it wasn't until the mid-'80s—at a point in my career as a sociologist when I could undertake such a project—that I suggested I help her tell her story.

In 1987, I spent almost three months at her home in Alexandria, recording her life. These twenty-five hours of tapes became approximately 720 pages of transcriptions. After I returned to Boston and began to write the narrative, there were regular taped telephone interviews for clarification and development. In December 1990, I visited the NAACP Archives at the Library of Congress in Washington, D.C., to verify some dates and events; in August 1991, I returned to Alexandria with the first draft of the manuscript, which we reviewed page by page. Reading the draft apparently stimulated memories in Ms. Hines and we recorded fifteen more hours of material. Those additions and modifications were integrated into the manuscript and the second draft was sent to her in August 1993, with encouragement to review it carefully. Clearly, she did. And when we met in Washington, D.C., in December of 1993 to discuss the final revisions, she requested a number of changes related to ethical and personal considerations: some names and incidents were deleted to avoid hurting people; some were deleted to protect her from the repercussions she thought possible in the still conservative and violent central Louisiana environment in which she lives; and some events that happened to her after our initial interviewing were added.

Through this process, I have attempted to produce a truly "intersubjective oral history,"[1] one that is the product of an ongoing collaborative effort between two women closely balanced in power. From the interviewing and writing to the choosing of photographs and the title,* every effort has been made to minimize the usual inequality of the relationship between scholar and narrator and to maintain an open, creative interaction between the two of us.

The experience has been invaluable. For a sociologist, doing an oral history provides the opportunity to observe in incredible intimacy and depth that interplay between "biography and history,"[2] which is the focus of the discipline. As Odette Hines tells her story, one constantly sees social constraints, especially those of race and gender, limiting her movement in the world. And yet, the power and effectiveness of her individual agency are undeniable. We see her maneuver in and manipulate hierarchies in which she is subordinate while we gain insight into the subtleties of operation of those same hierarchies. She is so effective, in fact, that the concept of "subordinate" seems inappropriate: Odette Hines projects no sense of subordination or disadvantage or of feeling limited. Hers is an identity of efficacy, forged within a family of confident black men and competent black women, nurtured by a vital African–American community (New York in the 1920s and 1930s). Odette Hines' identification with and dedication to black people permeate this narrative. And that identification, typical of the narratives of black women,[3] is one of the factors that contribute to her sense of self.

One is reminded of the critical importance and influence of subcultures

---

*"All is never said" is a proverb of the Ibo people of West Africa.

with distinct world views and norms. Odette Hines' knowledge of blacks in the United States, founded on her own family history and expanded by her reading of African–American history, has given her a self-affirming view of race relations in this country. When she is discussing the period of enslavement, for example, we hear her respect for her African-born, forcibly mated great-great-grandmother "Mary;" her admiration for her father's mother, who had been an enslaved child worker in a house just outside Richmond, Virginia; and her cherishing of the doll and cocoa set that had belonged to her great-great-grand-mother "Aunt Nell," an enslaved cook. On the other hand, Odette Hines refers to the white elite "First Families of Virginia" as the "British Mafia in America" because their position was based on the theft of land from the Native Americans and the forced labor of Africans. In Odette Hines' mind, as in the minds of many African Americans, the historical categories of people considered good and admirable and those considered evil and worthy of disdain are the inverse of what is usually taught in American history. This inversion serves her well.

Her conceptualizations about women, too, deviate somewhat from those of the dominant culture. Odette Hines grew up in a community where the ideal of womanhood—even for the privileged women who were her models—was not to be only a housewife, not to be passive and mindless. The women around the young " 'Dette" were holding jobs, creating schools, founding summer camps, traveling independently, and running their own businesses. Her ideas about womanhood, then, although not completely opposed to traditional Western conceptualizations, nevertheless deviate: they assume women's competence and ability to effect change in the world. These distinct ideas rooted in her African–American subculture also serve her well.

Working on this narrative, becoming closer to and learning more about Odette Hines than I had in the previous twenty-five years of our friendship, I came to realize that her decision to house Civil Rights workers, as extraordinary as it was for a person in her parish at that time, was not in fact such an exceptional act in the context of *her* life at all. Odette Hines was part of a generation that came of age in the radical 1930s, that pushed hard for change after World War II, and that embraced and brought wisdom to the aggressive energy of the younger activists of the 1960s. Her decision to provide housing for us and the welcoming attitude she brought to that decision were entirely consistent with the way she had lived her life: with passion, with a constant and profound commitment to black advancement, with conviction and strength.

The following narrative, however, is not just a Civil Rights memoir, not a recounting of her "public" life only. Odette Hines courageously shares her private world, too, including both past and recent private pain. The strength she has demonstrated throughout her life manifests itself again in the way she has chosen to tell her story. As a result, her narrative provides a complex and textured portrait of an extraordinary twentieth-century American woman.

J. R.

Acknowledgments

AS AN INSPIRATION and through her active involvement, Karen Fields has been very much the godmother to this book. Her *Lemon Swamp and Other Places*, which she wrote with her grandmother Mamie Garvin Fields, is a model for collaboration and for the successful capturing on paper of the vitality of a person and the music of the spoken word. Professor Fields' constant willingness to talk through issues and problems, her consistent encouragement and enthusiasm for the project, and her knowledge—of people, of this country, of the strange and wonderful process of doing an oral history—have been critical to the quality and completion of this book. Her contribution has been immeasurable.

Elaine Hagopian and Michael Williams (of Simmons College), Everett Hoagland (of the University of Massachusetts at Dartmouth), Kurt Wolff and Egon Bittner (professors emeriti of Brandeis University), and Alan Klein (of Northeastern University) have been sources of support throughout the work on this book. They have read sections of the manuscript and made valuable comments; they have offered friendships that nourish the spirit as well as the mind.

In Alexandria, Harold Williams, Louis Berry, and Dorothy Hobdy helped the project by clarifying events, names, and dates. I am grateful for the time they so graciously gave. I am grateful, too, to *Abafazi* and the *Journal of Women's History* for publishing Chapters VI and X, respectively. The secretarial assistance of Sarah Avery, Catherine Potter, Sarah Koolsbergen, and Denise Rebeiro has been enjoyable and expert. And the financial assistance of the Simmons College Fund for Research, the American Philosophical Society, the Devereaux Charitable Foundation, and a Wellesley College Research Grant has been invaluable.

PATERNAL FAMILY

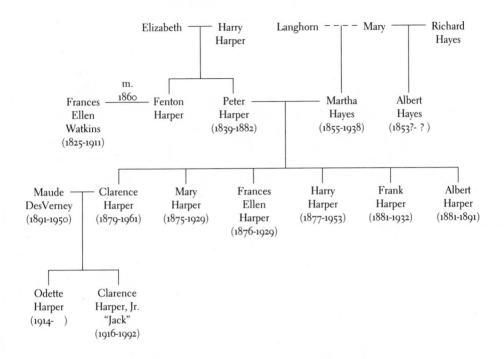

Elizabeth ── Harry
            Harper

Langhorn ──┬── Mary ── Richard
                       Hayes

Frances ── m. ── Fenton   Peter ──────────── Martha   Albert
Ellen   1860   Harper   Harper   Hayes   Hayes
Watkins   (1839-1882)   (1855-1938) (1853?- ?)
(1825-1911)

Maude ── Clarence   Mary   Frances   Harry   Frank   Albert
DesVerney Harper   Harper   Ellen   Harper   Harper   Harper
(1891-1950) (1879-1961) (1875-1929) Harper   (1877-1953) (1881-1932) (1881-1891)
                                (1876-1929)

Odette   Clarence
Harper   Harper, Jr.
(1914-)   "Jack"
            (1916-1992)

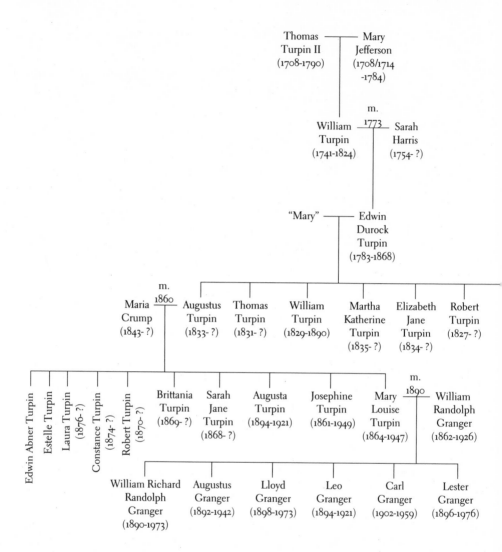

Thomas Turpin II (1708-1790) — Mary Jefferson (1708/1714-1784)

William Turpin (1741-1824) — m. 1773 — Sarah Harris (1754- ?)

"Mary" — Edwin Durock Turpin (1783-1868)

Maria Crump (1843- ?) — m. 1860 — Augustus Turpin (1833- ?)

Thomas Turpin (1831- ?)

William Turpin (1829-1890)

Martha Katherine Turpin (1835- ?)

Elizabeth Jane Turpin (1834- ?)

Robert Turpin (1827- ?)

Edwin Abner Turpin

Estelle Turpin

Laura Turpin (1876- ?)

Constance Turpin (1874- ?)

Robert Turpin (1870- ?)

Brittania Turpin (1869- ?)

Sarah Jane Turpin (1868- ?)

Augusta Turpin (1894-1921)

Josephine Turpin (1861-1949)

Mary Louise Turpin (1864-1947) — m. 1890 — William Randolph Granger (1862-1926)

William Richard Randolph Granger (1890-1973)

Augustus Granger (1892-1942)

Lloyd Granger (1898-1973)

Leo Granger (1894-1921)

Carl Granger (1902-1959)

Lester Granger (1896-1976)

MATERNAL FAMILY

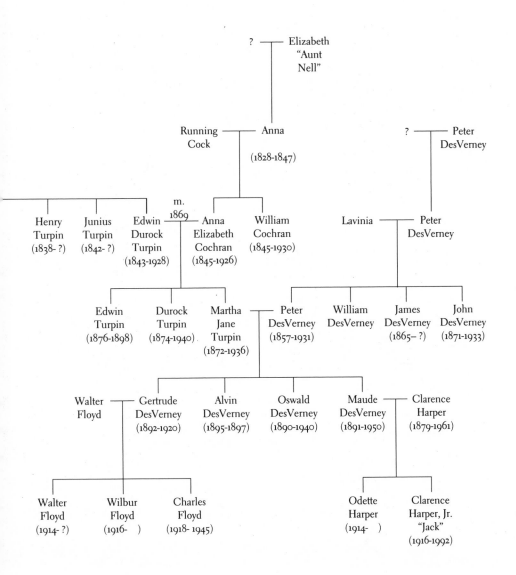

All Is Never Said

I

Home

"Jada, Jada, Jada Jada Jing Jing Jing"

I WAS BORN AND RAISED in the house in the Bronx that my great-grandfather had built in the 1860s. For the early years of my life, my whole world was that house and the neighborhood around it.

One of the earliest memories I have is Uncle Oswald's return to that house from World War I. He was my mother's brother who had been in Europe with the 15th Regiment, an all-black regiment with a white colonel, a Colonel William Hayward. I remember standing on the first landing of the steps in front of the house with my brother and three boy cousins. I couldn't have been more than four or five. We were all preschoolers. We stood there with great anticipation all bundled up in winter clothes, each of us holding little American flags. The adults were all out there too. As I remember, the older relatives had stayed home all day looking after us and cooking. The middle-aged people and young adults went to the parade in Manhattan. They'd come home full of excitement. The soldiers had marched to the band of James Reese Europe of the black 369th. But everyone was home now. It was shortly after nightfall—I remember the street lamp was on—and there we were, all rowed up on the first landing of the stoop.

And when the car drove up, a big touring car with my uncle, his buddies (all officers) and Colonel Hayward, there was such excitement! I can remember the screeching and screaming and the hugging and the kissing and the just contagious family joy at the soldiers' returning. Most of our neighbors from across the street—Italian, Polish and Irish—were there too. All the kids got thrown up in the air and bounced by all the soldiers. I can remember being thrown up in the air by Uncle Oswald and Colonel Hayward and the others. This was a *real* celebration. But it was the family part that was so impressive. That memory has remained a powerful one for me. My feeling about what a family is and how much a family can love each other comes from that memory. At times it's been a real source of strength.

Years later, when I was about to be shipped to Europe for the Red Cross during World War II, I told my parents—who were, of course, quite unhappy about my going into the war—I told them that they could look forward to welcoming me back. Somehow that didn't make them feel better. But I meant it. Uncle Oswald's return to us, the glorious joy of welcoming back a member of the fold, that scene is the foundation of what family means to me.

My feeling about those early years is that I was happy. I took for granted the security, stimulation, and joy of living in what is now called an "extended family." When I was very young, there were four generations in the house. There was my great-grandfather, Durock Turpin, who had built the house, and my great-grandmother, Anna Elizabeth Turpin; my grandmother Martha Jane Turpin and her husband, Peter DesVerney. There was Uncle Durock, the elder son of my great-grandparents; Big Aunt Jane, great-grandfather's sister; Little Aunt Jane, widow of great-grandfather's brother Henry; Mama's sister Gertrude and her husband Walter; Mama and Daddy; my brother Jack and I; and the three sons of Gertrude and Walter. That's a lot of people, isn't it? But the house was large, large enough for family members from outside New York to be always coming to visit and to be comfortably housed there. And large ·enough to be the family funeral home. Anytime *anyone* in the family died, the body would be shipped to that house and put on display in the front parlor, a room that could be shut off by a large sliding door set in a wide arch. As a child, it seemed to me there'd be a new body there every Friday. But great-grandfather was the patriarch. He ruled not only that household but the entire family. And he took responsibility for burying everybody.

He'd had that house built in 1869 when he married Anna Elizabeth Cochran. In their early years in that house, great-grandfather had a barber shop up in the Williamsbridge area. This was a largely black area north of our house, but his barbership was for whites. He'd travel back and forth with his own horse and buggy. Great-grandpa and Great-grandma had married in New

York but both had come separately from the same plantation in Goochland County, Virginia. He was the youngest of nine children of a white Virginia planter and an African woman this planter had bought in Baton Rouge and later married. Another one of their children, Henry, was one of the carpenters on the house. And a third was Big Aunt Jane, who was a widow and lived with us. Their white father's name was Edwin Durock Turpin. And, after buying my great-great-grandmother off of a slave ship in Baton Rouge, he renamed her "Mary." What I remember most is that my great-grandfather just adored his African-born mother.

Great-grandmother, Anna Elizabeth, was the daughter of a black American-born woman named Anna and an Indian named Running Cock who had bought Anna from this same planter. Isn't that something? Turpin owned slaves while he was married to an African woman. Anyway, the Indian freed Anna and married her. But she died in a fire when her two children—Anna Elizabeth and William—were still very young. The Indian father didn't feel he could raise a girl by himself, so he sent Anna Elizabeth back to the plantation to be raised by his deceased wife's mother, Aunt Nell, who was still the enslaved cook of Edwin Durock Turpin. (Running Cock kept William with him.) The little girl became a little worker, removing suckers from tobacco and doing chores in the house. Since she was free, however, wages were paid to her Indian father. I still have a doll and a cocoa set that belonged to her grandmother, the plantation's cook. That's how this little farmed-out girl, my great-grandmother, became the playmate of the planter's children, one of whom was my great-grandfather. So, you see, my great-grandparents had known one another since childhood, and it was when they married that great-grandfather went to the Fordham area of the Bronx to buy property to build a house on.

Great-grandfather loved to tell the story of how he chose that particular location. He had come up to Fordham and was surveying the area, looking at land on each side of the road. He saw a plot he liked and went over to the other side of the road to get a good look at it. A white man who had a house on the same side great-grandfather was standing on came up to him and said, "I understand you're going to buy land but you certainly don't want to buy across there." And Great-grandpa, who physically had taken after his white father (he was quite fair with cobalt blue eyes and blond hair), wanted to know why. The man said, "Because niggers live over there." So Great-grandpa just said, "Oh.

Is that so?" And proceeded to buy property right next to this disparager of black folks. Great-grandpa built his house there and lived in it with my great-grandmother, whose skin was brown and whom he lovingly called his "little black Betty." He really enjoyed what he had done and enjoyed talking about it, telling us this story with a great twinkle in those blue eyes. The house is still there, actually. It's on 187th Street between Washington Avenue and Park Avenue.

My grandmother Martha, my mother Maude, and I were all born in that house. Three generations. In fact, we were all born in the same room, the guest room, which was also the "birthing room." And my eldest daughter, Gretchen, almost made it. She was born in Fordham Hospital, but, two days later, she and I were back in that same room.

It was a three-story house with a cellar and another elevation called a "summer kitchen" between the cellar and the first floor. The house was set on two lots so there was lots of space around it—a big backyard and large side yards. The front of the house was right at the sidewalk. Altogether there were about fourteen rooms. On the first floor, there was the front and back parlor, a dining room, an alcove that was used as a kind of library, two bedrooms behind the back parlor, and another bedroom near the kitchen. Upstairs there were five bedrooms. But there was only one bathroom in the whole place. And, before my time, the house didn't even have that. Originally, it just had a washup place and a portable zinc tub. Later, the stationary tub was put in.

On the back of the house was a porch outside the first-floor bedrooms and a veranda above the porch. In the evenings before dark, the adults would sit on the veranda, facing the yard with its trees and flower beds. And we kids would usually join them. There was a specialness to those evenings. We'd choose a lap to sit on. There were plenty of wicker chairs out there but we preferred a cozy lap and loving arms around us. A record would be playing on the Victrola and, if it was too dull for our youthful taste, we'd asked for a jazzier tune, like "Jada, Jada, Jada Jada Jing Jing Jing." And one of us might slide down from a lap and do a dance on the tiled floor of the veranda. The grownups would always laugh and give us hearty applause—which would encourage another child to slide off a lap and dance or recite a "pome." Whatever we did, it would be warmly received. Then we'd fake sleepiness in order to get ourselves carried up to our bedrooms. And the game was that when you were put onto the bed, you'd open your eyes widely and giggle and be called "You little rascal!" by the grown-up who'd been pretending to believe your fraud. Those evenings were special.

The porch underneath was where my grandmother had the table and chairs for the tramps who would come from the New York Central railroad tracks. The family never sat there; it was just for feeding these nomadic men who were called tramps and hoboes in those days.

Also, on this back porch was a long window box where herbs grew. One of the herbs was mint that would be pinched off for Great-grandfather's mint juleps. Part of his plantation legacy was an abiding faith that mint juleps in summer and lemony hot toddy in winter did wonders for the "system."

Underneath the back porch, near the entrance to the summer kitchen, I had my children's-sized furniture: a set of chairs and a table that folded up as a bridge table would. This area was all paved. One time, when I was eight, I sat down on the table with my fingers curled under the table top. I was laughing at something, I remember. And the table folded and cut the tips off my fingers. Just the tips of the two center fingers, about a quarter of an inch. I must have really cried out because the grown-ups were all around me immediately. My great-grandmother, Anna Elizabeth, put the disconnected tips back on to my fingers and wrapped them in cobwebs—she believed the cobwebs were curative and would make the tissue adhere—and they rushed me to the doctor's. I was very bloody, a real mess. But the doctor was able to stitch the tips back on. One of my warmest memories came out of the horrible event: it's the memory of my brother Jack staying at my bedside that night to hold my arm up. The doctor said it had to be kept elevated. So Jack kept my lower arm pointed toward the ceiling while I slept. He was only six; and he stayed by me all night. Later, there was some kind of infection. They had to cut into the fingers and drain them. I missed about six weeks of school. But the other students would bring my lessons to the house—the school was right up the street—and the teacher, Mrs. Mary Mahrs, would come at the end of the week and work with me. It all worked out OK. I'm alright now. It was my right hand but today you can scarcely find the scars. Time does heal all.

Since I was the only girl, I had the room over the library to myself. The four boys—my brother and three cousins—were in two bunkbeds in a larger room over the front parlor. That was the parlor where the bodies of relatives would be put on display. As I said, relatives from all over the country would ship dead people to our house to be "laid out" in the bay window of the front parlor.

These bodies would be banked with flowers, and purple crepe would be draped over the double front door. The tall pier mirror had to be covered with sheets so that the body would not be reflected. That was considered bad luck. The body stayed there for a three-day period and then was taken to the church where the minister would preach over it. From there, it would be taken to Woodlawn Cemetery and interred in a large family plot. And all the people from the funeral would come back to the house and there'd be a quiet lunch with very good food.

As kids, we'd try to avoid those bodies. To get to the second floor where our bedrooms were, we'd have to go up the stairwell next to the front parlor where the bodies were. We'd run past the parlor as fast as we could, whispering, "Dead people in there!" The boys were not crazy about the fact that their bedroom was right above that front parlor. And mine was almost over it. But none of us dared say anything. Sleeping over dead people was a way of life.

Fortunately, all those funerals were interspersed with many joyous celebrations. On the first of May, we had a special feast to welcome spring. Great-grandpa knew the official first day of spring was March 21st, but he thought May 1st was a more fitting day. So that's when our family celebrated the coming of spring. We'd have a great feast that was always exactly the same: stuffed baked shad, fresh asparagus just drenched in Hollandaise, mashed potatoes, glazed carrots, hot homemade Parker House rolls, a tossed salad, and iced tea and lemonade. For dessert, there'd be both lemon meringue pie and mile-high chocolate layer cake. Wonderful! Shad is a boney fish and there was always a great ceremony about getting "the bones out for the children"—who, on special occasions like this, ate in the dining room with the adults.

Birthdays provided another reason for celebration. And in a house with that many folks, there were birthdays galore. We even had birthday celebrations for our parrot (unimaginatively called "Polly") and for the disagreeable cat, Xantippe. And we celebrated Great-grandfather's sister Kate's birthday too, even though she was long dead. This was a family that really liked shared "occasions." The funeral occasions, though, we kids could have done without.

One of my favorite things about my bedroom was that it looked out to a lovely mulberry tree. It had come to grow on the side of the house in a very interesting way. When my mother's mother was a very little girl, she was playing just outside the house and was offered some mulberries by a visiting cousin. Apparently, she had on a very pretty pinafore. All excited, she called to her mother inside the house, "Look what I have!" Her mother was horrified about her staining her pinafore and called out, scolding her. My grandmother dropped all the mulberries by the side of the house. And, the next spring, a little shoot came up that, by my time, had grown into a huge mulberry tree reaching all the way up to my third floor bedroom window.

In back of the mulberry tree was a cherry tree and, in back of that, an apricot tree, a pear tree and then another tree which Great-grandmother always called a Japanese tulip. It was really a flowering tree that is part of the magnolia family. The blossom had a blush of pink which shaded almost into a red or maroonish color. It was lovely. A hammock hung between the magnolia tree and the pear tree. All of us and sometimes even the neighbors loved to relax in that hammock.

In back of the house was a wonderful, wonderful grape arbor with Concord grapes that the Italian families across the street would use to make wine that they shared with us. They lived in two sets of three attached houses that Grandfather DesVerney had built. He was a contractor.

The fruit trees and flowering trees around the house were just delightful. And we used all the fruit, too, except the cherries on the cherry tree. We would get so mad at the robins because they would come and peck each cherry. They'd get a little biteful and then they'd go on to the next one. We couldn't get the cherries down fast enough. When we'd shake them down, they'd have a little bite in them and that would really infuriate us. But my family would put up the other fruit and it was always on shelves in the summer kitchen. And there would be Smithfield hams, potatoes hanging in open mesh bags. There was a kind of opulence—not because they were wealthy but because they were so conservative, so frugal. They stored more than most people. I know that because when the little white kids who were my playmates would come over and see all the food stored, they'd exclaim over the hams and preserves. Our family always bought in quantity too. If it was something you were going to have to use over and over again, the idea was to buy a lot of it, and, that way, it would be cheaper. Folks, in those days, went to the store every day to get what they wanted. They didn't have good refrigeration. And we went daily, too, for perishable items. But for things that would last, we'd always buy in bulk.

My family was conservative about clothing too. I remember Big Aunt Jane, my great-grandfather's older sister, sitting forever in the curve of the bay window with this big woven hamper full of all the socks and stockings and sweaters, aprons, shirts, drawers, whatever needed mending. And she'd neatly darn and mend everything. I guess I never wore anything that didn't have a patch or two. But it was beautifully done. It was so different when I married Jimmy and moved here to Louisiana. His mother thought of me as very extravagant because I insisted on buying toilet paper by the case. "That girl spends money like water," she'd say. And I had a darning egg to darn Jimmy's socks. She snatched the thing away from me! She said proudly, "He's never worn a pair of darned socks in his life. He's never worn anything darned!" And yet this was a woman who had scrubbed floors and had lined her own worn-out shoes with layers of cardboard to get him through medical school. But my frugality came from my family's frugal habits.

At the same time, though, I felt very indulged at home. Besides all the kind relatives, my mother had chosen three good friends to be my godmothers and they were also extremely generous to me. All of my godmothers were fairly comfortable—not rich but comfortable. Godmother Mattie was the secretary of Judge Charles Toney, the first black judge in New York. Godmother Hattie was W. E. B. DuBois' secretary at the NAACP. And Godmother Ethelle— who spent her last years here in Louisiana with me—was a designer of clothes and hats, the owner, with her mother, of her own boutique in Harlem.[1] (Godmother Ethelle's brother was Happy Rhone, a famous bandleader of that era, and had provided the capital for their business.) When she came here suffering from Alzheimer's disease, I was happy to be able to take care of her because she'd done so much for me when I was a child. There were trips and clothes and the theater. All three of my godmothers were wonderful. They and my great-grandparents, grandparents, aunts, uncles, and parents were *very* good to me.

I was slapped only one time as a child. Daddy slapped me. And the family was so upset with him, he never did it again. I was maybe two years old. They put black-eyed peas in front of me on New Year's Day, as is still the custom among black people. Eating them is supposed to bring you luck for the year. Anyway, they looked like little bugs to me. I just didn't want to eat them. And my father felt that you should eat whatever food was put in front of you. And he gave me a smack across the side of my face. On that holiday, his mother was present, in addition to all these other relatives of my mother who lived there. She and all the rest of them jumped on him for hitting me. "Clarence, you've left the print of your hand on that child's face!" I think they tried to humiliate him. So that never happened again; I never had another spanking in my life. I got punishments but I was never struck again. But maybe that experience had good end results. Maybe it's why today I always eat what's put in front of me. I accept food if it's edible, whether I'm going to enjoy it or not. If it's offered and it would be impolite to refuse, I eat it. And I think that's the best way to live. So maybe that one time I was slapped taught me a good lesson.

My brother and cousins got spankings all the time though. Over somebody's knee, they got a spanking maybe with a switch out of the yard or the flat of someone's hand. Nobody ever brutalized anyone though. The adults wouldn't have done that. But the spankings helped the boys remember what was expected of them. And not being punished physically made me feel more special, I guess.

But I think the main reason I always felt special was because I was the only girl with four boys. I was taken places the boys didn't go, more attention was given to my clothes, I was just treated as though I was special. I was very protected. Now, some of that might have been because I was sick a good part of the time—I was in and out of the hospital with bouts of pneumonia and bad tonsils—but, at the time, I didn't associate the indulgences with being sickly because I just didn't think of myself as sickly. I don't even now with a nurse coming in here every day. It's just not the way I conceived of myself. I have never thought of me as being sickly. And I get annoyed with people who want to be sickly, who dwell on it all the time. But now I realize that some of that special treatment probably was because of the illnesses. They said things like, "Now don't overtax yourself," all the time. The first of the bouts with pneumonia was when I was six months old. I was evidently falling apart pretty early. But the attention just made me feel important. And I continued to feel like that the rest of my life. At the time, though, I thought I was treated that way because I was a girl. I haven't thought about it before, but all that special treatment may be where my particular arrogance comes from.

The boys sometimes used the fact that I never got a spanking to their own advantage. When they'd done something wrong that the adults might discover, they'd tell me, "Don't tell them *we* did it! Pretend it was you." They felt I could get away with anything. And the other kids in the neighborhood thought that, too. I remember when I was very young, seven or eight, before one of the apartment buildings was put up, the kids used that sloping vacant

lot to ride sleds on the crusty snow and then roast potatoes. They'd build a bonfire and I'd always get delegated to get the potatoes. And instead of getting
them out of the house, I went to Steve's Grocery Store on the corner and stole
them. I apparently must have been sweet-faced or maybe dumb-faced. And I
was very well liked by the shopkeepers. So I'd go in and just say, "Hello, Mr
Steve." And he'd say, "How're ya doing, Sook?" (Sook was my nickname; it
was short for "Sugar.") And he'd offer me some candy. He'd reach into one of
those jars that had Mary Janes or something and give me a handful. And I'd
stand there and talk to him across the counter and steal potatoes from the cro-
cus sack on my side. I'd stuff them into my heavy winter coat. Then take them
back to the other kids and we'd roast them. It was routine. I was the official
thief. All the kids, including me, seemed to know I could get away with it.

When I think of that neighborhood, I think mainly of the playing, the other
children, the girls' club. Right across the street lived six Italian families in the
houses that Grandfather Peter DesVerney had built. These are the people
who would make wine from the grapes in my grandmother's arbor. Danny
Tenestito, Pasquale Borghese . . . all their parents were from Italy. There were
some Czechoslovakians in the next houses; I played with their daughter, Han-
nah. Working class people. But in the apartment buildings that had gone up
were lower middle-class folks . . . school teachers, registered nurses. And Mar-
garet Tombes' father was the curator of the Bronx Zoo. There were some Irish
and Scotch kids: Marie Fitzgibbons, Kitty Moran, Rita Campbell; some Italian kids: Vivian Benefacto, Aurora Perone; and I had one WASP girlfriend: Barbara Knapp. At the time, I didn't think about their ethnicity; it wasn't important to me. But as I recall their last names, I'm realizing who was what.

When I was about ten or eleven, we formed a club, the "American Girls'
Club." All of the girls I just mentioned were in it and a few more whose names
I can't remember. And they let me be the president of it. We would meet and
eat from house to house. And we'd go skating, had little projects where we
would make things for our parents for Christmas or Mother's Day or something. But we mainly got together and ate. I was the only black member of the
club but that was never an issue in that neighborhood—guess because my
family had been there forever; we had not "invaded" the neighborhood. Race
was never an issue among my playmates, but, because my family was very
proud of who they were, they transmitted that knowledge and pride to me.

For example, when I was very little I had a black doll and I knew she was

beautiful and I just loved her. Now, this was before Marcus Garvey popular-
ized the idea of black dolls. Do you know how I got it? Someone had given
me a large China doll with a blond wig and blue eyes. My father painted the
doll brown and sent away for a black wig and a set of brown eyes. You know,
when you open the skull of a doll, you can stick the eyes in. So he put some
dark eyes in it and put on the black hair. And I had an African–American doll!
Nobody else had one. They didn't even make them then. All the kids thought
the doll was perfectly beautiful. I didn't think about race at that age. I just knew
it was my doll and it was beautiful. But, for a child, I think it was a powerful
message. My family was very engaged in being what they were and not what
somebody else was. Although they had all kinds of appearances, there was
never any confusion about what they were. And they were more than clear;
they were proud, almost arrogant.

So we all played together very comfortably. I remember playing the game
"May I?" with kids on opposite sides of the street. And "Simon Says." The girls
roller skated, played "Jacks," and jumped rope, of course. The boys played
stickball in the street. Everybody rode bikes but I couldn't because of being
half sick a good part of the time. I didn't feel left out of the bike riding, though,
because I was preoccupied with things I liked to do: painting, drawing, and
once I was in school, writing. I loved telling stories and writing stories. I talked
and wrote about what I had seen, mainly. And I seemed to look for more than
most people, and, therefore, saw more. I wasn't so much interested in fiction;
it was mostly the business of being a kind of raconteur and chronicler. In
school, I loved composition and whatever I would cook up would be read to
the class. But I always wrote at home on my own, too. My family kept me well
supplied with paper and pencils and paints and watercolors. The boys would
get card games, marbles, jigsaw puzzles, things to play with. I'd get things to
work with. I never felt left out of their activities because I was doing what I
wanted to do. I drew and painted and wrote. That was my recreation at home.

Our street was really our playground. There was little traffic because it was
a side street between two main avenues. There was no reason for any traffic
on that street unless someone was coming to one of those houses. Every weekday afternoon, the girls would walk their dolls in their doll carriages. In the
mornings, we'd play in the yard and in the dirt. Often our backyard was full of
children making food out of mud and pebbles and stuff. But, in the afternoons, we went in and had a bath. All the kids in the neighborhood had a bath

in the afternoon. And we'd put on fresh clothing and the girls would then take out their doll carriages and walk up and down the street talking with one an-other. You did it just like the grown-ups. Many of the mamas had new babies and we imitated them. I can still see my wicker carriage. We had changes of clothes for our dolls and pretty blankets, pillows, and coverlets. And we'd walk and talk until we were called in for dinner. This took place every afternoon except Saturday and Sunday when there were other things to do.

A fascinating thing happened one of those afternoons. I was with one of my girlfriends whose family would be called "lace curtain Irish"—although, as I said, I didn't think about ethnicity at the time. This girl always had the most beautiful dresses. Very often, in my household, while you got a bath and your underwear was spanking fresh each time, you might put on the dress that you had on yesterday 'cause it was just for this stroll, really. This one time, after I'd had my bath, I went to the home of this friend to wait for her through her bath. And when she came out of the bath, she put back on the same underwear she'd had on, really grimy underwear that had been put back on many times, apparently. And then she put on this beautiful little organdy dress. That really did something to me. To this child of a registered nurse, it didn't matter what was underneath. What mattered was what you saw on the outside. It was dis-tressing. I had always thought of that particular little friend as very glamorous, interesting. I looked up to her a little, I suppose, because she was pretty and physical attractiveness always works. And she was very pleasant and warm and nice. And I liked her because her family was nice to me. That family had a special look about them. But that incident really affected me. I don't know. I think all folks do this labeling, generalizing. Just like one bad experience with a black person makes some white folks say, "All blacks are this or that," that incident affected my attitude toward whites. I think it made me think that white folks were not always what they appeared to be. She was willing to put this beautiful little dress on over this grimy, really *grimy* underwear that she'd been putting on for days and days. There was such an emphasis in my house on clean bodies and clean underwear. And to her, that didn't matter. It was what you saw on the outside. For me, this incident suggested that to whites the appearance of things is what counts. The glamour of her attractiveness went smash because I realized this is what she *really* is: dirty underneath.

Not all of our play was as benign as "May I?" and walking our dolls. There were ugly things that went on too. My brother and three cousins developed a game, a kind of contest to see who could land the best wad of spit in the center of Angelo the shoemaker's cap as he walked by our house. They had him timed. They knew that everyday he'd leave his shop around the corner at noon to walk over the hill to his home in "Guineatown" for a midday meal. Guineatown was the area around Arthur Avenue and Bathgate Avenue where there was a concentration of Italians. Pushcarts lined both sides of the avenues, manned mainly by Italian vendors hawking a whole range of wares. Daily, Angelo would walk to his home there, eat lunch, and then return to his shop. Everyone knew him because everyone patronized him. In those days, your shoes got half-soles and heels at least a couple of times before you stopped wearing them. Everybody in the neighborhood made use of Angelo's. So my brother and cousins would get up on the first landing of the front steps and, as Angelo passed, they would have this spitting contest. I didn't participate in that because I wasn't sure of reaching my target. But I watched and was as guilty as the rest of them. So, finally, the poor man complained. And, at first, my great-grandmother was indignant: "What do you think we're raising in here? They wouldn't do anything like that! Not *my* children!" But he insisted that that was what was happening. So she decided, I guess, that all children will do something sometimes, and she planted herself in an area where she could see what was going on. We couldn't see her. And she caught us. She seemed to think I was an innocent bystander. So I didn't get punished but the boys did get spankings for that. The two older culprits were also required to help the shoemaker for a time by sweeping up his shop. And, of course, all four of them had to apologize.

Another thing that was ugly was the taunting of an old Irish lady who was an alcoholic. She didn't live there but would sometimes wander into that block. And the fun seemed to have been to follow her and say, "Old Lady McGuire, your house is on fire." And the kids would walk behind her until she turned on them, and then they'd all scatter like they thought she was going to do them some harm. She never did, of course. She was just a pathetic old alcoholic. But the kids thought that was humorous. The mothers who were more conscientious wouldn't let their kids engage in that. But there were these others. . . .

Most of my memories are of play. The only responsibility we had as children was going to the store. But, as you would imagine, a house that size was a lot of work. When the two generations of grandparents were alive, they ran the house and did most of the work. As they died and my mother went to work when I was twelve, we got Miss Frances to help us around the house.

There was a daily schedule for housekeeping. I remember that the wetwash had to be ready to go on Monday morning. A commercial laundry around the corner had these big washing machines that would get the white things very, very clean and smelling like Clorox. But they didn't call the chemical "chlorine" then; it was called "jumelo water." All the bedsheets in that period were white and they'd come back pale blue. Before my time, there were washtubs made of slate right off the summer kitchen, which was also the laundry room. It had ironing boards and a coal stove too. The flatirons were heated on it. By the time I knew anything about it, they'd worked up to the electric irons. I can vaguely remember all those ladies ironing in the summer kitchen.

The wetwash would come back Monday afternoon or Tuesday morning damp dry, and would have to be hung out right away or else it would mildew. The hanging out of the laundry was something everyone participated in. When one person would get tired of hanging stuff, the other would say, "I'll hang it." The pulley clothesline ran from a kitchen window to a big pole that was like a telephone pole. So, in very cold weather, you didn't have to go outdoors to hang out your clothes. You could stand in the window with a sack full of clothespins and hang them. On Tuesdays, everything would be ironed. My grandmother did most of the ironing when she was alive. Then Miss Frances did it. They had a press about four feet long and they folded a sheet and put it through this press. All the linens were done that way; it wasn't that much of a chore.

Laundering curtains for all those windows was another matter. Curtains had to be lace if you were a certain stratum. But lace curtains were so much work! First, they were handwashed and heavily starched in the big slate washtub downstairs. Then they had to be stretched. You couldn't take an iron to them; they had to be stretched dry. We had these big rectangular wooden frames. They had to be large because the windows in the house were so large. All around the frame were pins, at about half-inch intervals, that stuck out like porcupine bristles. So getting the curtains onto the stretchers always meant pricking your fingers again and again. Not just me, the older women too. It was such an unpleasant task.

Personal underwear, like your panties and things, you were expected to wash daily after your bath. Those things didn't go into the wetwash. The men didn't wash their personal things, though; the women—my grandmother and great-grandmother—did it for them. The men wore knit vests and boxer shorts in summer, long johns in winter. None of those required ironing. They were nicely folded and put back into their bureaus. No, the men didn't do any housework. After dinner they'd get up and go and sit and read the newspaper or listen to the radio. Or they'd step out on the back porch to puff on a cigar. (Great-grandmother allowed no smoking in the house.) The women did all the cleaning up. And that was a task because there were so many of us and because the cooking utensils were heavy iron skillets and dutch ovens.

The children's main responsibility was the daily shopping. Because refrigeration was poor before the thirties, certain items had to be purchased daily. We'd get milk twice a day, in fact. It was delivered in the morning to Steve's Grocery Store, the same Steve who was the victim of my thievery. The milk was in a large can delivered at dawn and it sat outside the store until Steve opened up and took it in. I imagine in the summer months, they must have made a later delivery so it wouldn't spoil. But, in the winter time, it just sat out there in the snow. Then each family sent the children out to get milk and a loaf of Bond bread. We had two sizes of these white enamel milk buckets that had covers and handles that swung across the pail's top. One held a quart and one held a half gallon. The milk was kept in a huge galvanized bucket at the store and the grocer had a big dipper he'd use to scoop it into your bucket. There was no way in the world any of these things were sterile; but that's how the milk was dispensed. Usually we'd get a half gallon in the morning and another quart or half gallon later in the day.

We also had to buy meats daily. The kids were sent to Pete's around the corner to get two pounds of beef and lamb for stew. We would not be sent to get a goose or leg of lamb or pork chops, meat that had to be carefully chosen. Just the stew meat. And, along with that, the butcher would give you a kidney or some liver for the cat. As I mentioned, my great-grandmother had this very disagreeable cat named Xantippe. Xantippe was the name of Socrates' wife who was supposed to be a rather shrewish person. And we had a dog that stayed in the yard. The butcher would say, "Don't you need a bone for the dog?" and he sent bones for him. He didn't charge for any of that. Getting the milk, bread, and stew beef was the shopping that we, as children, had responsibility to do. The selecting of vegetables and all other food items was left to the adults.

In my time, the house had steam heat fired by a gas furnace. Before that, it was steam heat fired by coal. There was a coal chute that went down into the coal bin in the cellar near where the furnace was. Before I was born, they used the fireplaces that were all through the place for heat, and they added to that with small oil stoves. I remember seeing one of those little cylindrical, moveable stoves with a handle on top.

In the summer, the women would always be preserving things, not only the fruits from the trees around the house, but they'd go out in the country and buy sacks of fruit and vegetables. The fruit or vegetables might be cooked in kettles on the big range, this mammoth, ugly-looking something that they kept clean and shining with stove polish, probably made by the same company that made Black Sambo Stove Polish, whose trade name I later challenged when I worked at the NAACP. This stove gave off really excellent heat, creating an inferno in the summer. But in winter, it made the kitchen the coziest room in that drafty house.

On a truly cold night, the adults would bathe the tots in a round galvanized zino washtub that had been dragged into the kitchen and placed right in front of this stove. Now, embossed on the stove's black iron door was the boast that it was "PEERLESS." And one time, one of my boy cousins got a little too exuberant during his bath and backed into that hot oven door. He got a mirror image of PEERLESS branded on his little backside. I'm told it took years to wear off.

During my youth, Miss Frances did most of the cooking. She came about three times a week, cleaning, ironing, and cooking. Before she came, my grandmother and great-grandmother cooked. My mother couldn't cook worth a toot. She never had to learn. First, there were all those senior citizens around the house and then there was Miss Frances. My mother was always more of a peer to me than a mother. I didn't really have a model of mother as a housekeeper. But I did get the message that housework is women's work—just not my work or my mother's work. Absolutely all the cooking and cleaning and mending in that house was done by women. The only time they didn't prepare our food was when we got something from the pizzeria or rotisserie. There were a lot of Italians in that area and you didn't have an Italian community without a pizzeria and rotisserie within a couple of blocks. At the rotisserie, they'd have fowls on spits and they kept turning as they cooked. So sometimes we'd buy a whole cooked fowl. And pizzas were very much a part of our lives. When I first came here to Louisiana in the late forties, no one had ever heard of them. I gave a pizza party one time with an entire Italian theme—we dressed Italian, I had tiny baskets shaped like gondolas for favors, and I tried to teach an elderly lady called Mama Fanny how to make pizza. It didn't come out too authentic but everyone loved it. And maybe about ten or fifteen years later, pizzas came to this section. But, at home in New York, we ate them all the time.

Eventually, we got an electrical refrigerator. They were first shown at the 1933 World's Fair and we got one. But when I was growing up, we had an oak ice box that had a water holder to catch the melted ice. That had to be emptied very regularly and that was a chore we children rotated. Because of the water, the ice box was kept out on the back porch where my grandmother kept the table and chairs for the tramps who came through.

It was from my grandmothers and mother that I learned the importance of caring about others—strangers and neighbors as well as friends and family. Great-grandmother and Grandmother always fed anyone who came to the house hungry. I guess the hobos told one another where they could get a meal because there was a steady stream of tramps who would appear on our back porch. And they were always fed well. The neighbors would say, "I don't know why you do that. You'll have every tramp in the world coming to you. They're just taking advantage of you." And Great-grandmother would say, "It doesn't matter. That's between them and their God. No one's going to come here and not be fed." Being frugal didn't extend to being stingy. She was lavish with food. She said that whatever you had came from the Supreme Being; you were just allowed to monitor it. You don't own anything. She did not believe that you should pass up anybody. And Mama's mother was like that, too. Any beggar in the street who asked her for anything got it. Her mother had indoctrinated her, I guess. People walking with her would say, "Why don't you give them the address of Home Relief?" And grandmother would answer, "I suppose they can find the Home Relief on their own. I'm giving them this." All of those women in my family felt that you were your brother's keeper. That's what it comes down to. And they instilled that in me. I think you ought to do as much as you can for people.

Mama ran what amounted to a psychiatric service in our kitchen. People— friends of hers, all the neighbors—would come in there with a problem and she would offer them a cup of tea and "a nice slice of pound cake." That and her conversation cured everybody. Her friends would travel from way down in

Manhattan to come and "discuss it with Maudie." Mama liked everyone. She found something that she decided to like in everyone and that kept her happy—including finding something to like in me. As a child and as an adult, I too found her wonderful to talk to. She would get me to do what she thought I ought to do by praising me. It was a good technique. She was really always my friend.

Yes, my memories of my early years are that I was happy, irresponsible really, indulged and very loved. And for me there was the warming wonder of being able to sit in the comforting laps of all those reassuring folks, being loved and loving them right back. For years, my father carried a photograph of me in his wallet with the words "My only daughter" written on the back. He was very much the fond father. And they were all like that toward me. I took it all for granted—the material security, the loving family, the warming neighborhood. But I think that laid a secure foundation that made me somewhat adventurous later on, something of a risk taker. And it made me want to care for them and others as I had been cared for. Now, I'm not saying my family was perfect. Some of my older relatives were rather stiff, Daddy had a problem with alcohol, and Uncle Durock was downright eccentric. But I am saying I felt good being me those early years. I was a happy child.

II

Family

"They were so diverse . . ."

I KNOW MUCH MORE ABOUT MY MOTHER'S FAMILY than my father's because of living with them. But, actually, the two families were intertwined; they'd known one another since the 1860s in Richmond. My father's father, Peter Harper, and my mother's grandfather, Durock Turpin, even owned a barbershop together there when they were young. And the connection continued in New York. Daddy's first teacher was my maternal grandmother's cousin, Marylou, the daughter of Augustus Turpin, great-grandfather's brother. So, you see, my parents were very connected long before they met and were married.

As I said, Great-grandfather built and presided over the house I grew up in until his death in 1928. He was the youngest of nine children of that Virginia planter and his African-born wife. He was still young when his African mother died, and he just idolized her. I remember his talking about how he'd wanted to marry a woman just like his mother. He had wanted that so badly that, as a young man, he'd traveled all the way to Baton Rouge—he went down by boat on the Mississippi—to the slave ship entry port where his mother had been bought by his father. I have a picture of him at the time he did this. He couldn't have been more than seventeen or eighteen by the look of him. He looked over the newly arrived African women but couldn't find anyone that reminded him of his mother. When he told this story to us, he would say, "The slaves were a mangy lot." So he returned to Virginia disappointed, without a wife.

For a while he worked as a barber in Richmond with, as I said, the man who turned out to be my father's father. It was after the Civil War, I believe, that he moved to New York, looked up Anna Elizabeth, his former playmate on his father's plantation, and married her in 1869.

Anna Elizabeth had come to New York from the Goochland County plantation years earlier when she was seventeen. If you were free, you had to get out of Virginia when you were sixteen or so or they might re-enslave you. The patrollers would round up free blacks every now and then, and if you didn't have adequate papers, and sometimes even if you did, they'd make you somebody's slave. It was unsafe for a young free black person to stay in Virginia. So Anna Elizabeth left.

She'd gotten some education on the plantation. The planter, Edwin Durock Turpin, had all of his own children and her, this free child of Running Cock and grandchild of the plantation cook, tutored in the basics of literacy and arithmetic. Then the white planter offered to send her to New York where she could better remain free. That sounds generous, doesn't it? I mean, she wasn't related to him in any way. She was born free only because the Indian who'd bought and married her mother had set the mother free. But Anna Elizabeth was bitter about that planter. I remember her calling him "that old reprobate." Because, to pay for her trip north, he'd sold her grandmother — the grandmother who had raised her after her mother died, the grandmother who was his cook for decades. It was when Anna Elizabeth was leaving for New York that her grandmother, who was called Aunt Nell, gave her the doll and cocoa set I still have. My great-grandmother cherished those items, knowing they'd belonged to the woman who raised her, and knowing, even if she might ever visit the plantation on which she was raised, she could never hope to see her grandmother again, because the old woman had been sold away to a Carolina planter to pay for her trip north.

Great-grandfather told many stories about his father, this strange man who bought and sold slaves, sometimes owning forty or fifty himself, while he was married to a black woman. He'd been born in 1783 of English descent. He was, in fact, related to Thomas Jefferson; his father, William Turpin, was Jefferson's first cousin.[1] His marrying an African woman was *very* unusual. In those days, the custom was for the southern planters to have a white wife and also a black mistress. But Turpin had no wife when he bought my great-great-grandmother "fresh off the boat" in Baton Rouge, as my family told it. He brought her back to his place in Goochland County, Virginia, renamed her "Mary," and lived with her in his home. Usually, the black mistress was maintained in a separate dwelling. Not so, in this case. After the birth of maybe three or four children, they journeyed to Canada and a marriage took place. When they came back to Virginia, somehow word got out that this dreadful thing had happened and, routinely, his neighbors—and other folks who weren't well-wishers—burned the place down. And he would routinely reconstruct it.

Now, it was my great-grandfather's feeling that his father was a gambler. Not that that was his main means of support—the plantation's cotton and tobacco were what kept him going—but he apparently enjoyed gambling regularly. Great-grandfather guessed that because, when the children would come downstairs in the morning for breakfast (and, remember, he was the youngest of those children), there would be stacks of silver coins on the table that would have to be cleared away. Some of those coins were melted down and converted into flatware for the dining table. My great-grandfather still had some of it at our Bronx house when I was growing up. But many of the spoons had bowls that had split away from the stems because there was no alloy in the silver and it was quite soft. Great-grandfather also had chairs from that plantation, chairs I now have here in Alexandria. These were part of the furnishings of the main house and were undoubtedly made by enslaved black people. The workmanship in them is just beautiful.

This white planter apparently treasured his African wife as a real companion. He dressed her beautifully, so the family story goes, in clothes that he imported from Paris. Or he'd have people make her clothes from pictures he saw in fashion books. He took her to church with him, an Episcopal church. And her children remembered that she had some kind of little carving in her hand every time she went to church. She never seemed to accept what was going on there. She would go to the church dressed in lovely European clothing but she had this little figurine that she always carried with her—an African figurine. She had, after all, been brought to this country as an adult. So why should she give up the religious beliefs she was raised with? They could all sit together because it was accepted that any slave could sit with his or her master in these churches. If slaves were alone, however, they had to sit in the balcony or gallery. But a mammy could bring in her master's children and sit with them in the white section. So, in that family group, the mammy was also the mama. All of them would go to church together. I can remember Great-grandpa and his sister, Big Aunt Jane, talking about that.

This planter also had a daily habit which seems repulsive today. One of Anna Elizabeth's duties was to empty out his night urine pot in the morning. But she was instructed to leave a small amount in a container on his bureau. He believed his own urine was good for his complexion, so he would smear it all over his face every day. Great-grandmother Anna Elizabeth would tell us this story with great disgust.

In fact, there was a certain disgust every time she brought up the planter. Her attitude was the opposite of my great-grandfather's, who looked up to his father. She saw this planter as a criminal because he was part of the slave system, a system she despised deeply. I remember her saying he didn't have any business selling her mother to the Indian because he hadn't paid anything for her in the first place. (She'd been born to his enslaved cook.) Because Great-grandmother saw him and everyone else who benefited from slavery as criminals, she actually felt superior to him.

This attitude of my tiny, fiery great-grandmother made a lasting impression on me. She viewed the Europeans who had invaded this hemisphere as marauding bandits. She'd learned enough history (from that tutor who'd instructed her along with the planter's children) to know that the English crown awarded Englishmen huge tracts of land here for eliminating Indians. And she knew those Englishmen became rich and powerful by using African forced labor to work their stolen land. Some years ago, when this planter's will was released to us by a Virginia historical society and I was discussing that side of the family, I hit upon a name for those First Families of Virginia; they were members of the "British Mafia." That's how I think of those ruthless, predatory early Jeffersons and Randolphs and Turpins. The British Mafia in America. I think my great-grandmother, Anna Elizabeth, would have said Amen to that.

So this very unusual couple—this white planter and his African-born wife—had, as I said, nine children: Junius, Henry, Robert, Augustus, Jane, Katherine, William, Thomas, and Durock, my great-grandfather. Junius, Henry, Jane, and Durock all came to New York. Henry was a carpenter and helped build our house. Big Aunt Jane was widowed very young so she came and lived with us. Junius passed back and forth over the color line so that he could work on Wall Street. And Grandpa ran his barber shop and, like the others, had some income from the plantation.

Besides my great-grandparents, I guess Big Aunt Jane and Little Aunt Jane had the most influence on me from that generation. Big Aunt Jane, as I said, took responsibility for all the mending and darning in the house. She was a very serious person who looked like what we think of as a spinster, but she was actually a widow. She was tall and gaunt; her neck collars were high; she was very severe. And she had glasses—I think they were called "pince nez"—with a watch attached. The glasses rolled up on a chain that disappeared very much like a measuring tape. The watch was attached to her bodice. And when she said she was resting her eyes, she would take them off and the spring would pull the glasses back to this attachment at her bodice. And the glasses would be there on her chest.

Big Aunt Jane was always ready to teach you something. But Little Aunt Jane was a much more frothy lady. She was petite and quite attractive—even as an old lady. She was Great-grandfather's brother Henry's widow. Little Aunt Jane seemed little, light of spirit, and warm; Big Aunt Jane was just the opposite. She was a very remote person. Little Aunt Jane used to play something called "cat's cradle" with us. It's a very intricate pattern of cord wrapped around both hands, all the fingers. You could work it into a bridge formation and create other designs. And you could transfer it backwards and forwards to another person, if you had enough skill. And that was a great deal of fun. She also played catch with us, and she taught us to pick out notes on the piano.

Big Aunt Jane was a person who used a lot of proverbs like "Waste not, want not" and "Early to bed, early to rise . . . ." She'd do a lot of quoting from the Almanac and Benjamin Franklin and Emerson. Teaching, she thought. She would hold us while she said these things and look at us rather lovingly while she recited some proverb. There was always something she was teaching us. And Little Aunt Jane was playing with us. And I think that we probably learned a little more from Little Aunt Jane than we did from Big Aunt Jane because what Big Aunt Jane had to say, I don't think any of us cared to hear. But anything that Little Aunt Jane had to say, we were willing to listen to. We felt so much closer to her.

Great-grandfather's brother Junius lived a strange life, as far as race is concerned. Like my great-grandfather, he got none of his African mother's phys-

ical characteristics. So he used that to get a very good job as a financial consultant on Wall Street, which he could not have gotten if they'd known he was
black. He was almost forced to do that. He'd been fired from a job as a floor-
walker at Wanamaker's when they discovered he was black. (He hadn't deliberately passed; they hadn't asked about his race.) Then he'd been fired from a
"colored man's job"—a Pullman porter on the railroad—because the white
conductor resented his appearance and the fact that passengers sometimes
mistook him for a conductor. So he gave up and decided to deliberately pass
for white in order to be able to keep a job. (It was so hard back then for black
men to get decent jobs; I think that's why far more black men passed than
black women.) But, he never rejected his family. He visited the Bronx house
all the time and stayed in close touch.

So Uncle Junius had this good job on Wall Street. Now, one of the portfo-
lios he handled was that of a wealthy white Boston widow with one son. When
she came to New York to go over her portfolio, she fell in love with Uncle Junius. At the time, he was a Don Juan character who had no interest in marrying anyone. And, in every way he could, he tried to discourage this woman—
a very lovely woman named Abigail—who was becoming so devoted to him.
And he finally told her he was black, thinking that would certainly destroy her
feelings. At first, she didn't believe him. So, to convince her, he brought her
up to Fordham to meet his family. But, after meeting them, she said she was
still in love with him and it didn't matter that he was black. By that time, I
guess he was involved and falling in love with her too. So they married; and
they remained married until he died in old age.

By the time I was on the scene, they were living in a very exclusive home
for the elderly on Fifth Avenue in Manhattan and they rode around in a chauf-
feur-driven limousine. And twice a month—I think it was on Thursdays—they
would come up to what was then Rogers Department Store on the corner of
Webster and Fordham, on the pretext that the store had items that they liked
to shop for. The chauffeur would let them out on the Webster Avenue side
and they would walk through the store, out the Park Avenue door, then the
two blocks to our house. They'd always bring me a licorice stick, which I was
quite fond of. The chauffeur was instructed to come back to Rogers Department Store for them a few hours later. They had another excuse for being in
that area too: a sister of hers was buried at Woodlawn Cemetery. So sometimes
they would visit the cemetery as well as the family. Then they'd walk the two

blocks back, go through the Park Avenue entrance of Rogers Store, hastily pick up some items they didn't really need, and be ready when the chauffeur came to pick them up at the Webster Avenue entrance to the store. They'd had no children of their own; they just had her son by her first marriage who was in on their secret and who, even after their death, continued to come to the Bronx and visit us.

Uncle Junius' funeral caused a scene I remember quite well. I was about eight years old when he died. I remember Aunt Abby, as I called her, coming to our house heartbroken. She said she didn't want the funeral without his family present. Yet, she couldn't risk his race being discovered since he was being interred in an exclusive, white cemetery. So she asked that all the family be assembled so that there could be a screening to see which women, under veils, couldn't be identified as black. I remember the commotion, the parading, the switching veils around. And nobody was offended by this; this was essential to do. They'd look at themselves in the mirror and say, "I don't think this is going to do. Here, you try it." Men were selected on the basis of how fair their skin was. All of this was because she was burying her "Juney," as she called him, in a section of the graveyard reserved for people from this elite home for the elderly, and she didn't want them later exhuming his body. The home was exclusively white and the graveyard was exclusively white. And I'm sure those folks expected to go to an exclusively white heaven.

So those were the people of my great-grandfather's generation that I knew best. My great-grandparents, Durock and Anna Elizabeth, had three children: "Uncle" Durock, Edwin, and Martha Jane, who was my grandmother.

Grandmother (I always called her "Mother Des"), she married Peter DesVerney, a man maybe of Haitian descent from Charleston, South Carolina. There were four DesVerney brothers who had moved to New York: James, John, Will, and Peter. Their parents, Peter and Lavinia, were free blacks in Charleston. The elder Peter was apparently a very competent artisan, able to maintain his family well because of his skill as a carpenter. There's a family story that the elder Peter's father (he'd be my great-great-grandfather) was the man who betrayed Denmark Vesey to the whites. I've never tried to verify that story; I guess, I don't want to find out for sure that it's true. Anyway, the four DesVerney boys moved to New York where Peter met my grandmother, Martha Jane Turpin, and married her.

I remember my grandfather very well and very warmly: a tall, dark brown-skinned man, a builder like his father. It was he who built the row houses across the street from us. He was great for taking me for walks, walks that would end up at the Bronx Zoo or the Bronx Botanical Gardens or the nearby Poe Cottage, where Edgar Allen Poe had written "The Raven." When we'd get to the Poe Cottage, we'd usually just walk around it. It's a little white cottage on Bainbridge Avenue, I think. Grandfather just loved Edgar Allen Poe. I remember going inside one time; there were certain times of day when the caretaker would allow people to walk through. I remember some kind of bird figurine in the cottage. And I remember the plaque on the outside. When we went on these walks, he always recited "Ulalume" or "My Beautiful Annabel Lee" or "The Raven" or some other poem he liked. He'd recite them so dramatically, I grew to love those poems too. Later, when I came upon those poems in school, I felt they were old friends. Walking with him was wonderful. And fast! He was a long-legged somebody and I had to skip to keep up with him. And I'd be saying, "You're going too fast." And he would always tell me, "No, you're going too slow!" It was great fun.

Grandfather's brother, Will DesVerney, was a Pullman porter and had been friends with A. Philip Randolph for years before Randolph decided to organize the Pullman porters. Randolph's wife, a lady we called "Aunt Lucille," was a close friend of my grandmother, Martha Jane. So the Randolphs visited our house often. Both A. Philip Randolph and Uncle Will were very charming people, but Uncle Will was more of a "fancy man," a dandy, not as serious or as intelligent as Randolph. And, strangely, Uncle Will's wife, Naomi, was also an intellectual, but absolutely nuts about Uncle Will. Both Randolph and Naomi were idea people; I would see them sitting and talking at the house for hours. Yet both of them loved my apparently lightweight Uncle Will very much. I've often wondered if Randolph's friendship with Will and Naomi DesVerney and all the knowledge about the lives of Pullman porters that he must have gained from it were part of the reason he chose to organize that particular labor group. Because, you know, he was never a Pullman porter himself.[2]

Now, Grandmother's older brother, whom we called "Uncle Durock," was absolutely unique in that family. He was a very talented painter but very eccentric. While I was growing up, he lived either in our house or very nearby, so I got to know him well. And found him fascinating—so different from the rest of the family! He had no interest in school, had no ambition, did not like to work except at his painting, and was not even interested in basic material comforts. His angular features, pale skin, and flowing white hair always made me think of Arturo Toscaninni. In his later years, his "uniform" was long johns under a cheap, flannel, jacquard-patterned bathrobe and a straw hat with the top cut out. Now, this in a family that was fastidious about clothing, grooming, and style!

All his life, he said there were two things that would kill a man: taking a bath and getting married. So he assiduously avoided both. I don't remember his ever taking a bath when I was growing up. And my great-grandmother, his mother, told us this story about him in childhood: The house had just gotten the stationary bathtub—this is probably the late 1870s or early 1880s because Uncle Durock got himself born around 1873—and the children, Martha Jane, Edwin, and Durock, were required to take baths, of course. Uncle Durock would go in, put the latch on the door, and could be heard taking baths. Now, this one time, he was taking a rather long time and his mother wondered what he was doing in there. She could hear the great turmoil; as usual, he was making a lot of noise taking his bath. So she decided to look through the keyhole to see what was going on. And she saw Uncle Durock with a long stick in his hand standing some distance from the tub, so no water would get on him. And he was creating this swish-swash of water with the stick so people would think he was bathing! She realized then he had never been in that tub. So he hadn't bathed as a child and he wouldn't when I knew him as an adult. He always announced that his sweat kept him clean. He was a horror to his father, my great-grandfather, who always referred to him as "Durock, that stinking cuss!" Actually, he didn't smell bad; he smelled like turpentine because he used that for his painting.

What he painted best was horses. He would go to the racetrack because he loved the horses and he loved to bet. He had gotten a reputation for painting these horses that were owned by the wealthy folks who were out at Belmont Tracks. He'd get commissioned to paint the horses because anyone who saw a horse he painted wanted their horse to be done by him, too. He was just excellent. But instead of taking the commission and buying the proper paints and materials, he'd make the skies out of ironing starch and laundry bluing and use the extra money to bet on the horses. He didn't care about the skies, only the horses. So the skies on all of his paintings have lots of cracks in them. But the horses were done very lovingly with the best of paints. He had his own priorities.

Despite his talent, he never really made much of a living with his painting. And he didn't want to do any other kind of work. He took up with a woman who had come to our house looking for work. She was a German woman, Clara Elizabeth Brooks, with one son, Herman. Her husband had deserted her and gone back to Germany. Great-grandmother felt sorry for her and hired her as a domestic. So, in the late nineteenth century, you have this odd arrangement of a black family with a live-in German maid. She and Uncle Durock became involved and, by my time, they'd moved up to the North End Democratic Club on the corner of Webster Avenue and Fordham Road as caretakers, which meant they lived rent free and she did all the work. They'd had to move out of our house; the older folks in the family couldn't countenance his "living in sin." He definitely was not on good terms with the family. As the years passed, they produced seven children in addition to her son Herman. And, at the North End Democratic Club, all ten of them were living in two rooms.

One time, when I was in my early twenties, my cousin Lester and I made one of our sneak visits to Uncle Durock and his family on a Sunday. (We had to go there secretly because the family so disapproved of Uncle Durock, no one was supposed to visit him.) It was the middle of the day and we were surprised to find Uncle Durock in bed. We asked if he was sick and he said, "No, just resting up. You know, I have to go to work on Wednesday." And "work" was a WPA project where they put smut pots around the park. That was the extent of his work. And I think that's the only job he ever had. But, because of the Depression, times were so tight, he had to have something. There had been other times, though, that he just had to come to the house and ask his father for some money. Invariably, my great-grandfather would give it to him, but the gift was always accompanied by a request that he not come back anymore: "Don't you darken my doorstep again, you stinking cuss!" This was said in a soft low whisper; Great-grandfather never yelled. And, for a while, Uncle Durock wouldn't darken his doorstep—until the next time, because this was a ritual. He always knew he could depend on his father.

That household at the North End Democratic Club was as unbelievable as Uncle Durock. Another time when I was there, the whole family was engaged in a very loud discussion about what colors the walls of the rooms should be painted. Each had a different color that they wanted. They were all very opinionated and they all had very loud voices. Uncle Durock, in great disgust, finally yelled out, "Paint the son of a bitch black!" And he proceeded to do so. The next time I visited, both rooms were entirely black, even the ceilings! It was a cave. It didn't stay that way too long, though; I think the owners of the building objected.

Before Uncle Durock had taken up with Liz—this would have been back in the 1890s probably—he actually made the local newspaper with his eccentricity. The family had gone to their country house in Elmsford; they'd spend some time there every summer. They'd left Uncle Durock behind to take care of the house. He was just finishing a large canvas called "The Coronation of Queen Victoria" which was to be shown at the county fair. He always painted in the cellar, and when he went to take the painting out of the house, he found it was too large for the cellar door. So he knocked out part of the cellar wall— which was the brick foundation of the house! His picture was simply more important than that wall. When the family returned, they were horrified. But he really didn't care. He knew they were artisans so the wall would be rebuilt. And it was, of course. All of this was reported in a local Fordham newspaper called the *Home News*, I think. The headlines read, "Eccentric Bronx Painter Removes Side of House." So you see, Uncle Durock's eccentricity was well known in the area.

He finally did marry Liz though. When their children were grown and she was dying in the hospital, her son Herman, who was a Catholic, begged Durock to marry her. He said he wanted their union "blessed by a priest." And there's no reason why it shouldn't have been; it should have been long before that. So Durock reluctantly agreed. But it was really, he said, against his principles. They were both so old by then; they were ready for the grave. But he still didn't want to do it. Nevertheless, he did. And she died soon after. Since he was widowed and all his kids were grown—they all married rather unambitious whites except Emily, who married a very competent black man—since he was alone, my grandmother let Uncle Durock come back to the house. And Herman would routinely come to take Durock to Mass. Durock acquiesced for a while—until he was evidently fed up. And one day I heard him yell to Herman, "You go tell those priests to take all their Masses and stick 'em up their . . . !" So that was the end of his very brief period of churchgoing. A few years later, when he was dying of old age in the hospital, he swore he was dying because he had married Liz and because the nurse had forced him to take a bath.

I just loved Uncle Durock. And I think his presence in our family was good for me. He let me know that not everyone in the world is social and pleasant and fashionable and well-groomed. He raised a question in my mind about the importance of material things. His very existence taught me that some people live with entirely different values than those the rest of my family promoted. And those people may be fine people. I liked him. I liked his honesty and his total lack of concern about what other people thought of him. Being around such a character and being able to see his good qualities helped make me very adaptable. Yes, I do think that Uncle Durock was a wonderful character in our family.

Grandmother's other brother, Edwin, was entirely different. He was quite handsome, I was told, and quite brown. Grandmother was very, very fond of him. But I never saw him. Long before I was born, he was murdered in a saloon in the Tremont section of the Bronx. Because he was black. And Grandmother never got over that. Edwin was a Beau Brummel: a very good-looking somebody, always beautifully turned out—in contrast to his brother Durock. He had the manners and presence of his father and the skin color and features of his mother. His brother and sister, Uncle Durock and my grandmother Martha Jane, were absolutely Anglo-Saxon looking like their father. But Edwin was much more like his mother, Anna Elizabeth, in appearance. (He'd married the youngest daughter of Great-grandfather's brother, Augustus. Yes, Edwin's wife, Laura, was actually his first cousin. She'd come to live in our house initially to attend normal school and become a teacher. And she ended up marrying her cousin. They'd had one son, Irving.)

So one afternoon, Edwin had taken the streetcar to what was the last stop in the Bronx at that time, the Tremont area. He stopped at a saloon before walking the mile and a half to the house. It was a saloon frequented by the Irish who lived in that section. A fight broke out, a racial conflict: "You can't come in here, nigger!" (The family heard the details because there was a trial.) And they killed him. Bashed his brains in. He was killed for being black and daring to go into that saloon.

After that, his wife Laura "went into decline," as the family said. She died of consumption (which is what tuberculosis was called then) not long after he was murdered. And my grandmother, his older sister, was devastated. It was awful for her; she'd adored this younger brother. His death had such a severe effect on her that, although all of them had been very sedate Episcopalian people, she sought a religion that she felt would give her more solace. She became a Baptist and she started going all the way down to Waverly Place in lower Manhattan, to Abyssinian Baptist Church. That's where it was then. She started that connection which was to have a tremendous effect on my life. And it was the murder of her brother Edwin that caused it.

Grandmother had a lot of things that hurt her deeply. Her son, Alvin, had been the child that looked the most like her. He died in infancy and she grieved for him all of her life. Then her brother Edwin was murdered. And, later, her daughter Gertrude died of an ectopic pregnancy. I remember her talking about her "poor Alvin," her "poor Edwin," and her "poor Gertrude." That's how I know Alvin and Edwin's names. They died years before I was born but Grandmother was still grieving for them, still talking about them, when I came along. She had a lot of things that hurt her.

So, of her four children, only Uncle Oswald and my mother, Maude, survived into middle age. I talked about my early memory of that jubilant scene when Uncle Oswald returned from World War I. But what he did after that is very shadowy, because the family never discussed his occupation. He had to be involved in illegal activity because he and Godmother Mattie's brother, Mel Frazier, owned "The Nest," a Harlem speakeasy. Such clubs had sprung up everywhere in the wake of the Volstead Act that prohibited liquor. The speakeasies bought their liquor from gangsters. In Uncle Oswald's case, I heard Dutch Schultz's mob supplied him. (And Godmother Ethelle's brother, Happy Rhone, provided the music at the club.) What other illegal activities Uncle Oswald might have been in, I don't know. I do know he did well financially, had a nice home, was always well dressed when he visited us. And I know his job was never, never brought up. What's interesting is that, although he lived outside the law, he wasn't ostracized or even criticized by the family. He was as completely accepted as any other relative.

At that time, most of the black racketeers came from the class of blacks that was more privileged. Today, it's not like that; today, the gangsters come from poor backgrounds. But, back then, they were men of some skill and training who couldn't get decent-paying jobs simply because of their race. Many of them had come out of World War I with the attitude that they had the right to as much opportunity in this country as anyone else. But doors were closed to them. One of the few areas they could use their abilities to make a good living was in the rackets. And because the black community knew how racial barriers forced some of our men to do this, blacks did not push these men to the fringes of the black community; they were part of it: often treated like respectable citizens; often giving big donations to charities and churches. Not at all the kind of pariahs to polite society that black gangsters are today. No, Uncle Oswald remained very much a part of our family.

Oswald's sister, my mother, had an office job in a New Jersey insurance company before she got married. She traveled all the way from the Bronx, through the Tubes, over to Jersey City every morning. But, when she married, she stopped working and didn't resume again until I was twelve. Mama married my father, Clarence Harper, when she was twenty-one; and he, too, moved into the Bronx house. As I said before, his family and my mother's family had a long-time connection. As I said, his father, Peter Harper, and my great-grandfather had owned that barber shop together in Richmond, Virginia. And Daddy's first teacher was Marylou Turpin, another of Augustus Turpin's children (Laura's sister and Lester's mother). She had enjoyed him as a student and always referred to my father as "dear, dear Clarence." Daddy completed a year at Virginia Union before leaving the South at nineteen. He did a lot of traveling as a young man—he told us stories about Montana and working on a ship in the Bahamas—then he arrived in New York when he was twenty-five. He settled into a "waiter-in-charge" job on the Broadway Limited and the Twentieth Century railroad trains. They were crack trains that ran from New York to Chicago and New York to Philadelphia and Pittsburgh. This was the Pennsylvania Railroad.

For a short time, when I was in kindergarten, Daddy tried to start a restaurant. We moved to 143rd Street in Harlem and he opened his restaurant in Sunnyside, Long Island. He had picked up cooking from the chefs on the trains. I remember their coming to our house and all the men making these fantastic meals: squab on toast, wonderful popovers. Daddy had this restaurant for about a year and a half. Then Aunt Gertrude's death caused us to move back into the house; her three boys had to be cared for and mother took that responsibility. I don't think the restaurant was doing very well either; he was trying to offer very fancy food and didn't have enough capital to put into it. But the main reason we moved back was the boys. And Daddy gave up the restaurant and went back on the trains.

As I said, Aunt Gertrude, my mother's sister, died of an ectopic pregnancy. She'd married a man from Georgia, Walter Floyd, who worked in a swanky white hotel in Manhattan called the Bretton Hall. The black men who worked there had various kinds of service jobs—bellhops, busboys, nobody could be a desk clerk or anything like that, in those days—and they were all from Georgia. Uncle Walter was from Augusta. These men had an organization called the Bretton Hall Boys that did everything: they did charity work, had a baseball team, gave annual balls. It was a big part of Uncle Walter's social life. When Aunt Gertrude died, everyone felt her sons had to have a woman's care. And Mama, Gertrude's only sister and with small children of her own, was the obvious choice. So my boy cousins got "Aunt Maudie" as their new mother and "Uncle Clarence" as a part-time father along with their own father.

And Daddy treated us all very, very well. He was as attentive as he could be. About every three days, he'd hold "school" for the five of us. He'd be gone on the trains for three or four days at a time. But whenever he came home, we'd have "school." First, he was met at the corner by these five screeching kids running up to him. There was the hugging and the kissing and then each one of us getting a nickel for an ice cream cone. We'd get the cones at Max's candy store around the corner and lick them all the way home. Then we'd have supper and, after supper, we'd have lessons. Daddy had a blackboard and he'd do spelling, drawing (because drawing was his hobby); we'd go over our lessons from school, and he'd give us new stuff, sometimes reading to us from an encyclopedia. He did this all the way through our elementary school. I really enjoyed it. We had the best time with him. Those classes are one of my very precious memories.

As I said, Daddy's family was from Virginia too. He was one of five children of Peter and Martha Harper. (Yes, the same names were on both sides of my family: both grandfathers were named Peter and both grandmothers were named Martha.) Martha Hayes had been born a slave on the Langhorn plantation outside Richmond. She married Peter Harper, a free man of free parents, who died young while their five children were still fairly young. So the two older boys, Harry and my father Clarence, had to contribute to the family money. (Frank was a baby and the girls, Mary and Fanny, weren't expected to work.)

Harry and Clarence would go to Jefferson Market in Richmond and shell peas to be sold at the Market. And one day they met a homeless waif named Bill Robinson who was shelling peas too and dancing to make money. They brought him home and Grandmother Harper took him in. But his vocabulary wasn't at all to my grandmother's liking; he used a lot of vulgar street talk. She told him he would have to stop talking like that or leave. But he wouldn't stop, so he was asked to leave the house. But he and Daddy remained friends and, years later, he became very famous as "Bojangles" Robinson. In New York, we used to visit him and his wife, Fannie, in the Dunbar Apartments in Harlem. Daddy was always quite fond of him and he of my father.

I said my grandmother Martha Harper had been a slave on the Langhorn plantation. And indeed she was. But she was more than that. She was actually the daughter of one of the Langhorn men and an enslaved black woman named Mary. Mary was married to a black man, Richard Hayes. I don't know if he was free or not. And Richard and Mary had a son, Albert, before Martha was born. So Albert was actually Martha's half brother, and there were white children on the plantation who were her half siblings too. Richard and Mary's marriage continued after my grandmother was born and Grandma took the names Hayes. One can only speculate about the horrible way my grandmother was probably conceived. And the pain that conception must have caused Mary and Richard, this black husband unable to protect his wife.

One of the stories I remember this grandmother—who I called "Grandma Harper"—telling about her childhood was when, as a small slave girl who was a house servant, she was the mannequin for fitting the clothing of the white children who were her half sisters. The seamstresses would place my grandmother—who was six years old but a working member of the household—they would place her on top of the table while they pinned on the fabrics. That way, they avoided pricking the precious white flesh of the children who were going to wear the clothes. She said that, at the time, she had long cascading brown curls and these other children, two girls, had very stringy blonde hair that they were always trying to get some curl into. They'd use curling papers but, when they took them out, their hair would still be limp and straight. So, this day, they were so annoyed with "Marthy's" hair—that's what they called her—that they picked up the sheers in the sewing room and whacked off the curls. They were all around six or seven then. And they were standing there impatient, I guess, at even having to wait through this fitting, even though they were spared the discomfort of it. They had become cranky as children do and just cut off the little slave girl's hair. But as soon as they put the sheers down, Grandmother promptly picked them up and whacked off *their* hair. And the

two little white girls went screaming out into the hall to their common grandfather: "Grandfather, Grandfather, have Marthy whipped!" He looked at them
and asked what had Marthy done, and was told that Marthy had cut off their
hair. And he said, "What have you done to Marthy?" because, apparently, he
had some fondness for this little Marthy. And they said, "Oh, we cut off her
hair," like it was their absolute right to do so. And he put his hand on Marthy's
shoulder and said to them, "Then I'll not have Marthy whipped." And as
Grandmother always reported this story, her final comment would be, "I think
the old man gloried in my spunk," as though she felt he had a certain pride in
her for having the gumption to do this.

Grandmother did get certain benefits because she was a relative of slave
owners. Someone in that family bought her a whole string of rental houses,
tiny three-room dwellings that are called "shotgun houses" in the South. And
she received rent from them throughout her life. It was supposed to be an expression of indebtedness for her service but it was assumed by everyone in our
family that it was because she was related to these people. She also had the use
of a charge at Woodward and Lothrop's Department Store in Richmond that
she didn't have to worry about paying. My fourth birthday was spent with her
just before I went into kindergarten, and I remember that she went to that store
and bought the most beautiful embroidered white organdy and pink satin
sashes for me and then had an elaborate birthday party at Aunt Mary's house.
Aunt Mary was Daddy's sister and was by then the Dean of Women at
Hartshorn College, a women's college connected to Virginia Union University. That's when I first met Mary McLeod Bethune[3] because she was a friend
of both my Aunt Mary and of Maggie Lena Walker, the grandmother of one
of my closest playmates, Maggie Laura. Yes, this is the same Maggie Lena
Walker who was the first woman banker in this country, the first woman
banker of any race.[4] Her son, Russell, had married Godmother Hattie — my
mother's girlfriend — and their daughter, Maggie Laura, became my chum.

Now, when Maggie Laura and I were around six, we had what we thought
was the funniest experience. I was visiting my relatives in Richmond and staying with Maggie Laura for a few days so we could play together. Maggie Laura
and her parents lived with her grandmother, Maggie Lena Walker, who was
called "Miss Maggie." That house, at 110 Leigh Street, was so large, it could
easily accommodate many, many people. Large and, I would say, a little more
lavish than it should have been. I remember gold faucets, velvet drapes, a bust

of Beethoven, another bust of Maggie Walker, a marble fireplace, and a Due-
senberg equipped with a wheelchair ramp. (By then, Maggie Walker was crip-
pled—with arthritis, I think.) Anyway, this evening, Mary McLeod Bethune
was coming to visit her friend, Maggie Walker. Her arrival in Richmond by
train was late, after bedtime. So Alphonse, the chauffeur, was sent to the train
station to pick Mrs. Bethune up. Miss Maggie had retired to a guest bedroom
in order to make her own bedroom, with its elaborate canopied bed on a platform, available to Mrs. Bethune. The housekeeper, Polly, had prepared the
room and gone to bed, too. We were all asleep when Mrs. Bethune arrived.

The next morning, Polly brought breakfast on a silver tray to Mrs. Bethune's
room. As she entered, the first thing she saw was Mrs. Bethune's wig (they were
called "transformations" then and were not as commonly worn by women as
they are today). She saw it hanging on one of the bedposts. And she dropped
the tray and came screaming out of the bedroom, "Miss Maggie! Miss Maggie! The woman Alphonse brought in here last night ain't no woman! That's
a man!" Maggie Laura and I ran into the hall and Miss Maggie was trying to
calm Polly down and Polly just kept screaming and screaming. And Maggie
Laura and I *laughed!* Polly had never seen a woman wearing a wig before and
apparently hadn't seen Mrs. Bethune under the bedcovers. Because she did
have a good deal of hair of her own. Maggie Laura and I just thought this was
hilarious. But Miss Maggie didn't and, for laughing at Polly like that, we were
severely punished: we were made to sit in the corner of a room for most of the
day. But we kept looking at each other and smiling and giggling. The pun-
ishment didn't make that scene any less funny to us.

But what's sad about that story, when I thought about it as an adult, was that
Mrs. Bethune's natural hair was really quite beautiful. I was surprised a few
years later when I saw how lovely her hair was. It was soft, full white hair like
the loveliest kind of cotton. I was perplexed then as to why she had covered it
up. But as I grew older, I realized that it was because only straight, long hair
was considered attractive by most people. And the wig was Mrs. Bethune's
concession to that standard of beauty. She really felt she had to hide what I
thought was hair much, much prettier than that wig.

(But Mrs. Bethune wasn't alone in making this concession to the prevailing
standard of beauty. In my youth, not only did most of us black girls have standing appointments at the hairdresser's to have our hair straightened with heated
iron combs, but a number of the Jewish girls at my high school secretly went

to black hairdressers too. I knew at least seven who regularly had their kinky hair straightened. And, recently, an Asian friend confided that she's seriously considering having her eyes altered. Lord help us! How did we get bamboozled into denying ourselves the right to look like ourselves?)

Anyway, I was in and out of Virginia throughout my childhood, so I got to know the South and my father's family pretty well. It was from Grandmother Harper that I learned what it meant to be a slave girl. We visited the Goochland County plantation a few times (Great-grandfather and his siblings inherited that land, divided it up and, eventually, sold it), and that, too, gave me a feeling for the lives of my ancestors in the early 19th century. I was fortunate, in many ways, to have grown up in that family.

They were so diverse, I think it helped me be able to relate to all kinds of personalities and cultural styles. They were mainly Southerners, but there were many from the Caribbean; they were all skin tones from deep brown to pale pink; they were artisans and service people and teachers. Most of them were quite charming and outgoing but a few were stiff and retiring. All of them were articulate and curious about the world. Because they were so social (except Uncle Durock, of course), the house was always full of interesting folks. And they stayed abreast of what was happening to black folks: there were always copies of the NAACP's *Crisis* magazine and the Urban League's *Opportunity* lying around. Very early, I was accompanying some of these adults to political meetings. As I said, they really believed that you are your brother's keeper, especially your black brother.

However, they did have the prejudices about groups of people that most Americans had at that time: they thought Chinese people were sinister, that Jewish people were crafty, they talked about the Irish "micks," and warned us away from "Guineatown." They got these ideas from the movies, I guess, because when interacting with individuals from these groups, they showed absolutely no prejudice. But I can remember remarks around the house. Somehow, I never believed them. Later on, as a young adult who had gained some awareness of the political function of such prejudices—mainly through my friendship with Carlton Moss—I became very outspoken at home and would say things like, "I don't want anybody here saying anything like 'Jew somebody down' again! I don't like it!"

And some people around us had color prejudice. Not my great-grandfather; he wouldn't allow comments that suggested dark skin wasn't as pretty as light skin. Remember, he had just adored his African mother and had gone look-ing for a wife just like her. When he didn't find a suitable African woman, he'd married my brown-skinned great-grandmother. Nor would he allow people to talk about "good" hair and "bad" hair. He said any hair that was healthy was good. Mama's hair was long and kinky—below her waist—and her hair was considered pretty in our family, largely because of him. I'm grateful to my great-grandfather for his ideas about beauty. Hearing them was good for my mind. If a relative made a comment that suggested less African features were preferable, he'd chop 'em down so hard! And his view was the one I respected the most, I guess, even as a child. I was lucky to have him.

But there were more distant relatives and some close family friends that thought that it was kind of nice that their fair skin gave them certain privileges. Some had never been ill-treated in public because they weren't identifiably black. And they liked that. But, because of Great-grandfather and something in me, I rejected these color preferences. I mean, how could I think anything was superior to anything else when the people I loved most dearly were all dif-ferent colors? Mama was brown, Daddy was yellow, my brother was brown, Grandfather Peter DesVerney was real chocolate, Great-grandfather was Nordic-looking. They're all a part of me. How could I not feel close to, a part of every tone of black person there is? They were all in my family.

I was protected or blessed or something. I was able to absorb their positive values—helping others, education, excellence—and deflect their prejudices. Growing up knowing relatives who had been born in or close to slavery, then migrated north, gave me a living history of the experience of black people in the nineteenth century, north and south. It's as if my own experience of what it has meant to be black in this country began in the mid-nineteenth cen-tury—because their stories are so vivid to me—and is now going into the twenty-first century. I can see how their histories have had a great influence on the way I've interpreted and reacted to the important events of my lifetime. I can see how, even today, they are still very much a part of me.

III

"Young Thinkers" and Others

"I was encouraged . . . to be very much out in the world."

FOR THREE GENERATIONS, MY FAMILY MEMBERS were the only blacks in the local public schools. But when my cousins and my brother and I were there, it just seemed normal. Some of the teachers had taught my mother, and everyone just knew us and accepted us. I began school at P.S. #5 on 188th Street in the Bronx in 1920. I seemed to be pretty good at academics, so in elementary school I skipped two grades. At that school, I have memories only of being treated very well.

At the same time, I was taking dance and music lessons in Harlem. That didn't last very long, though, because I'm just not musical. I went to Grace Giles' Dancing School on 7th Avenue between 130th and 131st Streets. The classes were held in a loft above the Lafayette Theater. Grace Giles was the protege of Florence Mills, a wonderful black performer who danced all over the world. I had this extraordinary teacher but no talent. When they had the dance recital at Manhattan Casino, Miss Giles just dressed me up fancy and let me pose. I remember in one number being dressed up as a vamp, a five- or six-year-old vamp. The other kids were dancing to "St. Louis Woman." Godmother Ethelle had made my costume: it was a burgundy-colored satin dress off one shoulder. And I had a rhinestone tiara. All I was asked to do was walk like a vamp. Another number was "My Sweet Little Alice Blue Gown" and they rigged me up in a blue chiffon costume and put me out front, but, again,

I wasn't required to dance. After the first recital, my parents stopped the dancing lessons; they realized they were wasting their money.

Then they enrolled me in piano lessons which lasted until I was eleven or so. My piano teacher was Jessie Covington, a marvelous pianist who was going to be a concert pianist until she gave up her career to marry Alfred Dent (who later became the president of Dillard University). I don't remember much about the lessons themselves, and I can't play today. But that's because, as I said, I'm just not musical. What I remember most is what happened after each lesson.

The Martin Smith Music School—that's where Jessie Covington taught—was located on 136th Street in Harlem and my father always took me to my piano lessons. He'd drop me off, and while I was having my lesson, he'd visit with his old friend, Red Allen, a "manufacturer" of bathtub gin. (These were Prohibition days.) Then he'd pick me up and be very nice with all the people because he was alright then, not too far gone. Then he'd take me to a nearby ice cream parlor called the "Sugar Bowl." And he'd tell me I could order whatever I wanted and he'd say, "Baby, I'll be back in a minute. I just want to go here and see . . ." and there was a rush of talk that would follow. I was bright enough to get something very big that would last a very long time. But there wasn't enough ice cream in the place to fill up the time I'd have to wait for him. He'd be back in Red Allen's—I knew that even then—and when he finally returned to the ice cream parlor, he'd be in no shape to get us home. I had to see that we got on the right subway and "El" trains, that we paid the correct amount, the rest of it. It was no good. I was a caretaker to my parent very early, the same parent who when sober was a wonderful Daddy.

After elementary school, I attended Paul Hoffman Junior High School, also in the Bronx. That was a special experience because the principal, Angelo Patri, was so extraordinary. It was unusual for a junior high school to have the things we had: a woodworking shop for boys, handsomely equipped kitchens for the girls, wonderful sewing classes, music classes, a huge gym, a heated pool, art classes, pottery-making classes. These are things that other junior high schools just didn't have; some high schools did, but no junior highs. And the students could choose their courses; that was unusual too. I took everything: art, dressmaking, cooking, and all the academic classes. I especially liked writing and English. And I was in what they called "rapid advancement" where you took a year and a half's work every year. So I finished in two years instead of three.

The principal, Angelo Patri, was a renowned child psychologist and understood the importance of children having self-esteem. He preached having pride in whatever ethnic group you were a part of and he especially emphasized Italian pride since so many of the students were Italian and there was such prejudice against Italians at that time. Many of these kids had come from the rather poor Italian area called "Guineatown," in the Arthur Avenue part of Fordham. They were the children of pushcart peddlers and didn't have much feeling of self-worth. And some had come from elementary schools where they'd been drilled in a poem called "Giuseppi, the Barber," a very insulting poem done in Italian-American dialect. And Mr. Patri just didn't want to hear any of that because he felt it contributed to the kids' shame of being Italian. At that time, many teachers were also telling us that the current-day Italians were not in any way related to the ancient Romans. Can you believe that? Some books said that too! So, at assemblies, Angelo Patri would say, "What's your name?" to some youngster. And they would say whatever Italian name. And he'd say, "Do you know. . . ?" and he'd go off on some accomplishment of the Romans. He was very insistent about making them know that this was a continuing race of people, that their ancestors had achieved a great deal.[1]

That was good for them in the same way that it's good for us and our kids to know what Frederick Douglass and Crispus Attucks and Martin Luther King did, and to know when they see a beautiful antebellum home that it's only beautiful because black labor created it. I still have these three chairs that were built on my great-great-grandfather's plantation—they're put together with wooden pegs—and I tell my children their forebears did this. And we'd go to New Orleans and we'd see the wrought iron in the French Quarter and I'd remind them that it was enslaved black people who did that beautiful work. It's been a special joy to me that my children have been to Africa and have seen the ancient cultures of West Africa and the even older cultures of Ethiopia and what was called "Cush." And, right now, we're trying to locate the ship on which Great-great-grandmother was brought to Baton Rouge from Africa. It's very important for us to know enough to reinforce black kids in the way that Angelo Patri reinforced Italian kids.

Now, there's another interesting event that happened when I was in junior high school. In that same area of "Guineatown" lived many people who weren't Italian. A number of Jewish families lived there also, including the family of one of my cousin's good friends, Julius Garfinkle. They lived either on Arthur Avenue or Bathgate. Julius was a teenager, a little older than I, and he was very active in school plays. There were a lot of tough kids in that area and Julius was one of the toughies. But he channeled his toughness into acting. They did "Macbeth," "Julius Caesar," many plays. Now, Julius had a very strong crush on Sylvia, the daughter of Max the candy store owner. (Max's store was around the corner and they lived right across the street from us.) But Sylvia became ill with "consumption." Tuberculosis was widespread then. She was sent to Otisville Sanitarium, the same place my brother Jack would later go. And she died there. Our family hadn't heard about her death until the morning after she died, when my grandmother went out to our backyard and found Julius stretched out in our hammock, just sobbing. He was brokenhearted that the girl he cared for so much had just died. Do you know who that was? He later became very famous as John Garfield. And he remained a very decent person. Later, when I was working for the NAACP and he was a movie person, I contacted him to take out a $500 lifetime membership.[2]

During those early years, there was also a lot of traveling: Daddy would plan trips for us on the railroad, and my godmothers were great for taking me along with them on their vacations. When I finished junior high school, Godmother Mattie took me to Haiti. But, frankly, I got absolutely nothing out of it. I didn't understand what all the "to-do" was about Cristophe and the Citadel. I was too young. (I only appreciated that as an important part of black history when I went back as an adult.) Then, when I was in high school, she took me to Cuba. I got a little more out of that trip. I remember the hotel and the people speaking Spanish, and I recall the wonderful music. But, for me, there wasn't much value in that trip either. I don't think I was too good at absorbing foreign cultures and places. A child traveling wants pretty much what she had at home. But I really enjoyed the places I saw later under the aegis of the Red Cross because, as an adult, I began to look for things and I made historical connections.

I made many trips within the United States because Daddy's job gave his family big discounts on train fares and also because our family really believed travel was broadening and necessary to our education. We'd travel every sum-

mer, to Chicago, to the 1933 World's Fair, to Oklahoma. I remember our first
trip to California in 1930: the trains were not air conditioned and all the dust
and soot blew in on you. The train must have been run by soft coal. I remember there were these four nuns in the car with us, and while we got
sweatier and just full of coal soot, they remained pristine-looking and clean.
And we just marveled at them; Mama said, "How do they do that?"

On another trip to California, we stopped off and saw the Petrified Forest
and Yosemite. Daddy would write out the itinerary, with instructions on everything, even which food to order on which train. He always routed us above the
Mason-Dixon line so we wouldn't have to deal with the Jim Crow trains in the
South. Mama and I would share a berth. It was so cozy and secure sleeping
with her. These trips were wonderful. My brother Jack didn't travel as much.
He wasn't as interested and often would prefer to stay home with his baseball
team than go on a trip. I was the nosey one.

As a child, I was also always being taken to lectures, plays, and political
meetings. All of us kids were—but not usually as a group. This child went with
this adult to this event. One of us would be singled out and we'd go. Sometimes we didn't know what was going on but we always seemed to enjoy these
outings. It was a very active family and the kids were included in the activities.
Mother began taking me with her to NAACP meetings when I was about seven
and she continued to take me throughout my childhood. They'd meet in various Harlem churches because the offices—the headquarters at 69 Fifth Avenue or the New York branch office on 135th Street—neither was large
enough for mass meetings. And Mama subscribed us to the *Brownie's Book*,
the magazine that DuBois put out for children. So I was introduced to the
NAACP at a very young age and, as I said, I was scribbling very young also. So,
you see, the seeds for my ending up as Publicity Director for their national office later on were planted pretty early.

Throughout my childhood, I was always attending churches. My family was
mainly Episcopalian, except for my grandmother who had converted to Baptist after her brother was murdered. I was christened at St. Philip's Episcopal
Church, a black church in Harlem, and I attended that church until I was
about six. Then, because my godmothers Hattie and Mattie were friends with
the woman who ran the kindergarten Sunday school at Mother Zion AME, I
started going there and continued until I was eleven. During that period, Paul
Robeson's brother, Reverend B. C. Robeson, was the pastor at Mother Zion.

But I didn't get to know Paul Robeson until I was on the Writers Project. Those two Sunday schools were like most, I think: it was mainly a matter of having a loving teacher who kind of led you in the right direction, gave you a grounding in morals about not lying or stealing. For me, I can see in retrospect that the churches were also important because they were black institutions. For a little black girl growing up in a white neighborhood and attending all-white schools, attending black churches helped keep me in touch with my racial identity and with my own people.

Those Sunday schools were okay, but the real excitement began when I started going to the Sunday school at Abyssinian Baptist Church. My teachers there were wonderful. I've stayed in touch with three of them: Thelma Byrd, a very wonderful somebody; Elizabeth Ross Haynes, who was an extremely knowledgeable social worker; and Ethel Carr, who just died in 1986.

Because of the social concern of the minister, Old Man Powell (Adam Clayton Powell, Sr.), this was a living church. By then, it was on 138th Street in Harlem. When my grandmother had started going there, it was down on Waverly Place in the Bowery, and Fats Waller's father had been the assistant pastor. Then it moved to 40th Street in the Tenderloin district. But the church was able to buy property and build a beautiful large structure on 138th Street in Harlem and that's were I went. It had to be large; by then, it was the largest Protestant congregation in the country. And one of the liveliest, I think. Our Sunday school didn't spend a whole lot of time on the Bible; we talked mainly about the current social issues of black people. It came down from the pastor that you had to be concerned about the civil rights of our people, so we'd be talking about the fact that no blacks were hired in the shops on 125th Street and things like that. Also, during that period the Depression hit, so we'd talk about folks' economic problems and the fact that blacks should be included in the government programs. You must remember that, before the Depression, conditions in Harlem were not bad.

A group of us formed the Young Thinkers club. We'd meet during the week, read and discuss books, we'd submit articles to the *Advance*, the church newspaper, we even picketed. I think the first thing I ever had published was in the *Advance*. I don't remember the topic, but all our articles were about contemporary social problems. We were always writing to protest about something. By then, Adam Jr. was back from Colgate and had become assistant pastor. He was six years older than I, older than all of us in the Young Thinkers, but he worked well with us, giving us books to read, making suggestions for our activities. Adam was someone who believed there should be a whole lot of joy in living, but, at the same time, he was very much interested in human beings and deeply concerned about injustices toward black people. It was he who organized the picket lines on 125th Street that some of us Young Thinkers joined. We were protesting the discriminatory hiring practices of these white-owned shops whose clientele was mainly black. Adam had a wonderful library and encouraged us to read by sharing his books. He'd bring a handful of books down to our meeting and say, "Here's something good to read." I remember the first time I read Aldous Huxley's *Brave New World*, it was Adam's book.

Another thing he did was to bring psychiatrists to the church to be available to anyone who needed to talk to them. This was during the Depression and he felt counseling and lectures on how to cope would be helpful. The church paid for that; the services were free to members. Also, during the Depression, I remember the church dispensed free food and clothing to anyone who came for it. Members would donate the clothing and the food was bought by the church. There wasn't any rigmarole about whether you qualified or not. If you came in the morning and it was there, you could have it. There was a lot of goodness happening in that church. My family's interest in social issues and sense of responsibility for others laid the foundation for me, but I think it was in the loving, activist atmosphere of Abyssinian Baptist Church that my social concern and involvement really blossomed.

During my teen years, my social life became much more black. As I said, the American Girls' Club in the Bronx was all white, except for me. During my teens, not only did I become active with the Young Thinkers but I also went to a much more integrated high school in Manhattan and was part of an all-black girls club called the "Rainbow Girls." Many of the girls in the club also attended Abyssinian Baptist, but it was more social than the Young Thinkers. I've stayed in touch with many of the women who were in the Rainbow Girls—Carrie McHenry, Bernice Richardson, Ruby Hall, Melrae Harris, Fannie Ansley, Marjie Dabbs; they're still my good friends today. I suppose my continued contact with those women, while I've lost contact with the women who were in the American Girls' Club, has to be attributed to the bonding around racial concerns. I sometimes wonder if it's possible in this country with its pervasive sickness around race, for a black–white friendship to be as honest, as true, and deep as same-race friendships.

Abyssinian Baptist Church hired me for my very first job at age twelve! It was to teach summer kindergarten from 9:00 to 12:00 each morning for five weeks. I received ten dollars a week. And that fifty dollars was adequate to pay for my summer camp. I went to Camp Minisink during August, a predominantly black camp that my grandmother, Mother Des, had helped found near Port Jervis, New York. The camp was under the auspices of the New York City Mission Society. It's a lovely place; I sent my own children there in 'sixty-one.

Do you know how I qualified for the job at Abyssinian? Mama took extension courses in the evening at Columbia. And from the time I was ten until I was twelve, she took me along with her to her classes on religion and philosophy at the Union Theological part of Columbia. (Among our teachers was Harry Emerson Fosdick. I still remember his saying, "If there is something you want from life, hold a picture in your mind's eye and move toward it.") Now, only she was enrolled; the classes were for adults. But at the end of the course, they gave me a certificate too! So I was really qualified to teach church kindergarten at age twelve!

One of the sad things I became aware of during my teens was the deep prejudice of black Americans against West Indians. Some people I knew called them "monkey chasers" and dismissed Marcus Garvey[3] and his movement because the people involved were mainly from the Caribbean. I can remember watching the Garvey parades from Godmother Mattie's window on 7th Avenue near 135th in Harlem. The parades were very, very colorful and the black Americans around me, including Godmother Mattie, were so disdainful. Except for A. Philip Randolph; he could see some merit in what Garvey was saying. I guess the idea of black unity appealed to him. And he admired the way they really put their pennies to some use and tried to start businesses. West Indians, generally, did this, not just the Garveyites.

My own memory of Garvey is one of just being annoyed with him. As a child — and that's when I first encountered him — I knew he was prominent and led marches and had some big organization. But that means nothing to a kid. What bothered me about him was that he played "jacks" too well. You see, I'd see him when I went to 129th Street in Harlem to visit my girlfriend, Fannie Ansley. Garvey lived right across the street from her. And we'd be out playing. The boys would be playing stickball or cops and robbers or something, screaming and yelling. The girls would be jumping rope or playing jacks or just sitting on the stoop, talking. And Garvey would come out of his house and go over to the boys. And he'd lecture them. He'd interrupt their game and tell them they didn't need to be playing, they needed to be "improving" themselves. (And that's what he called his organization, wasn't it? The Universal Negro *Improvement* Association.) He would lecture them sternly. The word to describe him is "pontifical." And they'd want to say, "Oh, man, get away from here." But they'd been taught to say, "Yes, sir," to adults. So that's what they would say to him: "Yes, sir."

Then he'd see the little girls: me, Fannie, Dorothy Hadley, Virginia Alexander. This is when we were about ten or so. And he'd come over to us. I remember one time, we were playing jacks. You know, you throw this little ball up and scoop up the jacks while the ball is in the air. And he'd just play with us. He never lectured us girls; he never told us we were supposed to be doing something else beside playing. He encouraged us girls to be numbskulls, really. I know he had women in his organization, but maybe they were just handmaidens, dressed up in their purple and white. It didn't seem to occur to him that girls needed to be taught. He wanted to develop the leadership of males. I didn't care about that at the time, though. What I cared about was that, like any adult, he was more dexterous than we were and kept beating us at jacks. He was pleasant enough; I liked him okay. But I wanted him to go away. He was just too good at jacks.

But I never picked up any prejudice against West Indians. At one time, I was even engaged to a West Indian. This appalled some of my family's friends. Not only was he West Indian but he was dark brown. Godmother Mattie said to my mother, "Maude, what is that child thinking of? What will the children look like?" But neither Mama nor I cared about the color thing or the West Indian issue. But, I must admit, such prejudice was very much a part of the New York black American community at that time.

There was a young man in the Young Thinkers who was especially opposed to West Indians, always saying ugly things about them. And it was later discovered that all his folks were from the Caribbean. These stupid attitudes of the time you live in and the people around you can do a lot of damage to folks.

The parties I went to as a teenager were mainly those given by people in the Young Thinkers and the Rainbow Girls. Not that I ever really attended the parties. You see, my father had this strange habit of getting me to the parties long before they started and then insisting it was time to leave just when people were arriving. Why he did that, I don't know. He had this idea that young ladies should attend parties at a particular time and that these parties were scheduled too late. The parties were usually scheduled to begin around 9:00, but I would have gotten there around 7:30. So I would help put the stuff on the Ritz crackers and help the hostess prepare. Daddy would have dropped me off and gone to one of his usual places to wait for me. And just as the first kids were coming to the door, he'd return, a little tipsy. "Daddy, couldn't I stay a little longer?" never worked. He'd tell me about the hour's ride home on the subway. "But this isn't a school night. This is Friday," I'd say. Then he'd tell me what I was scheduled to do on Saturday. As I say, he was a very persuasive, very charming man, my father. And I ended up thinking, well, maybe he was halfway right. I didn't want to agitate him either because of his inebriation. You do become your parent's parent. But I still resented it. I would hear afterwards about the interesting things that happened: who played spin the bottle and who got to kiss whom. But I never got to be at any of those parties.

My move from junior high school to high school was a big social jump because I went from predominantly white Paul Hoffman Junior High in Fordham to mildly integrated Wadleigh High School in Manhattan, a school that prepared girls for entering Hunter. The curriculum was only college preparatory: Latin, French, history, three years of science, three years of math. I went there not only because it was good academically but also because my close friends, my black friends, were going there. When I was in junior high school in the Bronx, I had sometimes visited P.S. 136 in Manhattan because Jessie Fauset, the black novelist, was teaching there and my girlfriends invited me to join them in her classes. These friendships that were based in the Abyssinian Baptist Church were very strong and were part of the reason I ended up at Wadleigh. The "brother" school, DeWitt Clinton High, was in another area of the city so we rarely saw the boys who went there. Most of us weren't dating yet, anyway. Boys were not a part of our school world and the boys in the Young Thinkers were more like pals. Some of us might have had crushes, but no one in our group was dating. There were girls at the high school—not black—who were more "progressive," shall we say. They'd meet fellas after school in the ice cream parlor. But not us. I gave a few parties in our back yard with lemonade and good food. I guess those were the only parties I got to stay through. But no dating for most of us.

The few folks that did branch out and were doing some dating horrified the rest of us. We had one dear friend who had always been unhappy because she had not known her natural father, her mother's first husband, and did not get along with her stepfather. She was looking for somebody to care about her and she became pregnant during high school. My friend Fannie and I told Mama about this—because you could talk to Mama about anything—and Mama was horrified. What upset Mama was her age, only fifteen. Fannie and I ended up accompanying the girl to the doctor who performed an abortion. The idea of an abortion didn't upset me then and it doesn't now. I've always felt women should have that right. In that circle of people, there were a number of Mama's married friends who went through abortions. It was not considered very chic, I guess, to have more than two children. Abortions were risky—although it was always a qualified doctor who performed them—but it was the only way to curb having more children than you could handle.

Every summer during high school, I worked. I contributed to the house and bought myself some things. Because Mama was working for the New York State Employment Agency, I had access to information on available jobs. One summer, I did cleaning work in a very expensive dress shop called "Polly's, 480 Park Avenue." People like Sylvia Sidney and Joan Crawford were the clientele. My main responsibility was to run the carpet sweeper and keep foot tracks off the wall-to-wall carpeting. I also put lovely linen napkins on a silver tray and put champagne in a glass to take to these folks that came in there to buy their dresses.

Another summer, Fannie and I got a job together in the garment district. We were hired for hand sewing. Our job was to chain stitch the loops on the sides of dresses where the belt would go through. These were expensive dresses and these loops had to be done by hand. We were told that we'd average some amount of money that was reasonably attractive to us, maybe twelve dollars a week or so. And we thought, how nice! But nobody told us that it was piecework and the amount of money we'd make was dependent on how much we produced.

So, Fannie and I sat together and began our first "factory" job. We'd make a loop on a dress and then talk. We were always very gabby and always had plenty to talk about. So we talked and talked. And occasionally made another loop. When the woman would come by to pick up the completed dresses, we'd sweetly say, "Not yet," and go on talking. And Fannie said, "I don't know why people complain about factory work. This is nice!" We just relaxed, had a good time, and occasionally made a loop. By the end of the day, we'd completed maybe half a dozen dresses apiece; and you were supposed to do, I don't know, maybe two hundred or something. They fired us that night! We were so surprised! It never occurred to us that no one would pay us for doing a little bit of sewing and a whole lot of talking. Teenagers can be so flaky.

I worked every summer. While there was no feeling of poverty in my family, there was a very strong work ethic. So everybody worked; and the money came in; and we lived well. But it wasn't a matter of 'I've got to find a job.' We teenagers liked being grown-up enough to contribute to the family. At that age, if you heard about a job, it was thrilling to see if you could go fill it. So I worked every summer, but there was nothing burdensome about that.

Thus, my high school years were very active: the Young Thinkers at Abyssinian, the Rainbow Girls, rather demanding academic classes, and various summer jobs to contribute to the house. Most of these things were in Manhattan and many were in Harlem. But Harlem was a very different place then from what it is now. People lived quite comfortably—even those who had service jobs—and houses and apartment buildings were kept in good repair all over. Back then, the borders of black Harlem would have been 125th Street to 145th Street. "Sugar Hill," Washington Heights, was then considered an extension of Harlem where well-to-do blacks were beginning to move in the 1920s. But when I was growing up, "Striver's Row" (139th Street) and the "Block Beautiful" nearby were the nicest areas that were all black. They had lovely Stanford White houses, trees and the people in that area were the professionals—writers, teachers, lawyers—and were always beautifully dressed. But everyplace in Harlem, at that time, was safe and clean and well attended to. It wasn't until the thirties and the influx of a large number of poor rural Southerners that apartments became overcrowded and the problems of poverty became apparent.

So the Harlem of my youth was very pleasant, much nicer than many other parts of New York—like the "Tenderloin" where the poor Irish lived—and I was entirely comfortable going in and out of it daily. It did mean, however, that an hour's ride each way on the subway was a part of almost every day's activities. I was fortunate not to have chores at home to do too: the older people and Miss Frances took care of the house, the cooking, and most of my laundry. I did love to sew, however, and from junior high on, I was always making something to wear for myself. But housekeeping was not something I was expected to do, and it's still not something I'm very good at.

Mama didn't do much around the house either. As I said, she was always more of a girlfriend than anything else. I realized I never really had a mother in her; I had a sister. Was she ever allowed to grow up fully in that environment? I've wondered if perhaps the reason Daddy moved us to 143rd Street and tried to start a restaurant was because he felt he needed to be more assertive, more independent than Uncle Walter had been. And I've wondered if his painting pictures all the time after we moved back into the house, might not have been one of the ways he escaped from a situation in which he was very much subordinate to his wife's parents and grandparents. Did that situation exacerbate his problem with alcohol? It certainly wasn't the cause—his father and his brothers had problems with alcohol too—but it couldn't have helped. I'll never know how my parents felt about living there. But I do know that one effect it had on me was that I was never made to feel that housework was what I was put on this earth to do. I was encouraged to be creative, to look pleasing, to think, to try to be charming, to stay informed about what's going on in the world, to help others (especially those less fortunate), to be very much out in the world.

And that's what I was doing in my teens and have continued to do—no matter what was going on in my personal life, no matter how much pain I've felt, physical or emotional. I've stayed out in the world, stayed engaged, and tried to help people where I could. At times, I think I've used service to others to escape pain, or maybe as a way of bouncing back, a kind of healing mechanism. I just know I've never stopped living a very social—in the broadest sense—life. And I can see that style already formed by my mid-teens.

From Wadleigh, I went right into Hunter College in 1931 as an English major. It may seem odd that I was starting college at the beginning of the Depression, but, for some reason, the economic strains of the society didn't effect our family. No one lost his or her job and our existence stayed as it had been. I was aware of the bread lines and people on the street selling apples, though. Being at Abyssinian kept me in touch with problems in Harlem.

Now, a Harlem character that gained prominence during the Depression was Father Divine. He had what he called "kingdoms" all over Harlem. They were soup kitchens where people could get very good, well balanced meals for just seven cents or a dime. I encountered him only one time. Jack and I had gone to visit my grandfather's brother, John DesVerney, who was an Episcopal priest in Quogue, Long Island. We heard that Father Divine was holding one of his camp meetings in Oyster Bay and drove over to hear him. He held these meetings outdoors under the trees. Along the side of the seating area were long tables covered with white linen and just full of wonderful food. And he preached and preached, mesmerizing the people, who seemed to keep coming in droves from every direction. And what was amazing was that no matter how many people came and ate, the tables stayed full of food. And he would bless it and preach on and on. He spoke a kind of gibberish that made no sense to us but perhaps it did to his followers. And the supply of food was endless. We left there baffled. Uncle John said, "What was that man doing?" Father Divine had created a very strange, mysterious atmosphere.

College, for me, was really like an extension of high school. Because I was still living at home and riding the subway to school, and because so many of the same people I'd known at Wadleigh went to Hunter—Fannie Ansley, Marjie Dabbs, Harriet Baltimore Brown, Dorothy Hadley—my life didn't change that much from high school to college.

My family had always expected me to go to Hunter because my grand-mother had gone there when it was called a "normal" school for the training of young women teachers. It was an academically excellent public school. But, for me, going to Hunter was something of a disappointment. Abyssinian had offered me a scholarship to Fisk but my folks wouldn't let me go out of town. I was tickled to death when I got the offer and I would have loved to have gone, but they—actually, it was the grandparents holding the reins on Mama more than Mama holding the reins on me—they didn't like the idea of my leaving home. Why would I want to go that distance? What was the idea? Plus, there was this business of my intermittent illnesses that they were calling St. Vitus' dance then. And they felt that somebody who apparently wasn't the strongest something physically needed to stay close to home. And anybody who'd been constantly monitored the way I was wouldn't have had sense enough to make too much of a squawk. So there wasn't much "to-do" about it; I just went to Hunter.

The summer between my freshman and sophomore years was an interest-ing one. Mama was still at the employment agency and she got a call about a job for an "attractive, light-skinned young colored woman" to do light house-keeping. At that time, it wasn't against the law to request a person of a partic-ular race, skin tone, and age. Since Mama thought her child was attractive, she sent me to this job in one of the nicest parts of Fifth Avenue. I was seventeen, I guess. The caller had said it would be mainly dusting and straightening up and that they would supply a uniform. So when I got there, to this very well-kept and elegant old house, I was ushered on in by an Oriental woman who looked me up and down. I saw some very stunning-looking women emerge from some of the doors, expensively dressed but with a trashiness about them too. Then I saw some men moving about, very distinguished looking folks. And I started to get this feeling that something wasn't right here.

I was taken into an office and interviewed by a man. The interview was as one would expect, until he asked if I would be nice to the guests. He didn't say "customers," he said "guests." And I asked him what he meant—"Who are the guests?"—and he and the Oriental woman exchanged glances. And then the lights went on in my head. This was a brothel! These people were so subtle and the place was not at all vulgar in decoration; there wasn't anything that would make you think of a bawdy house. But I had picked up—I think it was because I was so blooming bookish, intellectually worldly though not street smart—I had sensed something was wrong the minute I stepped in the door. Mama had sent me to a whorehouse! So when he asked if I could start work right then, I said, "No, would tomorrow do?" and I got myself out of there. And then, I told Mama, "Maudie, you know what . . . ?" She was so upset because anything could have happened.

Then she sent me on a real job that I ended up enjoying immensely. I was a babysitter, what was then called a "mother's helper," to a woman, Helen Deutch, on Riverside Drive. Essentially, I babysat all day for her two boys and then put an egg on toast for them for supper. But to make their day interesting, I'd take them out to the park. And to keep from having to traipse all over the world after them, I'd tell stories. After a while, other children who were in the park with caretakers began to gather around and listen to my stories. And, when it rained, the superintendent of a building two doors down from the Deutch's offered to let me use an empty street-level apartment so the kids wouldn't get wet. And the attendants of the other children brought them in there too. Well, the parents started coming down to see what was going on. Because they liked how I handled the kids and told stories, they asked if I would continue to entertain their children also every afternoon. I realize now that I may have caused some people to lose their jobs because, for part of the day at least, they were no longer necessary. But they hadn't been doing anything with the children, anyway; they weren't as interesting or as stimulating as I got to be eventually. And I began to collect fees from the parents of all these little kids. There must have been nine or ten of them. My employer, Mrs. Deutch, never knew I had this little racket going. It turned out to be quite lucrative and lots of fun for me. I've always liked talking with children. Later, in Italy, when I had time off from Red Cross work, I'd often spend time with the Italian kids. And I would have a headstart program in my backyard here in Alexandria long before the federal Headstart.

After that summer, I returned to Hunter for my sophomore year but was not able to finish it. I got sick again. And this was the worst it had ever been. Four years earlier, when I was fifteen, I had missed some school because of the hurting, some twitching, aching all over. I wasn't hospitalized but I was in bed for about a month. They were saying it was St. Vitus' dance. Now, at nineteen, in addition to the aching and twitching, there was this awful business of the legs giving out, too, and a raging fever. So, at first, they said it was rheumatic fever and put me in Brooklyn Hospital because Randolph Granger, one of my doctor cousins, was attached to it.

The pain in my joints was so crazy they couldn't even let a sheet touch me. And their procedure for handling that was to put a cage over the bed and a sheet over the cage. So I was covered but not touched. The pain was just excruciating. And they still weren't sure what it was. At one point, they questioned me about whether I'd traveled to South America, thinking I might have picked up some tropical disease. Then, they thought it might be polio. Later when I came to Louisiana, the renowned specialists at Oschner Clinic said I had sickle cell anemia. But, in the seventies, they concluded it definitely wasn't that. Doctors can't always pinpoint disease; they're fumbling a lot of the time. Anyway, during the "it might be polio" period, they put my leg in a cast because it was drawing up. They did this sometimes to people with polio, stuck them in a cast. And they left that cast on for months. A sore was developing on my heel and they wondered if there were sores further inside, so they took the cast off. And when they did, there was nothing much but the bone. All the skin came off just like a snake's skin, all dried out from the fever. It was ghastly.

Besides the hurting and the atrocity of this leg, my most vivid memory of that hospital stay over fifty years ago is a very peculiar one. I shared my room with a very old woman who was apparently close to death. When people were not expected to last, they would close the curtain all the way around. Both of us had our curtains pulled around our beds—that's how bad off I was. But the curtain between our beds was sometimes slightly parted and, as sick as I was, I was still nosy and it picked me up to look at her. But then one time, when her gown was being changed, I saw the most disturbing thing: her pubic hair was gray. I became so alarmed and upset. It had never occurred to me that that hair would turn gray. Somehow that made me feel so sad: the dramatic changes caused by the aging process! All those old people I'd been living with must have gray hair there too. It was profoundly distressing to me and I don't, even today, fully understand why. But it is my most vivid memory of that hospital stay. People were visiting me all the time; doctors and nurses must have been constantly coming and going; but, aside from the hurting, this incident is what stands out in my mind. Like Countee Cullen's poem about his visit to Baltimore:

> Now I was eight and very small,
>   And he was no whit bigger,
> And so I smiled, but he poked out
>   His tongue, and called me, "Nigger."
>
> I saw the whole of Baltimore
>   From May until December;
> Of all the things that happened there
>   That's all that I remember.

Seeing that age changes every part of our bodies, even the most private, is what I remember most about that stay in Brooklyn Hospital.

Because my parents couldn't afford to keep me in that hospital, I was moved by ambulance to St. Luke's after about two months. A friend of Mama's who had been a butler to some millionaire for years had been given lifetime use of an endowed hospital bed at St. Luke's by his employer. So he allowed my family to use it as long as I needed it. St. Luke's was an excellent hospital, but they couldn't figure out what was wrong either. I did, however, begin to feel less pain there and the fever lowered. It started to seem like I might not expire after all. I even felt well enough to start scribbling again, and, believe it or not, I figured out a way to make some money while I was in the hospital. I wrote trashy love stories for romance magazines!

It happened like this: I'd run out of things to read and somebody lent me a

True Story or *True Confessions* or something. And the magazine was having a contest, inviting readers to submit stores. So I read a couple of their stories and figured out the format. And I just wrote junk. You know, "my sister's husband made eyes at me" kind of junk. I wrote the story longhand and Fannie or Ruby typed it for me, signing some fake name. The magazine accepted my first story and paid me for it. So, of course, I wrote another and another. Altogether I sold probably five or six stories. They paid by the word—maybe two cents for every three words—because I remember counting words and adding more junk just to make more money. I got plot ideas from conversations with other patients. Since I no longer had the curtain around my bed, folks would come and tell me their business and I would embellish their stories into titillating plots. It was all lots of fun.

I also wrote some serious fiction—under my real name—for the *Pittsburgh Courier* newspaper. My stories were taken to the *Courier* by Rienza Limus. He was another one of the Richmond orphans my father's mother had taken in. He and Daddy had been friends since childhood and he was now writing for the *Courier* and trying to organize a waiters' union. So he became my connection to the *Courier*.

I remember writing a short story about something that had happened to my father. When he was in Butte, Montana, in the middle of winter, he'd gone into a saloon. At that time—the 1910s—in some parts of the West, there was more prejudice against Asians than against blacks. Daddy had on a winter coat and fez-type hat. As I said, he was a light brown color, what blacks call "yellow," and had something of a Mongolian cast to his bone structure and features, something like Elijah Muhammed. The bartender refused to serve him. Then he took off his hat and they could see his kinky hair and their attitude changed completely. They served him with no problem when they realized he was black and not Asian. I wrote it as fiction but it actually happened to Daddy. And it was published in the *Pittsburgh Courier*.

I also wrote some political pieces for the *Advance*, the paper of Abyssinian Baptist Church. So I stayed busy once I felt a little better. And I'd never been really depressed, not even when I thought I was going to die. I didn't like being sick, of course, and, as a teenager, I was annoyed at having to be in the hospital, but, at the same time, I loved the attention. I guess everybody thrives on attention. And I also believe that if you act out happiness, it kind of leaks into you. So, emotionally, being very sick didn't get me down. And getting things published—even the trashy stories in trashy magazines—was exciting and fun. I was also fortunate in never feeling isolated in the hospital. There was a steady flow of people coming to see me. Despite being immobilized, I had a surprisingly active social and intellectual life. I'm sure that kept me from getting depressed, too.

I was in the hospital for about seventeen months. Then I went home to recuperate. But my first "home" wasn't our house in the Bronx because my legs still would not work and I couldn't handle stairs. So Godmother Ethelle took me to her apartment on Morningside Drive where everything was on one level. I stayed there for three months before going back to our house in Fordham. I continued writing throughout that period and kept trying to walk before the legs were ready. I remember, when I got home, my brother Jack would discover me on the floor outside my bedroom, having tried to make it to the bathroom alone. And he'd help me up lovingly but with great exasperation, saying, "Don't you know you just can't walk yet?"

Slowly, the legs became stronger. When it was felt by the doctors that I was able to work, I was given a job with the WPA's National Youth Administration. Mary McLeod Bethune was in and out of our house because whenever Aunt Mary, Daddy's sister, would come up from Richmond, Mrs. Bethune would come to see her. So she knew I'd been writing and she was impressed with the pieces for the *Pittsburgh Courier*, especially. So she gave me a job with the NYA for which she was President Roosevelt's advisor on black issues. This was 1935 and the NYA was part of Roosevelt's response to the Depression. I was twenty-one. Our office was at the corner of 135th Street and 7th Avenue in Harlem and our main goal was to keep young people in college. So there'd be counseling and a stipend of about $22 a month for any student who came in and registered with us. I remember a lot of paperwork on that job.

And even more on my next one. Less than a year later, I started working at Ellis Island. This was part of the WPA, too, and was probably a make-work job, but the project was very important to some people. What we did was to try to track down the original names of people who'd arrived at Ellis Island and been forced to accept an Anglicized version of their name or a completely different name because the immigration person found their real name too difficult to pronounce. People wanted to retrieve their family names and our job was to search through the records and, using their information about the date of arrival, try to verify the original name so that all their records could be legally changed. For the families involved, it was very important but for us, the workers, it was tedious, painstaking work.

Throughout both these jobs, I was taking night courses at Hunter and continuing to write. All my friends knew I really wanted to be a writer. And that's how I got into one of the most important and stimulating situations of my life: the wpa's New York Writers Project.

IV

The Writers Project

". . . right where I wanted to be."

THE BASIS OF WHAT I AM POLITICALLY TODAY was laid during my two and a half years on the WPA Writers Project. The activist orientation of Abyssinian Baptist Church had set me in a certain direction, but the people in and around the Writers Project clarified my thinking and explained the reasons for the injustices I'd been protesting at Abyssinian in a much fuller way. I learned the depth of the problem of racism at Abyssinian, but I learned the reasons for this exploitation and how it tied into class exploitation from my friends at the Writers Project. It was one of the most important learning experiences of my life.

I wasn't really eligible for it. It was created for writers out of work because of the Depression who had no other means of support. Living at home with two working parents made me ineligible in itself. In addition, I had a full-time job on Ellis Island. But all my friends knew I really wanted to write and knew the Ellis Island job was not very challenging. So when they heard about the government creating this project for writers, they knew I'd be interested. The question was, how to make me eligible.

It was actually Mary McLeod Bethune who gave me the details of this project. But she was not working with it herself and had no entree. It was when I talked to my friend Irené Augustine that I got the idea for how to make myself eligible. For years, Irené had worked in Braithwaite's typing school in Harlem. But she'd recently taken a job with Home Relief as an investigator and she had moved from the home of Walter and Gladys White at 409 Edgecomb to 116th Street.[1] She knew how the WPA worked and knew I had to be in need of a job and without support to be eligible. So we concocted a story about my being from Oklahoma and staying with her while I looked for a job. My fictitious parents' names were Winston and Winona Harper and they were back in Oklahoma and very poor. So I applied. Walter White helped in some way. I think he wrote a recommendation or something because I remember sending him a plant to thank him for his assistance. And out of that gesture, a friendship developed. Walter was head of the NAACP by then but still very involved in the literary world. He'd been a novelist and had become something of a literary engineer, hooking up people who were interested in writing, always promoting black writers in any way he could. Despite his help, however, I didn't get a job right away. I remember going into an office weekly to renew my application. But they finally placed me on a black history project. I was delighted.

Many of the people on the Project were already very well known—perhaps Claude McKay was the most famous[2]—but all had been very active, capable writers who'd lost their livelihood because of the Depression. There were blacks and whites, men and women—although I was the only black woman. And I was also the youngest one on the Project. It was all a very heady experience for a fascinated fraud like me.

Our offices were down at 110 King Street in a dilapidated brick building in Greenwich Village. A number of WPA projects were housed there. The Arts Project was on the top floor, where the skylights were. And we were on the fourth floor, I think. Our space was nothing special: they partitioned off this large open loft area into cubbyholes with plasterboard or something and put a desk in each cubbyhole. There were lots of glazed windows; that was the only means of ventilation. Remember, there was no air conditioning then. It was a drab place, really, but I never thought of it as being drab. To me, it was exciting because of the people in there. Writers, wonderful people who were writers. I was right where I wanted to be.

The objective of this particular project was, as I said, to write a history of blacks in New York. We got information all kinds of ways. We all spent a lot of time in the 42nd Street Library, going through history books, old newspapers and magazines (the black press was especially helpful), using census material, using absolutely anything we could get on whatever topic we were working on. We researched the history of old churches using their records. We wrote histories of fraternal and social organizations. If people were still alive who'd been associated with any of these institutions, we'd interview them and the interview material would become part of our data. We wrote about the New York race riots during the Civil War and in the 1880s. And I remember working on the history of Fraunces' Tavern, a black-owned tavern in Greenwich Village that George Washington had frequented. By our time, it was white-owned, but in the late eighteenth century it had been a lively mecca for some of the most prominent men in New York. Today, there's a plaque on the property because of its historic significance.

We got a lot of information from what were called "state clubs." These were organizations of people from various southern states—like the Georgia Club or the North Carolina Club—that would help new migrants from those states. These groups were exactly like some clubs of whites, say from Germany, who would help German immigrants adjust to the United States, except that they were made up of American-born blacks helping more recent migrants from their own part of the country. These clubs had records from the nineteenth century and they provided a wealth of information. The minutes to their meetings detailed all their activities, who they helped, and how they'd done it. Digging up interesting information was exciting in itself. And documenting the centuries of injustices to blacks in New York fueled our already developed political anger.

Although most of the writers on the Project would have preferred to be doing their own work rather than this history, I don't believe anyone was bored. The information we were discovering daily was always fresh and surprising and often tied into contemporary problems. Everyone on the Project was very talkative and social—except Claude McKay, who was somewhat isolated—and they shared whatever information they'd gotten daily. The black people on the Project included McKay, Waring Cuney, a very pleasant person, Joel Rogers (who published as J. A. Rogers), Carl Offord, and my closest friends, Ralph Ellison, Roi Ottley, and Carlton Moss. And the whites included Harry Kemp, who'd had great success with a book called *Tramping on Life*, Helen Boardman, a historian from the Midwest and the only nonfiction writer in the group, Larry Gellert, and Lela Russinky, who, with her kohl-rimmed eyes and gypsy-style clothing, was very much the bohemian Greenwich Village poet.

Roi Ottley was the supervisor of the Project. I'd known him before because he was one of Adam's friends—about ten years older than I. Adam's closest friends were Frank Steele, Dick Kinnard, and Roi Ottley. That quartet was always together. So I'd known him since I began at Abyssinian Baptist Church. He always seemed to have a lot of ex-wife and alimony problems, even before the Depression. But he was an absolutely charming man. By the time of the Project, he was in his mid-thirties and living with Joel Rogers, who had never married. Rogers was in his fifties, but I think what bonded them was their common West Indian heritage as well as the fact that they were both writers. As an administrator, Roi was good in that he gave assignments and then let us do them the way we wanted. As a person, he was handsome, likable, a man who, shall we say, enjoyed women immensely. Such men make a point of being charming and likable and fun, don't they? And Roi certainly was. When the Project was over, and we'd all scattered to different jobs, our research was placed in the Schomberg Collection. But Roi gathered up much of the material and used it in his book *New World A-Coming*, which became a best seller. Basically, he was a good scissors and paste somebody.

I'd known J. A. Rogers before the Project too.[3] He'd lived in Paris when my distant cousins, Mary Lou Granger and Josephine Washington, made a European tour. These were two daughters of Augustus Turpin, my great-grand-father's brother. Mary Lou had been my father's first teacher and was the mother of Lester B. Granger, one of my favorite cousins. Anyway, after Mary Lou's husband died, these two sisters decided to tour Europe and they stumbled upon J. A. Rogers when they were in Paris. He'd become their tour guide, taking them all over Europe. They were both in their sixties then, both retired teachers. And, when we were on the Project, Rogers kept talking about these two "elegant ladies" he'd escorted around Europe; he was apparently very impressed by them.

On the Project, Rogers was an excellent worker. He was an extremely thorough researcher, one of these people who'd dig and dig and dig. But, then, sometimes what he exhumed, he breathed different life into. After he dug up information, he fantasized over it, and what he published was what he fantasized. He worked very hard, but his writing is just not factual. He later became very well known for *World's Greatest Men of Color*. Like Roi, he was very personable. Rogers was tall, fair-skinned, with a good physique even as an older man. All of these people sold themselves well. All of them were outgoing and charming. Except Claude McKay.

McKay was downright grumpy. Abrasive, sullen, and silent. But I thought he had every reason to be. He'd had such success during the Harlem Renaissance with *Home to Harlem* and then went completely downhill. By the time of the Writers Project, he was in his fifties and living in a cellar. Not a basement apartment, a cellar. And his health was gone; he looked chemically ill. He seemed angry most of the time. And his anger was entirely justified, in my opinion; after what he'd contributed to the literary world, he shouldn't have been living in a cellar and barely eking out an existence. It was very sad to see.

Ralph Ellison, Carlton Moss, and I were a little clique. We often did research together and had lunch together. And our conversations were as much about the politics of the day—especially the things that pertained to black people—as about our research on the Project. I learned so much from them! They were very knowledgeable about history, social issues, how this country works, how the *world* works, really.

Ralph was a warm, bright, feeling somebody.4 A direct, very probing person, always wanting to get down to what the thing actually is. Nothing superficial about him. He was *very* pleasant to be around but very angry at the whole human condition at the same time. I remember that when we would walk from the offices at 110 King Street to the 42nd Street Library, he would invariably find some darn thing to kick. This is how he let out his frustrations, I think. He would kick it and kick it as we walked, not very conscious of what he was doing because he'd be carrying on a serious, insightful conversation all the time he was doing this. Years later, I reminded him of that habit and he'd forgotten he'd done it: "Did I really do that?" Ralph was continuously agitated by what was happening in the world yet he was a person full of fun, full of witty things to say. If you can be angry and affable at the same time, that's what he accomplished. Such enjoyable company, but with a "What the hell is this?" kind of stance toward the social conditions of the times.

We'd often walk up to the library and ride the subway back. It was a good walk—two or three miles, I would guess—but we'd do it to save a little money (one whole big nickel). At the subway entrance, there would invariably be somebody selling those dancing paper dolls. They'd been cut out of paper in an accordion, pleated arrangement. And there were very fine strings that were operating them. But you couldn't really see the strings because of the way they were positioned. And they would dance and those folks would sell them. These dolls recur in Ralph's book, *Invisible Man*. And it was on these trips from the library that Ralph saw them.

One time, Ralph, Roi, Carlton, and I got ourselves arrested. What an adventure! We were in the Horn and Hardart Automat on Broadway near the 42nd Street Library. We'd just done that walk and stopped in the automat to get something to eat. It was one of those inexpensive places where you put your nickels in the machines and you'd get a sandwich or coffee or whatever. Upstairs was W. C. Handy's publishing company. As we'd gotten in line, Will Handy, W. C.'s son, came down. So we gestured for him to join us. We all got our food and we were in single file to go to a table to eat. And as we approached a table—Roi was in the front of our line—a white man with his tray of food approached the same table. In a heavy Georgia accent, he said, "Don't sit there. I'm going to sit there." And we looked at him and we ignored him because we were closer to the table and there were plenty of other empty tables for him to sit at. As we started lowering our trays onto the table, he said, "I said, don't sit there, nigger," looking mainly at Roi because he'd been in the front of our group. And Roi just looked at him again and sat down. You know, to hear this kind of talk in New York, this was crazy. The man repeated, "Nigger, I told you not to sit there," several times and when Roi just continued to look at him and didn't budge, he hauled off and socked Roi. And suddenly everybody was in the fray. The women in the automat were screaming and jumping up on the chairs as though mice were loose in the place. All of us in the group were at that man. Roi and he were really tangled but I was swinging at him too with my shoulder bag.

So the management called the cops and the next thing I know, we're all in the paddy wagon on our way to the 53rd Street Police Station. The Southerner was in the same paddy wagon with us, but I guess the presence of the cops with billy clubs kept the fighting from starting again. We didn't realize it when we were in the paddy wagon, but all of the people in the automat were walking to the police station too. Many of them were unemployed folks who'd come into the place for their cheap cup of coffee, so they had the leisure time to walk on around to the police station and see what was going to happen. They were mostly white but it was clear in the automat that they'd sided with us because they'd been eating in automats with black folks for I don't know how long. An automat was not like the Waldorf Astoria, where I would later not be allowed to ride the passenger elevator. It was just an automat. So the other customers and the cops, too, were on our side.

They held us for a while at the station waiting for the judge to come and hear the case. They put Roi and the Southerner in a cell and the rest of our group was asked to just sit on a bench and wait. I guess we were regarded as participant–spectators or material witnesses or something. Anyway, the judge finally came. I don't remember his name but he looked like he might have been Jewish. And he patiently listened to this man meticulously explain what had happened. That all he'd wanted was a seat. That he'd reasonably explained to the "nigger" that he'd chosen that seat. That the nigger just wouldn't pay any attention to him. And, finally, he had just lost his temper. He was from Georgia, after all, and he was just not accustomed to sitting at a table with any niggers. He spoke very southern and in very superior language. And the judge just listened to him, nodding his head up and down while the Southerner was saying all this. And when the man finished, the judge asked him if that was all he had to say. And, when the man said, "Yes," the judge said, "Well, that's going to cost you $30. . . ." And the man from Georgia said, "Well, if that's all, I'm glad to pay it!" And he whips out his three ten-dollar bills. And the judge said, ". . . and thirty days." And all these people who'd come from the automat to support us let out a cheer. We all whooped! We were delighted!

So the mob of us left the police station in very high spirits and went back to the Horn and Hardart where the management treated everyone in our little group of black folks to whatever we wanted to eat. It was partly because they were very fond of W. C. Handy who worked upstairs, and his son had been a part of all this. But they also wanted to apologize to us for the incident. It turned out to be a real celebration. And the next day, the *Amsterdam News*, the black newspaper, covered the story with a headline reading, "Society Girl Arrested." Why I got in the headline, I don't know. And how the daughter of a waiter on the railroad could be a "society girl" is beyond me. But that's the way they saw it. I thought it was all pretty funny. My parents, of course, were absolutely appalled.

Not terribly surprised, though. By then, I had done so much picketing and protesting in Harlem with Abyssinian Church people, they'd become somewhat accustomed to my activism. But they never liked it. On the one hand, they knew something needed to be done. They agreed it was outrageous, for example, that the stores in Harlem that depended on a black clientele refused to hire black people. And, during the Depression, they were appalled at the widespread eviction of people unable to pay their rent. This custom of putting all of a family's possessions out on the street angered them tremendously. And they thought it should be protested. They just wished someone else other than their daughter would do it. You know, "Why do you have to do this? It should be done, but why do *you* have to do it?"

They had that same ambivalence toward my politically conscious friends, especially Carlton Moss.[5] They respected his talent and his mind, but they weren't so sure about his ideas. They knew he was reaching me a lot. I was living at home through this period and they were seeing me grow in my political awareness dramatically. Carlton was really putting the political puzzle together for me. He helped me understand how the world economic system works and where the U. S. fit in. He showed me the importance of the colonies to the world economic system—and, at that time, most of the Third World was still colonized—and he showed me the importance of racism to colonialism and to the American economy. For years, I'd been concerned about the problems caused by poverty in this country. But it was Carlton who helped me understand that class inequality and poverty were not aberrations of the system, they were a necessary part of it.

Carlton explained all the ugly little things that had always nagged me— everyone calling Chinese people "Chinks," and even my family talking about "Jewing people down." When I was younger, I would say to my relatives, "Don't say that," but I never understood why such expressions existed. Carlton helped me see how all of this works to divide and subdue, and help the powerful retain their power and advantage. Then, I guess, I became slightly preachy at home. I can remember straightening out my very religious grandmother, Mother Des, who'd become a Baptist after the murder of her brother: "How can you say those things when you're supposed to be a Christian?" I'm sure I became very annoying to them as I became more politicized. You can see why my family was somewhat ambivalent about my growing awareness. As I've often said, the political perspective I have today, fifty years later, is the one I gained during this period of my life. And Carlton Moss was undoubtedly my most important teacher.

His technique of teaching was to make you really look at something. I would see things in a very superficial way, and Carlton would pick them apart. He was always teaching; one could say his style was even a little pedagogical. He pushed you to reason, to look hard. It wasn't a matter of, "You accept this because I said it," but "You take a look and see if you agree with what I'm saying." A tremendously patient person.

Carlton was well known in New York because he was the first black person to have a regular radio series. He wrote and directed these skits that were fiction but social commentaries too. Actors played the parts—black actors—and while very amusing, the show taught in a subtle way. I remember the theme song for the show was "Love, Oh Love, Oh Careless Love." Carlton had also been involved with Orson Welles' black production of *Macbeth* at the LaFayette Theater. As I said, all of these people on the project except me had been quite successful in their fields. So Carlton had become a New York celebrity mainly on the basis of the radio show. When it ended, he went on the WPA Theater Project. But that, too, folded and he was reassigned to the Writers Project.

While on our Project, Carlton was working with John Houseman preparing a stage production of Richard Wright's *Native Son*. They'd had problems casting the role of Bigger Thomas. One day, Carlton and I were walking together up Broadway to the 42nd Street Library and he was expressing his concern about the casting of the role: "I don't know how we're going to find anybody to do Bigger Thomas. Because people will just walk out of the theater unless the actor is someone with such personal magnetism that they don't get angry with what he's doing but sympathize and stay because they care about what he is." And he was grousing along. And we bumped into an actor Carlton had worked with on the WPA Theater Project, Canada Lee. Lee had been a prizefighter before becoming a performer, and he was large and so likable! Carlton introduced us and the three of us chatted a while. I was charmed. As Carlton and I walked away, I said to him, "What would be wrong with Mr. Houseman casting Canada Lee as Bigger Thomas?" And Carlton said, "Damn, that's right!" And he went straight to Houseman's apartment on Central Park West and they hired Canada Lee, who turned out to be marvelous in the role.

So Carlton had enjoyed great success as a writer before coming to the WPA Projects. And although he might have interpreted his ending up on the Projects as failure, he had absolutely no bitterness in him. He worked hard at the Writers Project, and did so with the most pleasant attitude. In the years since the Project, he's been a documentary film maker and a professor in California. I cherish the friendship we still have today.

Being on the Writers Project led me to other kinds of wonderful experiences. Because of a typist on the Project, I got to know Paul Robeson. I'd known about him for years, and, as an adult, I'd seen him perform. I might have even seen him when I was attending Mother Zion Methodist Church: his brother was pastor there and I'm told Paul Robeson visited the church regularly. But I know I'd heard a lot about him when he was an outstanding student—Phi Beta Kappa—and star football player at Rutgers. My cousins, the Grangers, knew him, especially Randolph, who'd spoken so highly of this gifted person of such high character. I knew he'd gone through Columbia Law School, and, of course, the whole world came to know him when he started to perform. So when one of the secretaries on the Project mentioned that he was rehearsing "Ballad for America" nearby and that she was in the chorus of the production, I immediately thought, now how can I include me in on this? I knew the whole production was under the auspices of the Theater Arts Committee (TAC) and was volunteer, but I also knew I had no talent whatsoever—a fact that'd been repeatedly reconfirmed during all those years of dance and music lessons. But with the optimism of youth, I went over to TAC anyway, hoping they'd find something for me to do. And they did: I was assigned to take notes at rehearsals. I was delighted—and thrilled to be able to be in the company of Paul Robeson on a regular basis. The rest of the cast and production staff—blacks and whites—were all wonderful too, all people socially concerned like Robeson, all talented, bright, and interesting. Mr. Robeson was everything that I'd heard: a remarkable somebody with a remarkable mind and talent. He had such a presence. Most important was what he stood for: wanting black Americans to be regarded as people. As *people*. And he did everything in the world to indicate that he was a person.

The rehearsals were twice a week, and, after rehearsing, there'd be lots of conversation. Robeson took part in all of that; he was a very accessible celebrity. We'd talk about the most recent injustices, how picket lines were going, whatever was a current issue. All those folks, like the people on the Writers Project, were very politically conscious and concerned. And sometimes I'd run into them on picket lines. You see, all these aspects of my life overlapped because the concerns of the people involved were the same. So it was not unusual for me to go to 125th Street to picket and meet up with people from the Writers Project, the Theater Arts Committee, Abyssinian Baptist Church, the NAACP, and sometimes the Communist Party.

At that point, the picketing in Harlem was about people being "dispossessed." When landlords didn't get their rent—and during the Depression so many people lost their jobs and couldn't keep up with their rent—the land-lords would take the tenant's furniture and put it out on the sidewalk, some-times in the pouring rain so the stuff was just ruined. We'd go and protest and sometimes try to put the people's belongings back into their apartments. And the police would come and there'd be a big fracas. The papers would cover that chaos; that was news to them. But they wouldn't write about how all these people got to be put out of their homes.

The reaction of onlookers to our picketing and protesting was mixed. Some blacks definitely had an attitude of "don't come up here and disturb what we have 'cause it's better than what we had before." But there were others who were determined to make changes, and I have to say that these were largely West Indian people who felt we ought to make things better. But the migrants from the South often felt the best way to handle everything was to accept it. This had been the case when I'd been with Adam's tribe picketing the stores for not hiring blacks, and it was the case during the Depression.

But the people out there protesting during the Depression were more di-verse; there were more different groups involved. It felt good. We were all revved up with the idea that we were going to change everything, it was going to be better. It was a very zestful, dedicated collection of people.

Not that I ever left "Adam's tribe." Throughout this period, I remained ac-tive with Abyssinian Church. I remember getting involved with Adam's con-cern about what was being called the "Bronx Slave Market." Black women from Harlem, desperate for work because of the Depression, would go stand on street corners in the Bronx and try to get day jobs as domestics. Some of us at the church did an investigation of the reports that these women were some-times not paid at the end of the day or were being paid in clothing after being promised cash. We talked to some of these domestics and reported back to Adam that, indeed, such things were happening. Later, when I went to work for the NAACP, I discovered that Ella Baker had done a similar investigation.[6] But, as far as I know, neither our church nor the NAACP was able to do any-thing more than expose this awful exploitation of black women. The "slave markets" continued, with all their ugly practices, until the whole economy im-proved because of World War II.

Progressive political thinking was everywhere in New York at that time. The turmoil caused by the Depression made people question, made people ac-tivists. There was so much going on! It was during this period that my questioning led me to some of the lectures and workshops sponsored by the Communist Party. They were, at that time, one of the few organizations concerned with the elimination of poverty and racism. Eventually I concluded, as many blacks did, that they were using black folks—but there's no question that they were helping too. As I said, they often sent picketers to 125th Street, and they'd helped tremendously with the Scottsboro Boys case in the early thirties. I took my very first course in African history at their Workers School. No one else in the city—not even in the colleges—was teaching African history! That course meant so much to me. And the discussions at their meetings were always stimulating and informative. You'd go to one and hear all that they were going to do, and it seemed like you'd better get in and do some of it too—like stepping up the protests against landlords throwing people out of their homes, against the crazy amounts of money Harlem retailers were making people pay for merchandise, against the repossession of goods bought on the installment plan. There were any number of ways that blacks were being gouged, and the Communist Party was involved in trying to stop it, so you got involved with them. Many blacks were on the fringe like that, never actually joining, eventually becoming disenchanted. It wasn't so much an embracing of what Karl Marx had to say as that we rejected what was going on in this country. And it sounded to us, in many instances, like Marx must know partly what he was talking about.

And, frankly, I think the secrecy of the Party held a little excitement for a young person. It wasn't illegal but it was hush-hush. You'd tell a little bit to your family, say, but not all of what was going on because you knew that the Party was being attacked from the outside. Being involved in something righteous but slightly illicit definitely had an excitement to it.

I met Klaus Mann at one of their meetings held in a Greenwich Village loft. Klaus and his father, Thomas Mann, the author of *The Magic Mountain*, had come to the U.S. for asylum because their lives were in jeopardy in Germany.[7] And, this day, Klaus was giving a talk on the situation in Germany. After the meeting, we talked and I discovered he'd been in the U.S. only a few weeks. So I took him on a tour of New York: the Staten Island ferry (only five cents in those days), the Statue of Liberty, all of it. And, years later, when I was in Italy with the Red Cross and Klaus was in Europe assigned to the army newspaper, the *Stars and Stripes*, he became my guide in Italy. He was a very wonderful person and, after the War, I was so sad to hear that he'd died in Europe.

Richard Wright visited the Project often, and sometimes I'd go to a Party activity where he was also a guest.[8] He'd become friends with Ralph through Langston Hughes. Hughes, by the way, was never on any of these Writers Projects; throughout the Depression, he fared well enough with his writing to keep going on his own. But Wright had been on a Writers Project in Chicago and was curious about what our Project, with its focus on black New York, was finding. He, too, was on the fringe of the Party, but, as he's written, he eventually became so disheartened, he just left the country. He became disenchanted with the Party and with the fact that this wasn't really his country. So he and Ollie Harrington went to live in Paris after the War because they couldn't stomach what was going on here. And when there were no real changes after black men had died in the War, it was really sickening for those people. Yes, I did come to believe the Communist Party was using the black cause, but I also know I learned a great deal from their lectures and even from their paper, the *Daily Worker*.

The *Daily Worker* was informative but it did exaggerate and distort. You read it and a little part of your brain was saying, "Now, this is an exaggeration. But this is maybe the way it has to be stated in order to give the right impact." None of us lost perspective, though. The essence of what the *Worker* was publishing was the truth. But they manipulated facts in order to make points. Despite the distortions, I learned about events all over the world that I otherwise would not have been aware of.

Reading the *Daily Worker* on the subway had another exciting element. The trick was to read it without the people around you knowing you were reading a communist publication. Even the people in the Party said not to be blatant about your interest in communism because it could bring harm to you. So I was instructed in this system of folding the *Daily Worker* in such a way that people standing over me swinging back and forth couldn't see what I was reading. I suppose that, too, made a young person feel clever and a bit illicit.

But the secrecy wasn't why I was attracted to the ideas of the Party. My search for solutions to the injustices I saw all around me was. I learned a lot from those folks. And I enjoyed them. For the most part, they were loving, humane people. And I can't express how much that first course in African history meant to me.

Two dear people that I met during that period were Abel and Ann Meeropol. Abel taught English at Dewitt Clinton, the brother high school to Wadleigh, and he was a songwriter. He and Ann were both very committed to im-

proving social conditions, and even Abel's songs, written under the name
"Lewis Allen," reflected his concern. One of his best known songs is "Strange
Fruit," which he wrote for Billie Holiday. He'd taken the name from a Lillian
Smith book that was later developed into a stage play (with Walter White's
daughter, Jane, in the lead role). In the late thirties, lynchings were still happening with horrible regularity in the South and the song was Abel's way of
expressing his outrage about that: ". . . the scent of magnolia sweet and fresh,
and the sudden smell of burning flesh. . . ." It's a very powerful song and I
think Abel was right that Billie Holiday's voice, with its incredible poignancy,
was the perfect voice for the song.

Abel also wrote "The House I Live In." And he and Ann and I were thrown
out of the Paramount Theater because of that song! He'd sold the song to a
movie company and they'd included it in a movie. I can't remember the name
of that film. But the three of us went together to the big opening of this movie
in which the song was featured. We sat there really looking forward to hearing his song on the big screen; we knew that Louis Jordan's orchestra, a very
popular black orchestra at that time, was going to perform it and we waited
impatiently. But Abel was shocked when he heard it; they'd watered down the
lyrics and taken the most important words out of the song! Abel had written:
"What does America mean to me? The house I live in. The people black and
white. But, most of all, the people. The people black and white." And they'd
taken all of that about the people out and substituted things like: "America
means a white picket fence and a garden in bloom." You know, all this in-
nocuous, meaningless stuff. They'd butchered it. And every time Abel heard
one of his lines messed up, he hollered, "Shit!" Over and over, he was shouting "Shit!"—in the middle of all these well-dressed, moviegoers, now. So it
wasn't long before the uniformed ushers descended upon us—in those days,
movie theater ushers were dressed fancier than guards outside Buckingham
Palace—and they said, "We're sorry but you'll have to leave the theater." And
Abel yelled, "But that's my song!" Of course, they didn't care, and, over his
very loud protests, the three of us were hastily ushered out of there. We were
all very upset, but what could we do? Even Abel, the composer, had no rights
after the song was sold. I'm sure that's still painful to him even today.

I'd lost contact with the Meeropols until about ten years ago. At that time,
there was a TV program on which the Rosenberg boys, the sons of Julius and
Ethel Rosenberg, were interviewed. They were talking about the loving peo-

ple who'd adopted them after their parents were executed and they said their adopted parents' names were Abel and Ann Meeropol! I was so excited. I called New York. The only Meeropol listed on the Concourse, where they'd lived, turned out to be Abel's sister. She told me he was living in Florida and that Ann had died a few years earlier. So I reached Abel in Florida and we had such a lovely talk. We haven't been able to get together but we've stayed in contact. Wonderful man. They were both just wonderful people.

All the time I was on the Project, I was surrounded by extraordinary folks. We all had similar political concerns; so we stimulated one another and helped one another grow. And it was great how the research I was doing fed into my other activities. Finding out what had happened in the past helped clarify what was happening in the present. And the broader perspective on society I was developing helped me understand both. It was the magic of investigating and knowing what had gone before and wanting to be a participant in engineering change. You'd get so devilishly mad at what you read and what you saw around you, you *couldn't* be complacent. Some people might have said you couldn't change what was wrong in this country. But after you have seen how bad things have been and were then, you were saying to yourself, "You sure in hell better!" So the research energized my activism even more.

But as the Depression eased and the war industries expanded, the federal work programs were slowly being phased out. Blacks were getting into the menial jobs of the war industries and into the non-war factory jobs that were being deserted by whites getting into the higher-paying war jobs. The first of the government work programs to go were the arts projects like theater and writing, of course. Knowing our project would be eliminated early, we all started looking elsewhere. I was *very* fortunate: I ended up as Director of Publicity and Promotion for the national office of the NAACP.

V

The NAACP

"Everybody in there had a sense of mission."

WORLD WAR II OPENED UP JOBS FOR WOMEN throughout the society, including in the largest civil rights organization. The army had scooped up Carl Murphy, the person in charge of publicity for the NAACP, and Walter White put the first woman ever into that position, Charlotte Crump. However, she soon married and she left the organization in less than a year. That's when Walter invited me to fill the position. As I said, a friendship had begun after I sent Walter a plant for helping me get on the Writers Project. After that, I saw him at political meetings or protests or, occasionally, for lunch. There was one particularly interesting lunch that he invited me to just before he offered me the NAACP job.

Walter called me at the Writers Project and asked me to join him for a lunch near the NAACP office. I met him at the office, which was then at 69 Fifth Avenue, and we walked over to Luchau's to meet Alexander Woolcott, the subject of the Broadway play "The Man Who Came to Dinner." Luchau's was a German–American restaurant, a smart eating place. I remember that the actor Eddie Albert, very young then, and his wife Margo came in that day. Woolcott was a stout, middle-aged guy who had great charm as a talker. While he and Walter and I were sitting there, Harold Ross, the editor of the *New Yorker*, came in. And Walter, who was very much the *bon vivant*, called to Ross to join us. Ross immediately came over to our table. During the conversation, Walter told them I was on the Writers Project and they asked what I was working on. I had just written up a biography of "Pigfoot" Mary, a black entrepreneur who'd done very well, and I had the piece with me on a legal pad in my bag.[1] Ross read it and said, "This is great. I can use it for a profile in the New Yorker." Oh, my! I would be published in the New Yorker! I was walking on air! So I went back to Roi Ottley in the Writers Project office and told him about Harold Ross wanting to use my piece for a New Yorker profile. And I was so pleased with myself. Roi said, "Harper, you can't possibly do that. The project has already paid for this. It would be unethical for you to publish it independently." So I said, "Oh, I didn't realize that," and I contacted Ross to let him know he couldn't publish the piece. I was so disappointed. Now, remember, this from the same Roi Ottley who would later take the work of the Project and publish it as his book, New World A-Coming, without acknowledging the Project or the individuals in it in any way. If I had only known that then!

But out of the friendship with Walter and his respect of my writing came the NAACP offer not too long after that luncheon. I was to handle all publicity and promotion for the national office. I began working at the NAACP in October, 1942. And the most beautiful thing: I was assigned to the office that had belonged to W. E. B. DuBois. I'd always had so much respect for him. He was—and still is—one of my heroes. When I was younger, I had been part of his daughter Yolanda's wedding to Countee Cullen. I barely remember it, though. I was invited to take part because of my grandmother's connection to Reverend Cullen's church. I do remember everything was very elaborate and there were mobs and mobs of people. I was part of this long line of women and children who preceded the bride down the aisle and threw rose petals along the path as we walked. Even before that—I was maybe fourteen or so at the time of the wedding—but well before that, I knew about DuBois. I'd read the Brownie's Book he'd published for children; I'd read The Crisis. And, later, all the people I knew at Abyssinian and on the Writers Project really respected him. So he was someone I'd admired for a very long time. So there I was, sitting in an office with his name on the door. I was so touched by being in what had been his space that, when the workmen came to take his name off the door and replace it with mine, I asked them to please let his name remain for now and come back in a couple of weeks so I could enjoy sitting in there and seeing his name a little longer. I just held him in the highest esteem—and still do today.

My office was right next to Walter's, with an adjoining door between them.

Our offices were near the front lobby where people came in. Then, behind that, there was this large open area that housed the typing pool. And to the back were more private offices. *The Crisis* office was back there—Roy Wilkins was its editor then and George Schuyler its business manager—and so were the offices of the Legal Defense Fund, which Thurgood Marshall headed.[2] Thurgood had his own legal secretary but he used the typing pool, too, as we all did. It was a huge floor we had at 69 Fifth Avenue in one of those old, scruffy, but solid New York buildings. This space was adequate, I guess, but the aesthetics really didn't matter that much to any of us. This wasn't just a job; we all felt we were on a mission.

The only other woman executive for a long time was Ella Baker.[3] (Later, Ruby Hurley and Shirley Graham joined the staff.) Ella was in charge of branches. She'd gotten the job the same way I did: E. Frederick Morrow, who'd had the job previously, went into the army. (Morrow later gave a speech for which he became known, "We Who Are About to Die," on the death of black soldiers who had no rights at home; and, much later, he would write *Black Man in the White House* about his years advising Eisenhower.) Ella was absolutely wonderful—a small, energetic woman totally dedicated to working on behalf of black people. She traveled a lot; I can't even remember if she had an office of her own or just a desk, because she was always on the run. A powerful speaker who talked without notes from her heart to the hearts of her audience. Very forceful, with a strong voice that projected even without a microphone. Her speeches weren't full of statistics, nor were they anecdotal. They were to the point, descriptive of what was happening to black people at that time, and essentially "Get up and get going!" in tone. I'd heard of her before I came to the NAACP. She'd been an activist in New York and she'd been associated with efforts to organize southern sharecroppers. She was known as a person with great integrity. At the NAACP, not only did she organize chapters, but another concern of hers was getting southern blacks registered to vote. Yet, with all that work, she was very human and warm. She especially liked children and always seemed to be caring for some niece or nephew in her home. What can I say? I just know I liked Ella. I approved of her. I respected her.

Years later, when Ella was working in Shreveport on voter registration for the Southern Christian Leadership Conference—this would have been in the late fifties—she came to stay with me here in Alexandria to rest for a few days. And she was the same Ella: giving her all, absolutely committed to making the lives of black folks better, and still not knowing when her tongue was hanging out. She was exhausted when she arrived! I was so glad she just rested for a few days. We talked politics a little. I always liked Ella's clarity of analysis and her respect for people, especially. But she mainly rested. (And enjoyed the shrimp salads I made for her; that was one of her favorite dishes.) But, of course, when she returned to Shreveport, where she was staying with some friends of mine, I heard she just began overworking again. Ella never stopped. What an extraordinary woman.

My job included a little bit of everything. "Publicity and promotion" meant far more than press releases and fund-raising. I did do all of the press releases, however: I'd write these long statements announcing our conventions, protesting some film or legislation, whatever needed to be said by the organization. Whenever the press called the NAACP, it was me they talked to. And that led to some silly situations. The press would call our office for all kinds of information about black folks. If we didn't have it in our library—and the NAACP library was fairly extensive—I'd send someone to the public library to look it up. Now it wasn't unusual for me to get a call a few minutes later from a research librarian at the public library asking me for the very information I'd just sent someone over there to get. Because the public library had very little on blacks and the librarians didn't know how to fully utilize what little they did have.

Anyway, I was the information person. And an organizer of fund-raising events for the national office. Everyone in the office was a fund-raiser, really, because I gave everyone blocks of tickets and they'd sell them. Everyone—the secretaries, executives, the women in the typing pool. But I was the person who set up the events. I remember setting up a benefit dance at the Savoy in December, our thirty-fifth anniversary dance, and Count Basie agreed to play free for us. Mobs came because he was so popular. Then I had the nerve to get him to buy a lifetime membership by calling him repeatedly. Really, the poor man had done enough by giving the concert. But my dedication made me overly zealous and I called him at home, every place. Finally he said "Yes, yes, I'll do it. I don't want you worrying me anymore." I got a $500 lifetime membership out of him, after plaguing the life out of the man.

Whenever there was a national meeting scheduled, I was the advance person who'd go into the city chosen for the meeting, arrange conference accommodations along with the local chapter, and write all the press releases and program materials. I'd also sometimes be sent out in New York City to represent the organization when Walter didn't want to go. I remember one very peculiar such event.

Now, this is during World War II, and England was concerned about how the Burmese people, whom they'd colonized, were going to react if England chose to use the Burma Road to move soldiers and munitions. But they didn't want to ask the Burmese people about this; they thought that if they could sound out what the people of color in the U. S. felt, that would be some kind of yardstick for what kind of cooperation they could expect from the Burmese. Sometimes I find white folks pretty laughable, and this was one of those times. Imagine thinking you could use black people in the United States to figure out what the Burmese were going to do. Anyway, the British government sent Sir Stafford Cripps over here on a submarine for what were supposed to be "secret" meetings with "colored" Americans. They got in touch with Walter and with my cousin Lester Granger, who was, by then, the head of the National Urban League.[4] Not surprisingly, neither one of them wanted to attend such a meeting, so Walter sent me to represent the NAACP and Lester sent Elmer Carter to represent the Urban League. The meeting was held at the Henry Street Settlement House in lower Manhattan. Sir Stafford opened the meeting by asking how we felt about the war. And we proceeded to express our feelings about the war: that black Americans were really forced participants, that we really weren't treated like full citizens in our own country yet we were sent to die for it, all the usual stuff. I'm sure that was not what Sir Stafford wanted to hear, but that's what he got. The whole idea behind this meeting was absurd, so why shouldn't we have just used it to our own ends? And "our own ends" meant using it as a platform to discuss the concerns of "colored Americans" (as we were called then).

"Colored Americans." By then, that phrase had become almost an oxymoron for me. I no longer felt like an American, like a citizen of this country. As a child I had, of course, because my parents did. I was entirely comfortable with the name of my little club in Fordham, the "American Girls' Club." But as I grew older, and read more of the black press, more international news, I began to feel less and less like we were Americans. My parents never stopped feeling like Americans, deprived Americans to be sure, but Americans nevertheless. But at some point, in my early adulthood, I just got to be aware that this was a false sense. As I matured and began to examine things, I realized that we really weren't citizens. Later, there was a moment when I rolled into

Genoa with the troops, and the Italians were throwing roses at us for having "liberated" their city, that I wondered, "Gee, maybe I am an American." But, before that moment, from the time my activism began at Abyssinian, through the Writers Project and the exposure to the Communist Party, all the time reading the Pittsburgh *Courier*, the *Afro-American*, the *Peoples' Voice*, and the *Amsterdam News*, through all that my position was increasingly that it was never intended for black people to become part of the American mainstream. We'd been brought here to be laborers and to stay outside the society. And in the thirties and forties that's where we were still: outside. By the time I was working at the NAACP, I *knew* I was not an American. Maybe Sir Stafford was on to something. Maybe we had more in common with the colonized people of Burma than with the white citizens of America. But, as alienated as I felt at that time, I didn't make that connection. And, in any case, we certainly could not speak for them.

Seems like I was always going to meetings and rallies. And many of them were at night so it wasn't unusual for me to get into the office midday rather than first thing in the morning. That was true for all of us. Our secretaries were excellent at taking care of whatever needed to be done in the morning. They really ran the office. In an organization like that, the daily work that really keeps the organization going is done by the secretaries. And one of the reasons the NAACP was so effective was because the secretaries were superb. Rochetta Randolph had worked with James Weldon Johnson. Walter had Catherine Frieland, just terrific. Roy Wilkins' secretary was Edna Johnson, an extremely responsible young woman. And there was Lucille Black, so conscientious. My secretary was Alice Baird, who was not only capable and efficient, but one of the nicest people! She later became Thurgood's secretary and he loved working with her, too. The secretaries were as dedicated as everyone else. When work just had to be done, they'd work overtime voluntarily. We all did that. We were all so committed, we worked much more than a forty-hour week.

Another part of my job was accompanying the executives to important events to record everything that happened. And that part of my job is what brought me here to Alexandria for the first time. I accompanied Thurgood Marshall on the appeal of a case in which three black soldiers, based at Camp Claiborne just outside Alexandria, had been convicted of raping a white woman. This trial, in the summer of 'forty-two, had created even more tension in a parish already seething with local whites' resentment of the behavior of the black soldiers from the two nearby bases, Camp Claiborne and Camp Livingston. In early 'forty-two, there'd been so-called "rioting" right down on Lee Street. These "riots" were actually an attack on black soldiers by the white police. I remember reading a *P M* article quoting an Alexandria white saying those riots were caused by "sassy Northern niggers." Anyway, a number of soldiers had been shot—ten or twelve, as I recall—and a much larger number beaten. The army just didn't support these soldiers as they should have. You have to remember that most of the officers were themselves West Point-trained Southern whites.

And that's why this rape trial became such an injustice, too. When a local white woman who worked on the base as a waitress accused three black soldiers of rape, they were convicted in no time. The local NAACP called our office and asked Thurgood to handle the appeal; and it was for that that he and I came to Alexandria in February of 'forty-three. We traveled by train, arrived in the morning, and went directly to Camp Claiborne. It was a desolate-looking base and the building where the appeal was to be heard was army sterile.

I sat out in the hallway outside the hearing room. Thurgood would come out periodically to get a smoke or something, they'd break for a minute, and he'd give me a briefing on how it was really going. Mostly, he was concerned, *very* concerned. He knew they were innocent, but he knew he was up against racist officers and the sentiment of the local rednecks. And he knew that, for black folks in the South, justice usually didn't prevail.

We'd had the details of what had actually happened before we'd arrived in Louisiana. It seems these three young men—Lawrence Mitchell, John Bordenave, and Richard Adams (I remember their names because I wrote about them so much)—the three of them were a little clique, always together. This young woman had taken a shine to one of the fellows. Now the boy—I don't remember which one it was—he very sanely didn't respond to whatever overtures she'd made. And she became very angry and accused the whole kit-and-kaboodle of them of raping her. She was going to fix him, fix all of them.

Thurgood's appeal couldn't, of course, bring any of this up. If he even suggested a white women was attracted to a black man, they'd have convicted *him* of something. He based his appeal on the contention that the U. S. government technically had no jurisdiction in the first instance and, therefore, the conviction in federal court was illegal. It was a long day, a tense, unpleasant day. And at the end of it we got right back on the train to New York.

The appeal was lost. But the case wasn't. It was revealed that the young woman had a venereal disease, and Thurgood argued that if there'd been any congress between her and these three soldiers, they'd have it also. And they didn't. That eventually got them off.

But I remember vowing, as I left Alexandria that day, that I'd never come back here. It was an unattractive, backward, barely civilized place, I thought. The only reason the boys were found guilty in the first place was because of the gang-up of the vicious local whites and the reactionary army officers. I remember thinking, "This is an awful place. This is no place to live." Isn't it ironic that I've spent what is actually most of my life—over forty years—in that very place?

I also accompanied Walter to meetings and took notes for him. Walter was another hard-working somebody with great integrity. The irony of his fierce dedication to the cause of black people, of course, was his white appearance. Both his parents were black Atlantans, but the best description I've ever heard of Walter was that of his second wife, Poppy Cannon. She said he looked like "an English lord," and he really did—not only because of his Nordic features but also because of his bearing and speech. He had the demeanor of a very well-born Englishman. Now, how he'd managed to come out of a working class black family in Atlanta without much cultural blackness, I don't know. But, politically, he was very black. And Walter used this white veneer to help black people. He'd even gone so far as attending Ku Klux Klan rallies in the South to get information for the NAACP! I'm sure some of his early experiences in the racist South made him as militant as he was. As a child, he'd experienced the Atlanta race riots in 1906, when whites attacked his family's house because they thought it was too nice for blacks to have. He'd grown up in a totally segregated city. And I think the most powerful experience for him was the way his father died. After being hit by a car, his father was taken to the white section of the city hospital, Grady Hospital, by mistake (because he was so light). He was still on the examination table there when some of his brown-skinned relatives arrived; and when the hospital employees realized he was not white, they immediately stopped working on him and moved him to the "Negro wards" in a separate, dilapidated building across the street. The care for patients there was much worse than in the white section, and he died in what were really squalid conditions.

Such experiences made Walter want to do something about what was going on. When he first came to New York, he focused on writing fiction—his novel, *Fire in the Flint,* was rather well received—and he was also an investigator for the NAACP. It was during that period that he'd been sent south to hang out with the Klan and find out what they were up to. He stopped doing that, though, after an incident in Phillips County, Arkansas, where they found out he was not white and he barely escaped with his life. When James Weldon Johnson died, Walter became the Executive Director of the NAACP and pretty much gave up his literary career.⁵

So Walter was the ebullient, capable head of the NAACP all during the time I worked there. We worked closely and, I would say, well together. And I learned a great deal from him. Walter lobbied in Washington all the time on bills that had to do with civil rights for blacks. And sometimes I'd go with him. I'd usually stay with Conrad Lynn's friends and Walter would stay in some other friend's home. We'd do that in order to save money. Walter was very good at lobbying. We'd walk through the halls of Congress, meet Congressmen in the corridors, and he'd lobby them right there in the hall. He had a rapport that was remarkable with these folks. He was not tall. His face was quite handsome. And these people wanted to hob-knob with Walter White— because he was a glamour personality. He was on a first name basis with a number of them. I remember his having conversations with Claude Pepper who, at that time, had jet black hair.

Then there were the times we sat in the visitors' balcony of the House or the Senate. You couldn't get on the congressional floor unless you were invited as a witness or something. But you could sit in the balcony and observe as long as you were very quiet. You couldn't even yawn too loud or you'd be asked to leave—even though at times the congressmen were just wrangling and making all kinds of insane sounds down there. Senator Bilbo of Mississippi was always filibustering against some legislation the NAACP supported. Bilbo would do such things as read letters his father had written to him when he was in college and read long passages from the Bible. Nobody would shut him up, he would go on forever, just talking in order to defeat bills he didn't like. And he had tobacco juice in his mouth which he'd spit onto the green carpeting. There were brass spittoons, but he'd miss. A very gross man, grotesque looking too. He seemed to have arms that hung lower than his kneecaps. There were times when he'd spot Walter up in the visitors' balcony. And he'd proceed to insult Watler, calling him a "half-white nigra with idiotic ideas," and things like that. He'd point up to us and say the most vitriolic things. Remember, this is the early forties when overt racism was entirely acceptable and would even get him more votes. Congressional immunity permitted senators to say whatever they wished, so Walter had to listen to these very personal attacks from Bilbo without being able to respond. But I don't think it bothered him that much; he had a wonderful sense of self.

One of the things Walter taught me was that if a black person acts like he has rights or ought to be treated with respect, often whites will treat him that way. At the end of one of those days when he'd been called all of the things Bilbo felt like calling him, Walter suggested we go to the movies. Having to take that kind of abuse had to be a bit of a strain, no matter how much you've tried to feather yourself with duck feathers. So he needed to relax, I think, and he suggested we go see "The Major and the Minor." At the theater, Walter walked right to the downstairs area that was supposed to be for whites only. And he stood there, with assurance, and waited to be seated. The usher, all dressed up in regalia, looked hard at me but went ahead and seated us. When we sat down, I said something to Walter about our being in that section, and he said simply, "You are where you belong," making it clear with his tone that he was not going to entertain my apprehensions.

Another time we were having lunch with Howard Deitz of MGM at the Shoreham Hotel in Washington. Walter was talking to him about improving the kinds of roles blacks had in films. The waiters and the various personnel in the restaurant—even the bus boys—were all white and were trying to see what ethnic group I belonged to. They had their doubts. I had on a very large, green velvet tam that covered part of my face, so they couldn't get a good look. But they were curious and I was uncomfortable because this was an all-white hotel and I didn't know what would happen when they decided that I was black. When Walter saw my discomfort, he told me, "Please ignore them. You'll find out. If you act as if you belong, and you believe you belong, you will never, never be bothered by those people. Even if you're brown, it makes no difference. In the first place, this is the U. S. capital and they wouldn't dare offend you for fear that you're somebody out of South America or Asia or Africa, a diplomat or something." And I took that tip and used it the rest of my life.

But, of course, it was a limited truth. It might work in Washington or New York because these are cosmopolitan cities with many foreign dignitaries, but it wasn't as useful elsewhere. Also, Walter's opinion was based on his own experience, and looking white obviously made it possible for him to be accepted places those of us who looked black simply could not go. Walter passed all the time. And he didn't call it "passing." He felt that he was an American citizen and he could do what he pleased. He didn't think it was deceptive for him to act like an American citizen. But he also knew that he had the prop of being fair-skinned. So no matter how black he felt inside, white strangers were not going to respond to him as they would to an identifiably black person. Still, his advice has often been useful to me. Often, but not always.

I tried to act as if I belonged one time at the Waldorf Astoria in New York, and it did me no good whatsoever. I went into the hotel to take notes for Walter at his meeting with Madame Chiang Kai-shek. She had living quarters up in the penthouse and I was scheduled to meet Walter there. I went into the lobby and walked toward the elevators for hotel guests. And, as I waited for the elevators, a hotel employee came and tapped me on the shoulder and said, "I will take you to the proper elevator." And he took me to the freight elevator. When we got there, I said, "Oh, but I'm not delivering anything." And he said, "We're very sorry but this is the elevator for colored people." And I said, "It may be for people delivering something, but I am not delivering." And he responded, "The only way you're going to get to where you're going is on this elevator." And I said, "Then I won't get there. But I'm going to call upstairs." So I called the penthouse and Walter was in there gabbing with Madame Chiang; and they both came down. When the hotel employee realized who I was connected with, he apologized like crazy. And I went up on the right elevator. But that didn't mean anything because the next black person that came in there was going to be sent right back to the freight elevator. And I knew this. So the success of "acting as though you belong" depends on how vulnerable the white people are in a particular situation.

Walter's whiteness affected not only how whites responded to him but also, at times, the way some blacks did. His identification with blackness couldn't overcome his skin color during the Harlem Riots in August 1943. Walter had given a party for Wendell Wilke, who'd decided to run for president again. The party was being held at Walter's apartment at 409 Edgecomb Avenue in Harlem. Mayor Fiorello LaGuardia was among the guests. LaGuardia was a wonderful mayor—really cared about the poorer people of New York, used to read James Weldon Johnson's poem "My City" every Sunday morning on the radio, a good mayor. Anyway, he was there, too. And in the middle of this party, the police came to the door and told LaGuardia that rioting had broken out on 125th Street. LaGuardia decided to go to the area immediately and he asked Walter to come with him. Because I was supposed to record everything, Walter asked me to come along, too. So I got taken out of the party.

The three of us got on the back of a sound truck that went right to the area. This was an open, flat-bed truck with low railings on both sides and a bench along the back of the cab where we sat. Along the retail area of 125th Street, crowds of people where shouting, breaking the pane glass windows of stores, in and out of the shops looting. Glass was flying everywhere. Confusion, just chaos. LaGuardia was standing up with a light on his face, shouting into the speaker system things like, "Please stop. This isn't going to do any good. Please go home!" And folks just shouted back for him to shut up and go home. So he asked Walter, as the "Negro leader," I suppose, to speak to them. And before Walter could get two words out, people shouted, "Shut up, white mahn, we don't want to hear anyting from you. What you got to do with it?" with great anger. Most of the rioters, the really angry people, were West Indians at that time. They may have known the name "Walter White," but they weren't listening really; they saw his white skin and responded to that. So Walter looked over at brown me and asked if I would try to talk to them. And I got up there and said pretty much the same thing LaGuardia had. And they did respond to me differently. People shouted back, "Womahn, get down off that ting and come jine us!" There was no anger directed at me. They just tried to get me to see things their way and do what they were doing. But they weren't thinking about stopping. They'd been angered by a rumor that a black youth had been shot by the police. And that triggered this expression of all their other frustrations. So they didn't listen at all. And we realized there was no point in staying there. Walter never talked about how he'd felt being yelled at by black folks for being "white." I'm sure he encountered that at other times too. But he never talked about it.

He got it privately, too. The person in the office who brought up Walter's color all the time was George Schuyler. While Schuyler was business manager of *The Crisis*, he published a satirical book called *Black No More*. In the book, black people could put on a salve and turn themselves white. And George would say that the people in this book still didn't get as white as Walter. George was always making snide remarks about how fair Walter was. I think it was partly because George himself was about as dark in pigment as anybody could be and was very proud about that. But he was critical of Walter not only because he was white in appearance, but because he was white in behavior, too. At office parties where there'd be nothing but black people, Walter was pretty much a lost soul. In any situation where he was not making use of white culture, he was lost. He wanted to be part of the black culture but, somehow, the facade he'd taken on after leaving Atlanta, he then couldn't shed. It was somewhat sad. It created a distance between him and blacks, a distance he definitely didn't want.

That wasn't true of any of the other executives. Thurgood Marshall was so much fun! He was highly respected for his abilities but never pedantic, never a know-it-all. Thurgood was capable of talking our vernacular, unlike Walter, and he was consistently black. Walter was conveniently white and carried it over to all aspects of his life. Socially Thurgood was marvelous, wildly funny, perfectly willing to be a clown. But he was the most serious person underneath that. And the most insightful. He could get right to the core of whatever monkeyshines there were, get to the root of a problem while other people were still trying to figure out what the problem was. He just had some kind of antennae that enabled him to see things for what they were. And then he'd work very hard to right a wrong, always using the pragmatic approach of a good lawyer. I just loved him. And I loved the way he and his wife, Buster, got along. They were so playful and warm together. Just a wonderful married couple. It was so sad she died so young.

At that time, the NAACP Legal Defense Fund was still part of the NAACP. As I said, their offices were in the same suite as the NAACP. So, through casual conversation with Thurgood, we were all kept abreast of legal developments. There's one case that really stands out in my mind. Contrary to what most people think, our first school integration suit was not in the South. It was in Hilburn, New York. And Thurgood won it. It came to our attention through Helen Hayes, the actress. It seems that on her household staff in Nyack were some light-skinned blacks who were descendants of Hessian soldiers. She was disturbed because their children had to go to a separate all-black school and she wanted to find out why this was the case. So in the fall of 1943, she and a committee from the Hilburn NAACP came down to our office. There was a strike and Thurgood ended up filing a suit. Governor Thomas Dewey publicly condemned school segregation and the NAACP won the suit. That's how the Hilburn school system was integrated. Of course, after that, Thurgood focused on school integration in the South. But that case in Hilburn, New York, was his first school integration victory. He was such a capable lawyer. And black in every way.

In a very reserved, controlled way, this was true of Roy Wilkins, too. Wilkins, at that time, was Walter's assistant and the editor of *The Crisis*. Wilkins had taken over Dubois' job after DuBois went to Atlanta. Roy had a strong personality and it was apparent to everyone that he wanted to eventually walk in Walter's shoes (which, later, of course, he very capably did). But back then, Wilkins cooperated with Walter, though he seemed to feel Walter had a little too much autonomy. And Walter certainly was autonomous: he was so charismatic that the Board of Directors usually just rubber-stamped whatever Walter suggested. And Wilkins felt there ought to be more input into what was going on.

Roy Wilkins was a very hard worker who had a background in newspaper work in Missouri. A charming man. All of these men — Walter, Roy, George, Thurgood — all of them had that quality. In order to do that kind of work, you have to start off with personal charm because that's part of what the public wants. They were very much like black preachers, I think, whose success is partly due to their being good actors, good speech makers, as well as their being people with very real convictions and a very real dedication. This was hard work that required a certain kind of personality and a whole lot of ability. Wilkins had both. Though far more reserved than Walter or Thurgood, Wilkins was a dignified, engaging, well-informed representative of the organization. And they all got along very well — partly, I suppose, because of their shared dedication to the causes of black folks. Everybody in there had a sense of mission; we were going to straighten out the world. And that kind of dedication, constantly fueled by the outrages against blacks in this country, made us all work very hard, made us all — in our different ways — very passionate.

Another part of my job was the monitoring of the media — films, newspapers, magazines — for words or images that were disparaging to blacks. Our best known campaign during this period was our boycott of *Gone With the Wind*. Our main objections were the "Mammy" roles that Hattie McDaniel and Butterfly McQueen played and the historical distortion that southern blacks supported the Confederacy. Films at that time, like today, cast black women mainly as servants or whores, and we had been objecting to that (to

Howard Deitz and others) long before that film came out. We saw these characters as stereotypes. And they were. But when I saw the film years later, I realized that Hattie McDaniel's character was actually the only really sound female in the whole blooming picture. She was guiding the other characters and
giving a little bit of wisdom and sense to the rest of them. That's what the
mammy role was, largely. These women had to run the house, and did not
have to act frail and incompetent. They were the brains, the female brains of
that era in the South.

I didn't get to see *Gone With the Wind* in its entirety until just a few years
ago when it came on TV. Before our boycott in the forties, I'd gone to see the
film at the Paradise Theater on the Concourse up in the Fordham area. I went
to see it during the day when the prices were lower, and I happened to end up
sitting with a lot of women. Now, early in the picture, Butterfly McQueen
talks about birthing a baby and has to deliver some very silly dialogue. And
these women around me, Bronx housewives, were talking across me. And they
were saying—and I was seated in the middle between them—they were saying, "Look at that nigger. Isn't she just like a nigger?" And they niggered and
niggered and niggered to death in their enjoyment of Butterfly McQueen because, "I have a maid just like that!" I finally got up to leave, I was so angered
by them, and I deliberately stepped on the foot of one of these women, saying,
"Oh, excuse me." Then I stepped on her other foot. That was my stupid personal meanness offered in protest. And that exit was fairly early in the movie,
so I really didn't see the film until it was shown on TV.

Prior to *Gone With the Wind*, our biggest film boycott was of *Birth of a Nation*. That happened long before I came to the NAACP, but I heard about the
boycott of this D. W. Griffith film that glorified the Klan and justified its violence against black people.

Film boycotts got the most national publicity, but we were constantly objecting to all kinds of offensive things in the media. Sometimes the protests
grew out of my monitoring newspapers and journals myself, and sometimes
out of people writing their complaints in to us. For example, one protest that
grew out of our receiving a letter of complaint was our objection to "Black
Sambo" stove polish. This was a black substance used for shining the big iron
cook stoves. The can had a black male figure on it and the words "Black
Sambo Stove Polish." So I wrote and told the company that the image and the
name were offensive and black people were not going to buy their product

anymore. Then I'd send out an announcement of the boycott to all of our chapters. I also had to write the Aunt Jemima people and tell them that the image was a stereotype and objectionable. In time, the company changed the image and made Aunt Jemima lighter—they thought we objected to her dark skin. That wasn't it at all; we objected to the mammy image.

A constant problem was the newspaper cartoons. If they depicted a black person, he or she was a buffoon and grotesque. I remember one strip of "Harold Teen": Harold Teen and his friends—all white adolescent males—are following a very shapely female down the street. In the first few boxes, you just see her back, and she has a nice body and pretty hair. And the big joke is when she turns around: it's a grotesque black thick-lipped face on top of this shapely body. That was supposed to be very funny. So I wrote to the people who syndicated the cartoon, to the papers that carried it, and to the cartoonist himself saying that this was offensive. Of course, there was no retraction or apology. That kind of thing was so pervasive and entirely acceptable then.

And the total lack of black models was too. The catalogue companies, the department stores, *Vogue, Vanity Fair, Harper's Bazaar,* none of them used black models. Even when a white company ran an ad in the black press, they'd use white models. An acquaintance of mine, Jimmy Allen, was a photographer for many of the big companies. He always photographed white models but tried to get some companies to use black models when advertising in black publications. He took photographs of my friend Fanny and me and submitted them to Cheeseboro Vaseline Company. He argued that if they wanted to sell vaseline to black people, why not use black models? Those photos got to the point of having copy written for them and they ran in a few black newspapers. But he was never very successful in his efforts. Nor was I ever successful in getting the Black Sambo people to change the name of their product or the Aunt Jemima people to take the image of the mammy off their bosses. We didn't really expect change in those days, but we had to keep trying.

One of the endless outrages of that period that has stayed in my mind was a lynching. In the early forties, lynchings were still fairly common in the South, and still going unpunished. But the NAACP did what it could. This particular lynching remains more vivid to me than any of the many I heard or read about because I was sent to Mississippi to investigate it. Our office had received an anonymous letter from a black person in Quitman, Mississippi, telling us two black boys, both fourteen years old, had been lynched and ask-

ing us for help. So the office sent me and Sally Crayton Canaday, a white volunteer who was a student at Columbia University. The plan was for her to get
information from the whites of the town and for me to get information from
the blacks. We rode on the train together as far as D.C., and then I had to move
to the Jim Crow car. We arrived in Jackson in the early morning and then
caught a bus to Quitman. We did all this acting as if we didn't know one another because, if she'd been identified as a "nigger lover" by the locals, she
wouldn't be able to get any information. So we didn't speak to one another
when transferring from the train to the bus in Jackson, and, of course, once on
the bus, she sat in the front with the whites and I sat in the back with the blacks.

We had very little information to go on. The person who'd written the
NAACP office had just said that these boys — Charlie Lang and Ernest Green —
had been hanged from a river bridge. The first place I went was to the black
undertaker who'd buried the boys. Since he'd seen the bodies and prepared
them for burial, he had to know something about the cause of death. But I got
no information. "The boys were in a car accident" was all he would say. Like
all the black people I would talk to that day, he was frightened. No one knew
I was with the NAACP, but people were afraid to talk to any outsider. They could
be lynched next. I tried to start up casual conversations with black people in
shops and on the street. "What happened to those boys we heard about?" But
I kept hearing about a car wreck, or "We don't want to talk about that. We didn't
have no trouble here. We're alright. Where are you from?" My northern accent didn't help. But I don't think they'd have talked to anyone. Their fear was
absolutely palpable.

I managed to get a ride out to the area of the boys' houses, in an area called
Shubuta. They were on a country road outside of town. I was to find out later
that that's where the incident began, right near their houses. But people would
not talk to me. Some shut their houses up and wouldn't even come to the door
when I knocked. The few who would speak just said they knew nothing or
they'd heard about a car accident. I got no information there either. I gave up.
I hitched a ride back into town — country people are very hospitable if you
don't ask the wrong questions — and went into the bus station to head back to
New York. There were no black hotels in Quitman, and what had become
clear in my many frustrating conversations of the day was that no one was going to let me stay at their house. Few black people in rural Mississippi of the
1940s would risk their lives by housing what seemed to be a trouble-making
Yankee. No one in this town.

I found out later that Sally, in the meantime, was having great success. She was originally from Alabama and had a real thick southern accent, perfectly acceptable to the whites of that town. She found a place to stay—she was there for three or four days, as I recall—and she got all the details of the murder.

It seems three children—a white girl of thirteen and the two black boys—were playing together just off a country road. All of them were small and undeveloped for their age because of pellegra. Poor people in Mississippi had such deficient diets. Anyway, these children were next-door neighbors, near their own houses, playing together as they regularly did. At one point, the ball they were playing with rolled out into the road and the little girl went to retrieve it. She stumbled and fell in the road and one of the boys went to help her out of this dirt road. Just as he was helping her up, along came a truck with some drunken white men on this Saturday afternoon. And they said, "Take your hands off that girl!" And they stopped and they castrated the boys right there. They used pliers to tear away pieces of the boys' skin and rammed a screw driver down the throat of one of them until it protruded from his neck. Then they hanged the boys from a bridge nearby, a bridge that had been used to hang four or five other blacks in recent years.[6] Sally said so many people seemed to know all the details of the lynching that the names of the lynchers had to be public knowledge, too. But there would never be any convictions for those murders. Not even a trial. Blacks couldn't press charges and whites wouldn't.

My adventure in that town wasn't over yet, though. When I went into the bus station, I discovered there were no more buses out until the next morning. Now, what do I do? No place to stay. Half the town aware that this meddlesome black Northerner has been asking questions about the recent lynching. And the bus station becoming increasingly desolate as it got later and later. It occurred to me that the only somewhat secure place in the station was the toilet—the toilet for "colored." At that time in the South, all bus stations had separate waiting rooms for blacks and whites. They even had separate ticket windows. In these small towns, the cubicles that the ticket seller was in had one window that faced the white waiting room and another window that faced the "colored" waiting room. And each waiting room had a toilet. Actually, I think the white side had two: one for men and one for women. But the black side had only one and it was for "colored"; it made no difference if you were male or female. So that's were I stayed for the night.

It was *so* dirty. They kept the white waiting room and facilities clean, but were very negligent about the black side. I leaned on the sink and leaned against the wall. The toilet itself had no lid to put down so I couldn't sit on that. But I did squat on my suitcase for a while. I didn't care that much about the discomfort though; I just wanted to get out of that town alive. As the bus station became more silent, I became more afraid, more jumpy at the slightest sound. I kept expecting the Klan to break down the door and drag me out. The Klan was very active in that part of Mississippi, and I felt very isolated. I was really scared, more scared than I would later be in the Po Valley in the middle of World War II with enemy planes overhead. I distracted myself by watching tiny bugs make their way up the walls of the toilet. And by singing some of my favorite songs in my head. (I didn't dare sing out loud and risk attracting attention to my hideout.) I remember being a little bit strengthened when I silently sang the Negro National Anthem, "Lift Every Voice and Sing," a melody I've always liked and words that really are inspirational:

> Lift ev'ry voice and sing,
> Till earth and heaven ring,
> Ring with the harmonies of liberty . . .
> Facing the rising sun
> Of our new day begun,
> Let us march on
> Till victory is won.

And I made it through the night. I came out of the toilet about a half hour or so before my early morning bus. And I was so grateful to get out of that town.

That experience is the reason I welcomed CORE to my home here in Alexandria in 1964. Black people in this town didn't want a civil rights organization coming in. They sounded like the people in Mississippi in 1942: "We're doing alright. We don't want any trouble here." But CORE said, "You're already in trouble." And I agreed. So despite the White Citizens Council being very active in this parish in the early sixties, and despite regular threats from whites, I let three CORE workers live with me while they began the civil rights movement in central Louisiana. Because I remembered hiding in that toilet all night in Quitman, Mississippi.

VI

World War II

"[They] wanted to make like the Red Cross was integrated."

THE WAR INTRIGUED ME. I wanted to know more about what was going on, about what war was really like. By the fall of 'forty-three, I realized I wanted to go overseas. My motivation wasn't patriotism—by then I wasn't particularly patriotic about anything this government did. But I was curious and adventurous, I suppose, and I cared deeply about the black soldiers, especially.

First, I tried to go as a reporter for the Office of War Information. But before my application papers were completely processed, Elmer Davis, the head of the Office of War Information, rescinded the order that allowed women to go overseas. Then I heard the Red Cross was interested in recruiting some black workers. Basil O'Connor was the director then, and he and his black assistant, Jesse Thomas, wanted to make like the Red Cross was integrated. Most of their volunteers were white women, what was called "upper crust" women. That's who they'd recruited and that's who constituted the majority of their workers. There were a few men, a few lower middle-class women, but it was mainly these elite white women involved. The pay was nominal and many of them waived it to give it back to the government for the war effort.

A small number of black women had already been recruited. I was part of the second group accepted; there were around seven of us. We went for screening and training in Washington, D. C. in late May of 1944. One of the first things I remember was my physical exam. Apparently the white female doctor had not examined many black people before, and it was clear she'd rather not have touched me. She managed to poke and prod me with utensils, never coming in contact with me with her hands. She used a pencil to examine my feet, separating my toes with it to see if I had athlete's foot or any fungus, I guess. I'd watched her examine the white women who preceded me in line and she hadn't used these instruments to protect herself from direct contact with the woman. But she made sure she never once touched my skin with her hands.

All of the training for the first eight weeks was at American University. The classes were integrated—there were about thirty of us altogether—but we lived separately: the black women were housed at the black YWCA in the District and the women's dormitory at Howard University. The white women stayed in the American University dorms.

Our training prepared us to set up and run clubs overseas for the soldiers, clubs that operated similarly to the USO clubs. In fact, part of our training was to go to the USO in Washington to observe how they operated. There again, we were segregated: the white trainees went to the white USO and we went to the black USO. This whole idea of an integrated Red Cross was ludicrous even during the training period.

At American University, we also improved whatever foreign language skills we had. I knew a little Italian from growing up in the Bronx and I'd taken French in high school. So I did more work on both of them. They also taught survival skills—how to cook in a helmet, how to pack your sack. And they taught all the skills that would be used for entertaining the soldiers: organizing dances, card games, how to set up barber shops and tailor shops at the clubs. We were told we were to dispense condoms, too, because when the soldiers came to the dances, so often that was the beginning of some kind of alliance with somebody. It turned out to be true; I came to realize that had been pretty well thought out.

The time went quickly. It was all interesting to be me because it was what I wanted to do; I was really looking forward to getting out there in the middle of the war. My parents, needless to say, just couldn't understand that. They came down to Washington every Saturday during my training. We'd have lunch at the restaurant in Union Station because it was the only restaurant in Washington that was not segregated. And the conversation was always the same: "Why are you doing this? Aren't you happy at home?" They couldn't understand when I told them I'd been very happy at home but I really wanted to know what was going on in the war. Because of my brother's bad lungs, he'd been excused from the draft and my parents were relieved about that. Then to have me voluntarily rushing off to a war just baffled and distressed them.

After eight weeks, we were all sent to army camps within the U. S. to have the experience of running a Red Cross installation for two weeks before being shipped overseas. I was assigned to Camp Pickett in Blackstone, Virginia. There was already a Red Cross club there so it was just a matter of my colleague and I—they sent a white worker and a black worker out together—continuing what our predecessors had done. Everything was segregated in the army, so I worked with the black enlisted men's club, the black NCO club, and handled mainly the black soldiers who came into the Red Cross installation.

There was a USO operating at Camp Pickett, so they handled most of the entertainment activities. What I ended up doing could loosely be called social work: I was available to the enlisted men to discuss their problems, I helped them write letters, played cards with them, generally gave "aid and comfort" as needed.

As soon as I arrived—it was on a Saturday afternoon—it got around that I had worked for the NAACP. Immediately, some men came in to talk politics. And I was more than willing to do that; in fact, I probably did much more of that at Camp Pickett than the Red Cross would have liked. But, to the black officers, these discussions were "aid and comfort." So I didn't hold back in any way. I remember many long and lively talks in various locations at the Camp about the plight of black folks.

In fact, it was during one of those discussions that the man who would become my husband and the father of my four children first saw me. It was my second night at the Camp, a Sunday night, and I was in the Officers' Day Room talking with a small group of officers about some of my experiences at the NAACP. Sitting on a table, I guess I was quite animated and had taken off the Red Cross pump to shake it emphatically to make some point. Jim Hines was walking by the room and noticed me. He later told me he stopped, listened for a while, and said to himself, "Now, that's a crazy woman. I believe I'll marry her."

He didn't come into the Officers' Day Room then, but the next morning, he came into my office and introduced himself. I was very impressed. He had these shiny white teeth and shiny eyeglasses and he just looked very nice. I found out he was a doctor and was from Louisiana. In the course of our talking, he said, "Oh, I understand that you have a date to go to the USO show tonight with my dental officer." And I said, "Yes, I do." Then he said, "You don't look like the kind of young woman who would date a married man." I asked, "He's married?" "Yes." So I said, "Oh, well, then I'm not going." It didn't really matter that much to me. We talked a little more, and, as he was leaving, he turned and said, "Oh, I'm sorry. I've ruined your evening. Would you consider going to the show with me?" I was delighted: "Oh, that would be nice." And, thereafter, all my evenings were spent with him.

He was absolutely charming. A totally outgoing person, full of energy, very much interested in medicine, loving music and the theater. So many of the doctors I'd known were very single-minded. But Jimmy's interests were really eclectic and I was impressed by that. I could never have anticipated how unpleasant things would become later in our marriage. Things were not alright even then, although I didn't know it. He'd begun our courtship by warning me against dating a married man. Within two weeks he would propose. He was magical. He was perfection. And, I was to discover years later, he was at that time already married.

But there was no hint of that at Camp Pickett. He was totally attentive and seemed to be as much in love as I was. I think he was; and he was certainly serious about marrying me—as I found out in the most enchanting way.

The weekend after my arrival at Camp Pickett, I was to go to Washington by bus to meet my parents, as usual, for lunch at Union Station. I'd told Jimmy about our custom and I'd gotten on the bus that Saturday morning to go to Washington. Jimmy, in the meantime, borrowed a car from somebody and drove himself to Washington, popping up at the restaurant in Union Station while we were eating. My mother was instantly charmed. My father was not impressed. He never particularly liked the men who had an interest in me; he just didn't think any of them were good enough for me. And now this pushy unknown from Louisiana who had the nerve not only to come uninvited to our lunch but to actually announce to my parents (announce, not ask) that he was going to marry me—well, this was too much for Daddy. "Young man, you're out of line! What makes you think my daughter's going to marry you?" Jimmy just turned to me and said: "Aren't you?" And I nodded and quietly answered, "Uh, hmmm." My mother was delighted; she thought he was an absolute jewel. My father was so upset he wouldn't even have a drink with Jimmy (and, as I've already said, Daddy was very fond of alcoholic drinks). But Mama, who never touched any alcohol, asked Jimmy what he was drinking, and when he said a daiquiri, she said, "I'll have one too." It was her way of showing her approval of him and of the idea of our getting married. She loved, especially, his warmth and his sociability. I remember, during that first conversation, her expressing her disbelief that he was an only child. To her, there was nothing in his personality that would indicate he was less than part of a big mob.

That lunch was the first time Jimmy had brought up marriage but it didn't surprise me. If you're in love and the other person's in love, you think that's the next thing. Marriage is just a natural next step if it's been a mutual thing. At least, it was in those days.

So we had one more week in Virginia and one more Saturday lunch with my parents in Washington before we were both shipped out. On the second Washington trip, a funny thing happened which shows something about how Jimmy handled racism, how this man raised in the oppressive South had learned to cope in indirect ways with the insults of whites. Jimmy was taking me by taxi back to the Y from Union Station. It was really difficult for blacks to get cabs in Washington at that time. All of the drivers were white and they just didn't want to pick up black people. We'd waited and waited, and, finally, one of them stopped. But the driver was absolutely nasty, talking about "niggers" and making all kinds of ugly, racist comments. Now, Jimmy had his medical bag with him, the black bag doctors always carried then. He said nothing unpleasant to this driver but he took out some surgical scissors and, while he talked very brightly to me, he loosened the screws on the ashtrays, the door handles, everything around the back seat that had a screw in it. I kept whispering, "What are you doing?" and he just whispered back, "Never mind, I'm going to fix this so-and-so." His talk remained very pleasant while he unconcernedly unscrewed everything. And when we got out of the cab at the Y, Jimmy slammed the door as hard as he could, and we heard everything fall. We fell out laughing. It was an imaginative and crazy way to address the driver's racism. I probably would have confronted him with my anger if I'd been alone. But this was vengeance with fun. I liked that.

Jimmy liked my craziness, too. He admired the adventurousness of my going to Europe. And he liked my unconventional ideas and even my appearance. For example, I changed the drab Red Cross outfit to suit my taste. Mainbocher, who'd designed the Navy outfits, had designed ours too. The cut was OK. And there was a white blouse used with the Red Cross pin at the throat that looked good. But the suit and coat were charcoal gray. Drab. And I didn't want to look drab. The separate wool flannel liner of the coat, however, was cherry red. So I wore just the liner flung over my shoulders. It was very, very gay, very happy looking. And Jimmy said I could be seen a mile away. But he said it with delight.

At the end of the two weeks in Virginia, we both got our orders for overseas. Jimmy left for England from Boston and my point of embarkation was Newport News, Virginia. There I had more training. We learned how to crawl under a barbed wire fence, how to scale a ship by rope, how to get into a lifeboat; we had target practice; we ran. You had to be in good physical shape.

In the early part of the training, they'd considered sending me to India. Red Cross installations were all over the world, everywhere GIs were. But as my departure date drew closer, they decided I'd do better in the European Theater of Operations (ETO) because of my health record, my having had rheumatic fever. They figured the heavy, wet weather of Southern Asia wouldn't be good for me. So my health and my facility with Italian got me assigned to the Red Cross in Italy.

We traveled in a convoy of ships. The trip took about twelve days because we went a very roundabout route to avoid German submarines and mines. We were not told the route we were taking because it was all secret for security reasons, but my guess is that we went by way of the South Atlantic.

My cabinmate was another black Red Cross worker, Evelyn Vaughn, a returnee from service in India. She was great fun. Evelyn was a person of great presence and of great theatrics, physically a very attractive young woman. She was also very clean and when we discovered that our toilet was not at all clean, despite supposed navy cleanliness, Evelyn felt great disgust and suggested we scrub it ourselves. I wondered out loud to her how in the world we can get some rubber gloves so we can clean this up. And Evelyn said, "What are you talking about? You can wash your hands after you get through!" And so I followed suit and we scrubbed and scrubbed in there with our bare hands. It was really quite nasty. But we did get it clean and we were both—but especially Evelyn—much more comfortable with it.

Now, as we were cleaning, we heard this clatter in back of the metal-lined shower stall. When we climbed up to look over the shower wall, we discovered that someone had thrown empty liquor bottles back there. Of course, there wasn't supposed to be any liquor on board, so whatever navy officer had occupied this stateroom could not just put his empties in the trash. Instead, he'd made use of this nice hiding place. Evelyn and I laughed at this ingenuity and I laughed even harder when Evelyn showed me what was in her traveling bag: there was more liquor than anything else. So it was perfect that she'd discovered where the empties went; she hid hers there too. But by the time Evelyn had finished her bottles, the space behind the shower had completely filled up and the noise of the clatter every time the ship swayed was awful. Evelyn said, "I just can't stand that anymore!" She called somebody in to investigate, acted horrified when they discovered that the previous tenants must have put all those bottles back there, and had the mess completely cleared out. Her performance was hilarious: shock, outrage, indignity. She was great fun. And she was very supportive of me. I got very sick on the ship, although I hadn't gotten sick before when I went to Haiti and Cuba by ship. I guess it was part war fear. Evelyn would say, "Hell, girl, a couple more days and you'll be straight." But I was over the rail the whole trip. It had to do with where I was going. I'd given all this big talk about wanting to go into the middle of the war. Now, I'm saying to myself, "Why am I here?"

On this trip, we weren't just being transported; we were supposed to function as Red Cross workers to the men on board. One young soldier, a little fellow about nineteen or so, died of some illness or fright or whatever you die of in the middle of war. And there was a burial at sea, a very impressive and very sad thing to watch. They encased the body in a sack of some kind, then wrapped it in a flag. And it was slowly slid down a plank into the sea. A great, sad ceremony I'll never forget.

In Italy, I was assigned to locations where there were a large number of men from the 92nd Division, the black division. I was in Naples, Rome, Livorno, Pisa, Florence, Genoa, and Milan. Anyplace I went, my job was to work in a Red Cross installation servicing all the troops in that area. But they would assign the black workers to places where black troops predominated. I never worked with a white worker overseas. Not once. And they claimed the Red Cross was integrated.

The facilities we used varied by location. After our army liberated an area, they would confiscate a large building to be used by the Red Cross. In some places, they appropriated palaces; in other places, *dopo lavoro*, the "after-work" clubs that had been built by the *fascisti*. Or it might be a schoolhouse or a hotel that we used. We'd live either in the facility, in someone's home, or in a hotel. The army would give upper-class Italians the option of vacating their home or remaining in it as servants to the Red Cross person. In Livorno, for example, I lived in a lovely villa where the woman of the house elected to stay.

I spent my first few months in Naples. Naples. When I think of Naples, I think of Roberto. Roberto was a little Italian boy who became my child for a while. He was about four when soldiers discovered him while they were going through the rubble of a bombed building. I'd been in Naples just a few weeks when the soldiers carried this dirty, emaciated, weak little fellow into the Red Cross office and said they didn't know what to do with him. His family had apparently died in the bombing. Taking him in my arms, I knew that if no one claimed him, I wanted him with me.

In Naples, the three of us black Red Cross women working together shared an apartment. The other women became fond of Roberto immediately. We all did things for him, took care of him, but I took main responsibility. I cut up discarded army uniforms and made clothes for him. He slept with me at night and went wherever I went during the day. And I made sure he ate well. Nobody objected to my putting all the army food into him his little body could take. And it was wonderful how quickly he began to put on some weight. The army doctors said he probably had TB, but he kept looking better and better and I became very optimistic. What a warm, pleasant child he was.

Soon he started calling me "Mama" on his own, and I was feeling he was my son too. I wrote Jimmy that I wanted to bring Roberto back to the States with me and Jimmy agreed to that. And I made some inquiries of the army about how I might legally adopt him. The reaction of the white army officers was to be dumbfounded: "Isn't he white?" they asked. They couldn't fathom a black woman adopting a little Italian child. After their initial shock, they said they had no jurisdiction over such matters. Whether they were telling the truth or just avoiding the issue, I don't know. In any case, they were no help. Fortunately, they were no hindrance either. In the chaos of war, no one thought of taking him away from me. So Roberto and I were together constantly. And he was a constant source of joy for me.

My other memories of Naples are somewhat vague. I do recall the city was still quite beautiful even after it had been bombed. The saying in Italy is "See

Naples and die" because it is an extraordinarily beautiful city. As we would do everywhere, we had set up the Red Cross Club with a barber shop, a tailor shop, an auditorium for movies, and a stage and dressing rooms for the USO shows that came through.

One of my tiny achievements in Naples was managing to make a lemon meringue pie for a soldier using just my helmet and mess kit. He said he missed that more than anything else from home. This was somebody almost ready to get a section eight, a discharge for being nutty—and it's easy to be on the verge of being nutty in the middle of a war and you're nineteen years old and this is your first time away from home. So I made him this pie. I got some eggs from a farmhouse, and lemons were easy to find because they grow there. The mess kit unfolded open into two pie plate tins. And you created an oven out of your helmet by putting sterno under the inverted helmet and using part of the mess kit as the top of the oven. The other part of the kit was the pie pan itself. And he really appreciated that lemon meringue pie. I must say I was rather proud of that pie myself.

Amidst the beauty of Naples, though, there was the devastation. Thousands of people had no homes, no food. The water system had been bombed so everyone, including us, was parceled out small amounts of water each day for drinking and washing. The hunger was the most painful thing to have to witness. People were desperate. One afternoon, the day after the main post office had been bombed, I was walking from the Red Cross club to the army mess hall to eat. There were these kids in the street around a bonfire. As I got closer, I realized they had skinned a dead cat and were cooking it to eat. This was the extent of the desperation. I couldn't do anything to help them. But I couldn't eat the meal served in the mess hall that day either.

Perhaps the reason I don't remember a lot about Naples is because it was mostly shocking and painful. Nothing in the Red Cross training had prepared me for seeing bombed out buildings, desperately hungry people, for having to grab Roberto, run to a shelter, and sit in terror through yet another bombing. I've noticed that I tend to forget ugly events in my life; I guess that's how I survive. And, as beautiful as the city of Naples was, on the human level, there was ugliness everywhere.

Except for Roberto, of course. Fattening up nicely every day. Getting good color in his cheeks. As attached to me as I was to him. Like most children, he thought riding in a truck was great fun. He really enjoyed our trip to Rome in the back of a British lorry. (There was much cooperation between the Allies, so it wasn't unusual for us to travel in their trucks.)

Being in Rome was something of a break. We worked as hard there as anywhere, but, because Rome had been declared an open city, it was never bombed. What a relief that was. I knew this was temporary for me, that I'd be moved north as our army moved north, but I was so grateful for this short reprieve from the constant bombing of Naples. And it was good for Roberto too.

Our other treat in Rome was being housed in the Excelsior Hotel, an elegant place with lots of space, and, my goodness, running water! I never thought being able to take a bath would be so precious to me. In Naples, we washed as best we could with a helmet full of water. But that first night in the Excelsior, with its hot running water and mile-long bathtub, I think I took three baths. And Roberto enjoyed the nice warm water, too.

Now, I had been receiving letters from Jim Hines ever since I first arrived in Naples. He was based in England then and writing me more than once a day, as he'd promised. There was a popular Pepsi jingle on the radio at that time that said you should refresh yourself at 10:00, 2:00, and 4:00 with Pepsi Cola. So he'd said he'd try to write me three times a day so I could refresh myself myself at those hours by reading his letters. And he seemed to be doing just that because mail would pile up. I was really the laughing stock of the places I worked because I would get these stacks of mail! But I was flattered and delighted.

From Rome, I went to Livorno. We traveled again by British lorries and Roberto, of course, was with me. I decided that in Livorno I would again try to adopt him legally.

In Livorno, again there was a Red Cross club with a tailor shop, barber shop, stage, and so forth. We'd established a practice of hiring entire Italian families to work for us. The scarcity of food brought this practice about. During the work day, any employee could eat at the army mess, but they couldn't take any food out of the place. The soldiers would pat people down as they left to see if they'd taken even a slice of bread. What you had, sometimes, was a mother or a father who ate nothing during the day because they couldn't eat knowing their kids at home were starving. So we hired the little girls to pick up in the tailor shop and the little boys would polish boots in the barber ship. And the parents were hired to do all kinds of work. So our civilian employees were often an entire family—mama, papa, and kids. And everybody got something to eat.

In Livorno, there was a new challenge: a boxing ring had to be set up. It seems Primo Carnera had agreed to fight one of our men. Carnera was a huge boxer who'd fought Joe Louis years earlier at Madison Square Garden. But, by then, he was paunchy and out of shape and had returned to his home town of Livorno. So I had to find out about the Queensberry rules of boxing, the legal size of the ring, and I had to get a referee to officiate. The fight didn't last long, though. Carnera was paired with a really smallish black soldier who'd been a professional boxer. Seconds after they started fighting, the soldier landed a good punch and the out-of-shape giant of a man was down for the count. End of fight! In the first round! But I learned a lot about boxing in preparation for the few minutes of entertainment for the soldiers.

As I'd planned, I again approached the Peninsular Base Service (PBS) about adopting Roberto. They, too, thought that this was "most irregular," meaning they couldn't fathom a black woman adopting a white child. But, in Livorno, I made a wonderful discovery: my good acquaintance from New York, Klaus Mann, was based there and was a reporter on the *Stars and Stripes*, the army newspaper. He'd grown up in Europe and was very familiar with Italy. When I told him about my problems trying to adopt Roberto, he thought he could help. He suggested going to the Italian civilian authorities because they'd have no problem with the adoption. From what I could see, I tended to agree. The Italians were not as racist as white Americans. I'd seen how well they responded to the courtly manners of the black soldiers. And I could also see their accepting attitude toward the Ethiopian war brides that were coming into the country. At that time, Mussolini had been waging war in Ethiopia, trying to colonize it. Some of the soldiers had fallen in love with Ethiopian women and were bringing them home. No one seemed at all uptight about that. The Italians took that all in stride. In southern Italy, their skins are very dark anyway. And the race issue just didn't seem to bother Italians the way it did white Americans. So Klaus was sure we could work out my adoption of Roberto. He got the papers from the Italian authorities and I filled them out eagerly.

While I was in Livorno, I got to see two other old friends, too: Roi Ottley and Huerta Neals. After the publication of his book, *New World A-Coming,* Roi was much in demand by the wire services. He was traveling around Europe for the Associated Press, as I remember, reporting on the war experiences of black soldiers. He'd heard I was in Livorno and came to my villa. I was living in the elegant villa of a woman named Gentille. Her family had owned a haberdashery company, and, when she'd been given the choice of vacating the house or operating as the housekeeper to the Red Cross worker, she'd chosen to stay. She was willing to stay, I suppose, not only because it was her home, but that was a way of guarding her lovely things. She was a very cultivated human being who spoke maybe half a dozen languages and played the piano beautifully. She treated me very well and I respected the person she was in return. I regarded myself as a guest in her home.

Now, one of the rules for Red Cross workers was that we could only socialize with military officers. Our job accorded us officer rank so we could not fraternize with enlisted men when we were off duty. Our Italian civilian workers were indoctrinated by U.S. authorities to respect this stupid snobbery. So when Roi came to my villa and Gentille saw he was not an officer, she turned him away. As he walked away from the door, he saw me though the window—I was sitting, reading in the living room—and he proceeded to make a big stir, so much noise. When I realized who it was, I let him in. Then I had to listen to him playfully reprimand me for getting so "high-falutin." I had to explain to him it was not my policy, that as a war correspondent he was the equivalent to any officer, but Gentile didn't know that. He was a very arrogant somebody, so I had to go through all that. It was a fairly brief visit: he had espresso, we chatted, and he was off to some other town.

Huerta Neals also turned up in Italy. He was one of the many doctors who were drafted into the army. He contacted me from Sorrento and invited me down for Christmas, the Christmas of 'forty-four. I'll never forget that visit. Huerta was attached to a black unit which had not seen a black American woman since they left the States. There were *senorinas*, yes, but no black women. I was extremely well received, but it was a bit too much. We had this excellent Christmas dinner the soldiers had gotten from the navy. The navy always served better food. The army "mess" *was* a mess. But the navy cooks were excellent. They were mainly black cooks. And since that's about all blacks could be in the navy, they were the best they could be. On special occasions like this, if the army was in a port city, the navy would share their good food. So this black unit had arranged a dinner for me that was all this wonderful navy food. And they hired an Italian combo with a tenor to entertain me after dinner. When he sang "Return to Sorrento," all the soldiers joined

in. It was very moving. I was the only woman at the dinner and they were ser-
enading me. Because I was a black woman from the States, and that made me
very special. And when I was leaving Sorrento, there was this exhausting
scene: all the soldiers came with their canteen cups so I would tilt the cups to
my lips and leave lipstick stains on them. I felt like a politician who has to
shake hundreds of hands; I had to leave the imprint of my lips on what seemed
like hundreds of cups. I was very touched by their feeling about a black American woman.

Trips like that were a break from the work, though. Where I spent most of
my time was in the Red Cross clubs. Besides the work being hard and emotionally difficult, racism was always an issue and often created a good deal of
friction in the clubs. Everyone made use of the Red Cross clubs—no matter
what the race of the Red Cross worker who ran it. As I said, they put the black
women in locations where there was a large number of black troops, but the
clubs were used by everyone—white Americans, East Indians, British, Brazil-
ians, Moroccans, any Allied troops that were in the area. But, without question, the interaction was most tense between white Americans and black
Americans.

The basic problem was the racism of the white American soldiers. In milder
forms, it showed in their attitude toward other soldiers of color and even toward the Italians. That's why the dances we organized for the black soldiers
were better attended by the local women than the dances we organized for the
white soldiers. Yes, the dances were all segregated. But that wasn't my doing.
It was because the army itself was completely segregated. It worked like this:
a company commander would call me and ask me to arrange a dance for "our
fellows." Now, each company was either all black or all white. So you arranged
the dance and you invited the young ladies of the community. (You were supposed to carefully screen out the whores. That was part of your job, to see that
that element didn't come to the club. And it was also part of your job, in case
they did come, to see that the soldiers got condoms.) So the mothers and aunts
of the young ladies would ask, "*soldati bianci?*" or "*soldati nero?*" And, if it was
a dance for the black soldiers, we'd get an excellent turnout because the black
men were so courtly and mannerly. The 92nd Division drew heavily from the
South, and these southern blacks deferred to elderly people and were very polite to all Italians. The white soldiers, on the other hand, had a terrific arrogance toward all Italians. No matter how educated and cultivated the person,

many of the white American soldiers regarded them as "wops" and "guineas" and lorded it over them. Many of those whites were people who'd had to make use of outhouses back in the rural South, but they still thought they were superior to the "wops." So the Italian girls preferred to come to the black dances. If it was a *bianci* dance, you just couldn't get much of a turnout of the local women. Because once they'd been exposed to white American arrogance, they didn't come back for more.

But it was the black soldiers that got the brunt of the white soldiers' racism. Part of the problem, I think, was the way the army itself was structured. The companies were, as I said, all segregated. But they had different tasks, too, different level tasks. The blacks were always engineers, maintenance men, cooks, that kind of thing. They were assigned to the tasks that serviced the white troops. This reinforced the sense of superiority of the white troops and the resentment of the blacks. But the basis of the problem was, of course, good old American racism. There were arguments daily and fistfights regularly, often right in the Red Cross club. About absolutely anything.

For example, one morning a black soldier came into our tailor's shop and gave his jacket to the Italian tailor to have buttons replaced. Before he'd left, a white soldier brought something in to be repaired. When the Italian tailor told him he'd get to it as soon as he'd put the buttons on the black soldier's jacket, the white soldier got angry. He felt he was entitled to have his clothes done first, that the Italian should set aside the black soldier's jacket. So he grabbed the black soldier's jacket out of the tailor's hands and said, "You don't do that first! Do mine! Let the nigger wait!" And then, of course, the black soldier took issue with that: "What do you mean 'wait'?" And then it gets to be fisticuffs. That kind of thing happened all the time.

This nonsense extended to the Red Cross club's snack bar where white soldiers frequently demanded preferential service. It was often, "Serve us. Let the niggers wait." The Italian employees would mutter "*pazzo*" under their breath, the Italian word for "crazy." And the black soldiers would be ready to fight.

After one of those days when there'd been some of this racial mayhem, there was a USO show in the evening with Phil Silvers and Frank Sinatra. For the USO shows, everyone was invited; the audience was entirely integrated with troops from all the Allied forces in the area. Because of what had happened that day, I asked Sinatra if he knew Lewis Allen's song, "The House I Live In."

Great-grandparents Edwin Durock Turpin and Anna Elizabeth Cochran Turpin, holding two of their children. Martha Jane (Odette Harper Hines' grandmother) is on the left and Edwin Durock, Jr. ("Uncle Durock") is on the right. Circa 1874.

Great-grandmother Anna
Elizabeth Cochran Turpin,
daughter of Anna and
Running Cock. Circa 1868.

Great-grandfather Edwin
Durock Turpin, Sr., son of
Edwin Durock Turpin and
"Mary." Circa 1893.

Maternal grandparents Martha Jane Turpin DesVerney and Peter DesVerney. Photographs taken in 1880s.

Maude DesVerney Harper and her sister Gertrude DesVerney Floyd, Odette
Harper Hines' mother and aunt. Circa 1912.

Three-month-old Odette Harper, held by her paternal grandmother, Martha Hayes
Harper. 1914

Maude DesVerney Harper, Odette Harper Hines' mother, holding her three-month-old son, Clarence Harper, Jr. (called "Jack"). 1916.

Clarence Harper, Sr., Odette
Harper Hines' father. Circa 1919.

Clarence Harper, Sr., Odette Harper
Hines' father, in the doorway of the
dining car where he was "waiter-in-
charge" on the Pennsylvania Railroad's
Twentieth Century Limited. Circa 1930.

"Uncle Walter" Floyd at a banquet of the Bretton Hall Boys. Floyd is in the second row, sixth from left. This was an organization of employees of the Bretton Hall Hotel in Manhattan who had in common not only similar service jobs but their origins in Georgia. Circa 1920.

"Aunt Gertrude" DesVerney Floyd outside the 135th Street office of
Harlem realtor, Phil Payton, for whom she worked as a secretary.
Circa 1913.

Uncle Walter and Aunt Gertrude's three sons, Wilbur, Walter, and Charles (left to right).

"Godmother Mattie," Martha Frazier Wiggins, secretary to Judge Charles Toney, one of New York's first African–American judges. Circa 1912.

"Godmother Ethelle" Rhone Jackson, owner of a millinery shop in Harlem, would spend her later years with Odette Harper Hines in Alexandria. Circa 1913.

"Godmother Hattie" Frazier Walker, secretary to W.E.B. DuBois at the national office of the NAACP and daughter-in-law of Maggie Lena Walker.

Odette Harper at age four.

Odette Harper at age fourteen.

Clarence "Jack" Harper, Jr., Odette Harper
Hines' brother.

Odette Harper at twenty. This photograph was taken by professional photographer Jimmy Allen to encourage the Cheeseboro Vaseline Company to use black models when advertising in black publications.

Abyssinian Church Sunday School in 1925. The pastor, Reverend Adam Clayton Powell, Sr., stands in the center. Eleven-year-old Odette Harper is to the right of Powell, in the third row, with a tam. Her brother Jack is to the left of her, with the bottom of his face hidden.

Odette Harper, in her position as Director of Publicity and Promotion for the national office of the NAACP, attends a mass meeting of the Negro Labor Victory Committee in the Golden Gate Ballroom in Harlem. Adam Clayton Powell, Jr., is speaking. She is to the right of him in the second row, the only woman without a hat. Circa 1943.

Red Cross volunteer Odette Harper with two soldiers in
Sorrento, Italy. December 1944.

The Hines family in 1953. Left to right, James III and James II (both called "Jimmy"), Terry, Gretchen, and Odette Hines.

The Hines family in November 1956. Left to right, Gretchen, Terry, Odette, Maggi, and Jimmy Hines.

1956 Christmas dinner for the Golden Age Club of the Bethune Branch of the Alexander YWCA. Standing on the left is Odette Harper Hines, then a member of the Board of Directors of the newly "integrated" YWCA.

Odette Harper Hines in August 1991

And he said, yes, he did. And I asked, "Do you know the version they put on the screen or do you know his original version?" And he said, "No, I know the original version." And I told him there'd been an awful lot of racial strife among the troops and asked him if he would sing that song. When he sang it, he looked out in the audience and said, "Come up here, fellow," to a white, then a black, and to a person from all the different groups represented there that night. And he put his arm around the shoulders of a black man and his other arm around a turbaned East Indian who, in turn had his arm around a soldier from Brazil whose arm was around an Englishman—and they stretched on each side of Sinatra across that stage, so many races of this world. And Sinatra sang the song through one time, then asked everyone to join in the singing. And, you know, those wonderful words that Abel had written— about all races and all religions being a part of America—singing those words together seemed to change them. For a while, anyway. I was very impressed by the way Sinatra handled that. But, of course, the problem was too deep to be healed permanently by a song. It was just a matter of days before the next fight.

No matter how tense or ugly my work with the soldiers, though, I always had Roberto around me, to play with, to hum to at night. He was a kind of nourishment; he was my joy today and a part of my dream for the future. I wasn't terribly impatient about the adoption. Klaus was confident it would go through and we'd gotten no indication that the application would be denied. The legality of my relationship with Roberto was just a matter of time, I thought. He was already my son.

But the adoption never happened. I lost Roberto. In the middle of a bombing in Livorno, I lost him. I hadn't seen it coming. He'd been fine. He'd been playing in an office at the club and it was closing time when bombing began. It was about 9:00 P.M. Livorno is a port city and our ships were out in the harbor. That's partly why the Germans bombed it so often. I grabbed Roberto and ran to the shelter. It was in the basement of a building near our office. The place was full of people, mainly local people, a few soldiers, no other Red Cross workers. We were packed in there—maybe fifty or seventy-five people. Tense, huddling. A soldier sitting near me had brought his bottle of cognac into the shelter with him. The more the bombs fell, the more he drank. He offered me some, but when I declined he said, "For God's sake, Harper, do *some*thing! Here, smoke this." And he handed me a big Cuban cigar. So that's where I smoked my first cigar. But the bombing lasted much longer than the cigar did.

I was sitting on a box with Roberto on my lap. There are the explosions, then silence. And you think that's the end. Then, all of a sudden, there are shattering noises. And you know that a building near you has been blown up. We'd been in there an hour or so when I looked down at Roberto and saw blood coming out of his mouth. He'd been fine and now he was hemorrhaging, and it was only moments until he was gone. I remember the people around me yelling in Italian, "Oh, my God!" Beyond that, I can't remember what I did or said because I was just numb. He'd been fine, I'd thought. He'd recovered from the TB, I thought. And then he was dead. Roberto had become my child. And suddenly, he was gone.

The bombing stopped shortly after that. The soldiers took Roberto. I was full of tears. The soldiers took him and they buried his body. In a war, you don't have a formal funeral. You don't have any of that. If a life is over, then it's over. And my only consolation was that Roberto had a little more life than the rest of the folks that'd gotten blown up in that building in Naples.

For a long period after Roberto's death, I stayed numb. Doing what I was supposed to do, like a machine, but cold inside, devastated inside. Klaus tried to console me by taking me sightseeing whenever we had free time. But I was barely present. He took me to Florence, all the sights there, to the Uffizi Museum there; he took me to the Ponte Vecchio, the "Old Bridge," to the Viareggio where the poet Shelley drowned. We even went to San Remo, on the Italian Riviera. But I wasn't good company. Klaus tried, though. And I appreciated his caring. But the loss of Roberto had left me with an emptiness, an emptiness that couldn't be filled by art and scenery, no matter how beautiful.

From Livorno, the Red Cross sent me to Pisa for a short time, then to Florence. As more and more of Italy was liberated by the Allies, the Red Cross followed. Our work stayed the same—giving aid and comfort to the troops. But, at times, "giving comfort" was very painful because you knew it was possible the young man would not be alive much longer. Soldiers from those areas were being sent into the Po Valley, where there was still fighting. And those guys didn't get very much cover from American planes. A lot of them didn't come back. It was a very sad thing, this was. When you heard a boy you'd been talking to had been killed, you had to try and dismiss it the next day if you're in a war. Because the war goes on and you have to deal with the living. But it was hard.

The boys would come and talk to us when they knew they were going into the Po Valley. They'd leave things with us, things they wanted sent home to their folks if something happened to them. And we always saw to it that their families received whatever it was they'd left with us. They'd leave pictures of themselves—we set up a photographer's studio in most of the Red Cross clubs—they'd leave cigarette lighters, mementos from the places they'd been. Not expensive things, just items that meant a lot to them. Black and white soldiers did this. When war was dangerous, people tended to forget about my race. And, really, the black Red Cross women were never the targets of racism anyway. I guess that was because we were there to help, and also because we were women and less threatening than black men. But, even among the men, when they were in battle, they usually didn't think race as much as in situations of more safety. The tensions of war can make you develop a nasty spirit and the racial thing was always available as a good basis for a fight when danger wasn't imminent.

But race wasn't always absent on the battlefields. Some of the black soldiers talked to us very confidentially and told of incidents where they were ordered by their white officers to move forward over an area they were certain was mined. The soldiers felt that such an order came out of the officer's animosity, his belief that black lives were not very valuable. Not only did they refuse to follow his command but they pushed him in front of them: "If anybody is going to get mined in this field, you're going to be the first!" The attitude of the black soldiers in World War II was very different, I think, from in World War I. In World War I, they were really patriotic, trying to prove themselves, getting the *croix de guerre* from the French for valor. But because nothing had improved for blacks in the States between the two wars, these black soldiers didn't have that same spirit. They were there and they were going to fight for their country but many of them didn't feel they *had* a country. And they certainly didn't have any special love for these officers.

From Florence, I went to Genoa. I'll never forget our entrance into that city. One of the few really happy scenes I remember from the war. We went in with the liberation forces—with the Partisans (the anti-*fascisti* Italians) and the men from the 92nd. The response to our entrance was unbridled jubilance. The Genoans welcomed us with shouts and tears, throwing rose petals and kisses. They were just ecstatic. In addition to the city being liberated, the army had recaptured an urn from the Germans that was supposed to contain some of the remains of Christopher Columbus. Now, the fascinating thing is

that anywhere you go in Europe, it seems to me, you're going to find some
fragment of Columbus. In Madrid, in a cathedral, they've got some part of him
buried in a crypt. But the Italians claim they have a part too, and it was in this
urn. It had been stolen by the Germans because the urn was jewel-encrusted.
But the Partisans had gotten it back. To celebrate retrieving the urn and the
liberation of the city, the Partisans created a very formal mock funeral pro-
cession led by an ornately carved, ebony, horse-drawn hearse with the urn inside on a platform draped in velvet. And the 92nd followed it.

The local people were so joyous to see the Americans (who, in this case,
were almost all black) and the Partisans, who were mainly responsible for the
liberation of Northern Italy because they conducted guerrilla warfare, which
was much more successful there than any conventional tactics. But the Italians of Genoa shouted gratitude to the *"Americanos"* — all of these black men
from the 92nd and a few black Red Cross women. And, for the first time in a
very long time, I *felt* like an American, I felt some pride in being part of our
country's effort. And I thought as we rolled in, "Gee whiz, maybe I am an
American."

In Genoa, I was taken to some of the torture chambers, places the *fascisti*
had made use of to extract information from people. I remember walking into
this one room with a floor covered with several inches of what I thought were
seashells. And I asked my escort, an Italian Partisan, why seashells would have
been brought to this room when there were probably plenty down at the shore.
And he told me these were not seashells, these were fingernails and toenails
from people who had been tortured in that building. A wave of revulsion
moved through me which I still feel today when I think about what I saw in
that room.

And then there was Milan. As usual, we traveled piled into the back of a
British lorry, sitting on the floor, bouncing along. Any time I was in a lorry, I
thought about Roberto because he enjoyed those uncomfortable rides so
much. I missed him. Really, I still miss him today. By then, we were all a little weary, but we were buoyed, too, by the progress the army was making. Before we entered Milan, we'd heard that Mussolini had been captured and
killed. But I never expected that macabre scene I witnessed in the central
square of Milan.

We walked in. I can't even remember now where we were walking from —
probably some army installation. But a group of us — some soldiers and I — de-

cided to walk to the square because we heard Mussolini was there. He was there? Had they put a dead man on display? Worse. They'd hung him and some of his men and his mistress up by their feet. Upside down, as a way of showing the disdain the people felt. His mistress was the only woman in this line-up of bodies and the lower part of her was completely exposed because she'd had a skirt on when she was killed and someone had deliberately torn off her panties. But I saw a local woman run up to the body and tie the skirt around the knees to cover her exposed genitals, this ultimate shame.

The square was mobbed. Thousands of people. Noisy, relieved, glad the despot was dead. They cursed and jeered at Mussolini. The Partisan guards tied to keep some kind of order but many of them were shoved out of the way by the local people, who wanted to get close to the hanging bodies. When they did, they fired shots into Mussolini's corpse. I saw one man punch Mussolini in the face. (The bodies were hanging so that their heads were just about on the same level as our heads.) And some people in the mob spit on the faces of the corpses, creating just gobs of spittle that glistened in the sunlight as it dripped off their faces. Some images you can't erase; this is one of them. I can still see glistening spittle hanging like tassels off these upside down faces. The death of Mussolini might have been progress in the war, but I could feel no joy at this grisly scene. It reminded me of lynching back home. I just felt sick.

This was late April, 1945, and by early May the war was over. But the horrors were not. In Milan, I received orders to go to Paris to work with the Red Cross there. But before leaving for Paris, I went to visit some Red Cross friends working in Viareggio. That place was full of troops on R & R—rest and relaxation. All of them were going to the States. Some would be reassigned if their time was not up, but all of them were going back home first. An American general had ordered that some mines that had been stored in Pisa be brought to Viareggio to be stored. I don't know why he wanted to do that. But the day I was there, these mines were being removed from the trucks that had carried them from Pisa. They were being brought into an army building, a school house that also housed the Red Cross club. At the time, the building was full of soldiers; it was their sleeping quarters and they were resting before going home. The army and Red Cross had hired Italian farm people to do some of the manual labor. As usual, we'd hired entire families—men, women, and children. Some of the Italian men had formed a long line to pass the mines hand to hand from the truck into the building. They knew they were mines;

you could hear them yell, "*Mina! Mina!*," as they passed them along. At one point, some jeeps that had just been serviced by the engineers arrived, and all the Red Cross people, including me, went to see them. We were all outside. And, suddenly, the whole building blew up. Someone must have dropped one of the mines. We saw bodies, limbs, heads going up in the air. Everyone in the building was killed. And all the Italians on that line were killed, just blown to pieces. After the explosion, there were dismembered bodies everywhere. Women. Children. Soldiers. Soldiers who had been on their way home because the war was over. Italians relieved because their country had been liberated. Entire families blown to bits. *After* the war.

This had to be the end of the horrors for me. I'd always thought of myself as strong, but how many hundreds of bodies had I seen? Naples, Livorno, now Viareggio. Roberto's. When I received my orders for Paris, I welcomed leaving the devastation of Italy. My commitment to supporting the soldiers was still strong, but I was relieved I could continue to do that without the sickening aspects of war surrounding us. And the two months in Paris were a reprieve. Not the end I'd hoped for, but indeed a reprieve.

Our living conditions were comfortable; the work was without the stress of bombings and combat; and Paris was a beautiful city. I was housed with another worker, Evelyn Adjar, at the George V Hotel on the Avenue de L'Opera. At one end of the Avenue was the Paris Opera House, and at the other end, the Louvre.

The work the Red Cross did there was the same as elsewhere: I played cards with the soldiers for endless hours (I'm sure that's why I can no longer abide card-playing), I saw that USO shows were booked, I counseled, and saw that the facilities ran smoothly.

Unlike in Italy, I felt the French didn't exactly embrace American blacks. Now, this was a departure from what Uncle Oswald had said when he returned from World War I. But this was my experience. I remember going into a store with Evelyn and they were very cordial, very warm, actually hugging us. Then they asked if we were from Indochina. When we responded, no, we were black Americans, they became very cold. This was curious because the French adored Josephine Baker. The subways in Paris all had toothpaste ads, and no matter what the brand was, it was Josephine Baker's face they used. But, then, she was a star, and even in the States, bigoted people often enjoy black entertainers. In France, it might also have been some anti-American feeling that we were experiencing. But I do know that they thought being Indochinese was much better than being black American.

Paris was a dream city. I loved to walk along the banks of the Seine, browse the bookstalls that had begun to reappear, go to the little bistros in Montmartre. Paris was just a wonderful place. I was there in late summer and, because the war was over, the Red Cross work was more like a nine-to-five job—with some leisure time for sightseeing. I even got to make a trip into the lovely French countryside. It was an emotional and physical rest. But then it was over. Then I was sent to Germany.

The circumstances were entirely different from the other places I'd worked. I traveled and worked alone. The country was newly occupied by Allied troops, so, of course, there were no installations for the Red Cross. And the local people were quite resentful of this occupation. My first night in the country, in a town called Geissen, was just awful. The army had arranged for me to stay with a German family and had told the family to prepare for me. But they just didn't. They put me on a horse-hair sofa that pricked me horribly when I laid on it. So I ended up sitting up most of that first night. It was a very clean house, they were very austere people, and they swore by all that was holy that they'd never heard of a Nazi, had no idea that people were being cooked in those ovens. "No, we don't think that ever happened. Why do they tell these lies about the Germans?" By the second night, the army had forced them to make me more comfortable. One of the family members vacated a bedroom, and I slept there. But their feelings toward me—and all the Allied troops, for that matter—were clear: you're here but we wish you weren't.

In Giessen and my next assignment, Wiesbaden, my job was the same: give the troops the same kind of support as I'd done elsewhere and also try to get information about what had happened under the Third Reich in those locales. We tried to find out about missing people and about the camps. It was much more difficult to service the soldiers without any Red Cross installation. I had to go to the enlisted men's tents and talk or play cards with them there. In Germany, too, I worked mainly with the black soldiers.

Wiesbaden was being used as a place for R & R for the soldiers. We could all go to the famous spas, take the baths, and have the massages. It was somewhat relaxing for all of us. But all the soldiers were understandably restless. They wondered if they'd be reassigned to Japan; they wondered, "How long are they going to make us stay here?" Of course, I had no answers, but, as always, I listened sympathetically.

In some instances, though, being sympathetic was not so easy. For example, one soldier asked me to arrange a layette for a young German woman who was going to have his baby. So I did that. Two weeks later, he came to me as angry as he could be: "Can you imagine this? My wife's writing me that she's running around with someone else! I want to see somebody about how I can get a divorce!" And I asked, "Are you planning to marry the German girl?" "Oh, no," he said, "I'm just mad at my wife. It's the idea that while I'm over here in a war, she's doing this!" The crazy male attitude. It was perfectly alright for him to be unfaithful. He felt no obligation to the German girl who was going to have his baby. And he was going to dump his wife because she confessed that she was seeing someone else. In a case like that, I'd just say, "I can't help you with the divorce. I don't know anything about that."

Some of our soldiers really exploited the local people. They'd be dating a local girl, and, if they found out her father was a Mason, the soldier would claim he was a Mason too. They'd make inroads any way they could and become engaged. Then there'd be someone sick at home they needed to send money to. And the girl's family would give the soldier the money. It really hurt to know that they were exploiting people. Even when we knew it was happening, we couldn't interfere. We were not there to judge, just to help the soldiers when we could.

Sometimes, the local girls would come to see me about the soldiers. That happened everywhere—in Italy, France, and Germany. The most common story was that she was pregnant, he'd left, and could I find him. Often, the soldier's leaving had not been his choice; he'd just been reassigned somewhere. And many of these men were truly in love with the women. So, if the pregnancy was verifiable, I would see if I could get a line on where the fellow was. Then I'd get in touch with him, giving him all the information, including her address. At that point, it was entirely up to him if he wanted to get in touch with her. Neither the army nor the Red Cross pressured him to take responsibility.

Years later, all of this hit home when Jim Hines, by then my husband of eleven months, received one of those letters from the Red Cross. Seems he had a child in Belgium he never knew about. Actually, the letter came to him at his mother's address here in Alexandria, and she read it before bringing it over to us. I urged him to respond to the woman, help her in some way. He could have; his medical practice was going well. But his mother would hear none of it: "This woman accusing *my* child of this!" When I argued that this baby was her grandchild, she dismissed that idea by accusing the woman of promiscuity. Then she threw the letter into our fireplace and forbade me to get involved because "these white folks will lynch my child!" Perhaps she was right. If local whites in the Louisiana of 1947 had found out Jimmy had a child with a white woman, he would have been ruined if not killed. But still, although I did feel betrayed by Jimmy and fear for him, I really wanted to help the woman. And I don't think my reaction was peculiar, considering what I'd experienced in Europe. I remembered all too well the shamed and desperate faces of those Italian, French, and German girls who'd come to me for help finding the fathers of their babies. Being at the other end of the search and not being able to help was just awful.

In Germany, most of the local girls showed a distinct preference for the white soldiers, especially the Aryan-looking ones. No one there ever admitted to being sympathetic to the Nazis, but they were really indoctrinated. There were exceptions, of course—but, generally, the German girls were not too keen on black soldiers. As I said, it was just the opposite in Italy. And somewhat different in France, too. What turned the French girls off about the white soldiers was the soldiers' preconceived notion that every French girl was a tart. The guys could be very obnoxious. They did have derogatory terms for the German girls, too, and they did believe that as white Americans they were superior to everybody, but I do think they respected the Germans more than they did the French or the Italians. So this better treatment of the girls combined with the girls' Nazi racism to make much better relations between the white soldiers and the local girls there than anywhere else.

So my work in Wiesbaden was mainly social support to the black and white soldiers in a particularly pleasant setting. This didn't prepare me for my last assignment. But, then, what could have prepared me for Dachau? Dachau. I cannot begin to describe what I saw: the ovens where thousands had died, hundreds of people barely alive, corpses, endless corpses. The army had to bury them in common graves. It went on day after day after day. I just did clerical work there, recording names of the dead when possible, recording the numbers and the names of people who were sent for rehabilitation. I did no counseling or social work there, no "aid and comfort." It was just a matter of assisting the army in its tasks of dealing with the horrors of that camp.

I lived in a farmhouse a good distance from the camp—these camps were never built near any towns or residential areas. The Nazis built them way out where you had to drive and drive to get to them. I'd be picked up in a jeep or lorry every morning and driven out to the concentration camp. Some days, I would deliberately stay inside the office all day, even when I could have taken a break from the work, even though the building was cold and ugly. Because to go outside was to see sights that just tore at my soul.

I have no sense of how long I was there. Whatever it was, it was too long. Because it was a terrible, terrible place to be. For a year and a half, I had seen war horrors. Dachau was, for me, the final straw. I'd had enough long before I'd seen all those people blown to bits in Viareggio, long before Roberto died in my arms. Seeing this evidence of the systemic, well-planned torture and murder of people at Dachau hurt me beyond what I could handle. When my Dachau assignment was completed, I asked to go home.

VII

Going South

"In the front of the train and the back of the bus."

THE TRIP BACK WAS INCREDIBLY COMPLICATED. We had to get rides on whatever military plane was available. I was taken by truck back to Paris, and my journey from there was, first, a flight to Rome, then to Casablanca where I had to wait a few days. What struck me about Casablanca was the anger and sadness of the people about being ruled by the French. And I didn't blame them. What was all this talk of the French about freedom and all this outrage about the fascism of the Germans when the French themselves still had their heels on the necks of these people? It was upsetting to see colonialism first-hand—the discrimination, the control, the superior attitude of the French, the exploitation of the Arabs in every situation. It was the raw injustice of one people ruling another, so similar to the situation in the American South.

From Casablanca, I went to the Ascension Islands, then to Natal in Brazil. From Brazil, the plane was supposed to go directly to the States, but there were weather problems and we ended up flying back to Paris! I'd been traveling for about eleven days and I ended up right where I'd started. This time, the Red Cross put me on a luxury liner docked in Le Havre that had temporarily been converted to a transport to bring people home, mainly soldiers but lots of others, including some of us Red Cross folks. This time, I made it home. After a week or so, we docked in Boston in early November, 1945. I took a train down to New York, looking forward to a wonderful reunion with my parents.

I walked into the house unannounced with my own key. Now, this was humorous in itself because, when I was living at home, I was famous for misplacing my key and having to ring the bell late at night and throw pebbles at the upstairs windows to wake someone to let me in. But I'd held onto that key all over Europe. I *always* knew where it was there. Because it was my connection to home, to safety, to all that love from my family. So I just walked into the house one day in early November and took everyone by surprise. What a reunion it was! What a warm reunion.

Now, what troubled me, though, was my mother's appearance. She had aged so much. And didn't look well. Had my activities, her worrying about my being in the middle of a war done this? It took a while for my parents to tell me that Mama had been diagnosed with angina. But, she said, except for some aching in her left arm, she felt fine. I was still concerned and felt some responsibility for this change in her appearance.

I talked and talked. They wanted to know all about my adventures in Europe and I did tell them lots that first day. But mainly about the more positive, upbeat adventures. It was a while before I could talk to anyone about the horrors I'd seen.

And I told them about Jimmy, how we'd written to one another regularly through all this, how we still planned to get married. And I told them I was supposed to call him as soon as I arrived back in the States. He was stationed back at Fort Huachuca in Arizona, but was briefly at home in Alexandria. I called him that very first day I was in New York.

We wanted to see one another as soon as possible, of course. So, on the phone, we planned on my going down to Louisiana for Thanksgiving. Now, when I told my parents, they weren't too thrilled by the idea. It would have been my first Thanksgiving with them in two years, and, remember, my father did not have the most cordial feeling toward Jimmy anyway. "Who *are* these people?" he asked, "You don't know them. It seems to me, if you're going to his parents' house, you should have received the invitation from his parents." All this protective etiquette after I'd been traipsing all over the world by myself! But you are your parents' *child* no matter what you've done. So, the next time Jimmy called, I said, "Jimmy, for me to get out of here without a lot of hassle, your parents have to invite me to come." The next day, a wire arrived from his mother to my parents. That eased their minds a bit, but Daddy, especially, was still not very happy about the trip. Mama would have preferred

I have Thanksgiving at home, but she was pleased about Jimmy and I planning a marriage.

When I purchased my train ticket in New York, I made a mistake I would pay for dearly: I did not get a round-trip Pullman reservation, only one way. I'd been away from the U.S. and its insane system of segregation in the South. No, that's no excuse. I should've known better. One of the incidents everyone was talking about when I returned to the States was when black troops in the South had to watch German prisoners of war being taken into the front door of restaurants that they, the black soldiers, could not enter. The German prisoners were fed like white American citizens and the black *soldiers* had to go to a back window and get carry-out food. So I knew that the South was still the South. I just wasn't thinking defensively enough.

Anyway, it was a two-day trip by train with a several-hour stopover in St. Louis, where you changed railroads. I arrived the Wednesday before Thanksgiving. Everything was very proper and loony. Jimmy had to go and stay at his grandmother's house because you couldn't have a young lady and a young man in the house. So I stayed with his father and mother, and Jimmy stayed at his grandmother's.

Thanksgiving was pleasant and uneventful. My parents were pacified with a long telephone chat. Jimmy's mother was clearly looking me over but we seemed to get along okay. The unfortunate thing that happened was that Grady Orange, the doctor with whom Jimmy planned to go into practice, had a heart attack the day after Thanksgiving. Because there were no black hospitals in Alexandria, Jimmy and I and Grady's wife, Ruth, and daughter, Barbara, drove him to Flint Goodridge Hospital in New Orleans that same day. (Now, there was a public hospital and one floor of Baptist Hospital where blacks could go in Alexandria, but neither were very good. Anyone who could afford to avoid them, did.)

After we installed Grady in Flint Goodridge, where he would recuperate well, Jimmy drove me back to the Alexandria train station for my late afternoon departure to New York. As I said, I had purchased only a one-way Pullman in New York. And when I went to purchase a Pullman ticket in Alexandria, they wouldn't sell it to me. I was wearing my Red Cross uniform and thought maybe that would help, but it made absolutely no difference to them. I was black; that's all that was important. And, in the South, the railroad companies would sell blacks tickets only for the Jim Crow coach car, a car that was always right behind the engine and had no berths. I later discovered how some blacks in the South got around this: They'd telephone the ticket office, introduce themselves with some white-sounding name, order the Pullman ticket, and then say they were sending their maid or their "boy" down to pick it up for them. Then they'd go down and get it themselves. Once on the train, if they presented the Pullman ticket, the porter would have to allow them to use the berth. But I didn't know this strategy then, and Jimmy hadn't realized until we got to the train station that I didn't already have my ticket. So, despite my protests and my uniform, the railroad people here in Alexandria were quite nasty and quite insistent that I was going into the Jim Crow car.

During this unpleasant scene getting the ticket, Jimmy ran into an acquaintance who was en route from New Orleans and had stepped off the train to stretch her legs. She was the sister of one of his Meharry classmates and also a nurse who'd worked with Jimmy when she was in training at Hubbard Hospital. She was now attached to the army and was wearing a lieutenant's uniform. We chatted briefly and then she went to her compartment in the back of the train while Jimmy got me situated in the Jim Crow car. Also riding in this car was an army buddy of Jimmy's. He'd functioned as Jimmy's orderly overseas, but he'd been a law student before his studies were interrupted by the war. He was on his way home to South Dakota and had a very decided, non-black Western accent. When Jimmy saw him in the car, he asked him if he'd look out for me, see about my bags and things. The young soldier seemed pleased to have me entrusted to him. Apparently, he and Jimmy had become good friends.

The Jim Crow car was just awful. Besides being right behind the engine — with all the noise and fumes that that means — they had oversold it. That often happened because usually there was only one Jim Crow car per train. So no matter how many black people were traveling, they'd all be put in that one car. They assigned us three to a seat although the seats were designed for two. And, because many people were traveling with children and babies, there were often more than three in a seat. I sat down beside a couple with two adorable babies. So, in that seat, there were five of us. But they had sold seats to more people than even this overcrowded seating could accommodate. And, as a result, some of the men, mostly soldiers, had to sit on their suitcases and dufflebags in the aisles and in clusters near the door.

People had brought food and thermoses because we couldn't use the dining car. Well, you could use the dining car, but you'd be required to sit at the end, at a table right next to the kitchen. And they'd draw a curtain around you—it was on an overhead track like a shower curtain—they'd draw that around you so that the sight of you wouldn't distress the white diners. The table sat four and would remain "uncurtained" if white diners were using it. And if a black person attempted to enter the dining car when the table was in use by even one white person, the black person was told he could not come in. To avoid all this humiliation, passengers in the Jim Crow car brought shoe boxes full of food onto the train: homemade biscuits, fried chicken, sliced ham, homemade pound cake, whatever goodies well-wishers and relatives could stuff into those empty shoe boxes. And good manners dictated that you offer the food to fellow passengers. But that meant the car was full of food smells, which was especially exciting to the goo-gobs of roaches that were everywhere because the railroad companies didn't keep the Jim Crow car anywhere near as clean as the others. This promised to be an eventful trip. But I couldn't have begun to imagine how eventful.

Soon after we'd gotten underway, one of the porters came to me with a message from the nurse Jimmy had introduced me to at the station: "There's a friend of yours. And she wants you to come back to her compartment." Since they'd been so awfully nasty in the station about my being anywhere except in the Jim Crow car, I asked the porter, "Is that okay?" And he said, "Oh, yes," and took me through a number of white day coaches to the roomette the girl had. The roomette looked like a ship cabin: it had a wash basin and a seat that converted to a bed. I think there was a second bed you could pull down too.

Anyway, this young woman and I talked for a while very pleasantly. I think she was trying to be friendly to Jimmy's fiancée. (I didn't ask her at the time, but I assume she'd gotten the roomette in New Orleans using the surreptitious telephone strategy.) We talked and talked and eventually the train pulled into some station. Through the window, we saw two white Air Force officers who waved at us—at the uniformed Red Cross lady and the army lieutenant nurse. We could see from all the insignia on their chests they'd been a few places, and we had a few campaign insignia on our chests, too. They were young officers and, in some cases, the war experience had washed away a lot of the crazy racism. And I think they were just relating to us as military and quasi-military people who'd also been overseas.

They gestured through the window that they'd bring us some coffee. Most railroad stations had a USO somebody giving away coffee and doughnuts to war returnees. So they came into the roomette with coffee and stale doughnuts. They were being nice: "This is what you did for us," they joked. Apparently, they'd had good experiences with the Red Cross. So they sat and talked for a while. It was very pleasant. But I noticed the conductor going back and forth outside our open door, doing a deliberately conspicuous parade thing, apparently becoming more and more enraged. The Air Force officers were telling war stories and I was still doing what I thought was my job—listening, yakking with people, and hoping that I could make them feel better.

When it began to get late, maybe eleven or so, I started to excuse myself to go back to my Jim Crow seat. The nurse said, "Why don't you see if you can pay the additional money and stay here? I'd love for you to." And I said, "Well, I've already made friends with some people in the Jim Crow car and I wouldn't feel good about doing that. They can't come back here. I'd feel like I was being disloyal. I'd better go back where I came from." So I left and started to progress forward through all these now dimly lit cars. As I walked through, most of the people were sleeping but some of the white soldiers were awake and they still related to my uniform: "Hey, Miss Red Cross, can you get me a furlough?" That kind of thing. But I knew where I was, I knew the craziness of the South, so I did not respond. Normally, we were supposed to give them a reassuring smile and say, "I'll see what I can do, fella," or something like that. But the scene at the station and the conductor pacing outside the roomette had put me on guard. I walked through the cars very tight-lipped.

The next thing I knew, that conductor was behind me, making sure, I thought, that I went all the way to the Jim Crow car. I just kept walking through, white day coach after white day coach, because they put the sleeping cars and roomettes at the back of the train so they'd be as far away from the discomfort of the engines as possible. Finally, I reached the Jim Crow car. But when I tried to open the door, I couldn't. This conductor, who'd been "escorting" me through the train, moved in front of me, took out his keys, and, in a surly manner, said, "I keep this Goddamn door locked to make sure the niggers stay where they belong." By that time, I was writhing but I said nothing—for I knew it wasn't smart to say anything. As we moved toward my seat, he asked to see my ticket. I said, "I don't have it. It's there, tucked in the back of my seat." (I'd left it stuck on the back of my seat when I went to visit the nurse.) He picked up the ticket, saw my destination, and snarled, "New York?

You're going to be a hell of a long time getting to New York!" And walked out. Now, all the soldiers in the car had been staring at us. And, after he left, they asked me what he'd meant by that. "Oh, nothing," I said, "I don't know what he's talking about." And I really didn't. And I didn't think it helped to specu- late aloud; it would just create more confusion. So I just dismissed his remark. But I was perplexed.

I settled into my seat and took one of the babies onto my lap. And we rolled along for another half hour or so. Then, suddenly the train stopped. Outside there was moonless, starless blackness. No station. No lights. No town. The people familiar with the route said this was not a scheduled stop. So we waited. The next thing we knew, the door to the Jim Crow car flung open and that same conductor escorted three huge MPs into our car. Whites always describe our men as being big and black and burly; well, these guys were big and *white* and burly. And they carried fixed bayonets! The tension in the car was palpa- ble. Think about it. This is the middle of the night, the rural South, 1945. They were still lynching black people then. And here come three huge, white MPs, bayonets in front of them, into a train car full of black people. And the con- ductor brought them right over to me.

He told the MPs to arrest me for being drunk and disorderly. He said I'd in- sulted his porter. Now, this black porter was standing right behind him and had made it clear earlier he had nothing but pride about what I was. But he was in a position where he could say absolutely nothing. And the conductor said I'd used profane language. It was *he* who had used the profane language, as everyone in the car heard. So the MPs said, "Come on, girl." I gathered up my things, trying to figure out what had happened—that the conductor must have wired ahead to the MPs because he thought I was under military juris- diction. On a train, a conductor has the same authority as a captain of a ship. And I was trying to figure out what to do. The eyes of the people in the car showed their concern. They knew the potential dangers of my getting off that train alone in the middle of nowhere.

The young law student Jimmy had asked to look out for me jumped up to help me with my bags. As he did so, he turned to one of the MPs, and, in the thickest uneducated southern accent imaginable, said, "Please, suh, kin Ah go 'long with her? She plumb crazy." These MPs were hillbilly types, probably had never been out of the state they'd grown up in. They couldn't see through the law student's performance at all. They weren't even suspicious of it. They agreed he could come. So the five of us walked through the crowded car, through black people's caring eyes, to the vestibule of the car where a cluster of soldiers were sitting on their dufflebags. One of them stood up as I squeezed by and leaned toward me, slipping something into the pocket of the Red Cross overcoat I had over my arm and whispering into my ear, "Use it if you have to, soldier." I knew it was a gun. The movement of his body and arm was so smooth and nonchalant, the MPs didn't see his hand go into my coat pocket. And, in the noise and confusion, they didn't hear his whisper either.

The MPs then got impatient with our fumbling out of the train, and began shoving me and the law student down the steps. As the train moved away, my fear intensified. We were out in the desolation of the night, one shed nearby, no railroad station, no nothing. I started babbling: "You have no authority to arrest me! I'm not military. I'm quasi-military." And they looked at me as if to say, "What the devil is that?" And I kept on, "You're going to be in big trouble. I'm Red Cross and I'm not under military jurisdiction!" And they seemed to panic and they decided maybe they were wrong. They were saying to one another that maybe they should turn me over to civilian authorities. And I realized that maybe the tack I'd taken wasn't too smart, I'd probably fare better at a military installation than in some small southern town. But I had told them the truth; they really didn't have authority over me. Anyway, it was too late. They had decided to take us into the town and let the civilian judicial system handle us. So they ordered us to start walking. We walked about a half a mile in this darkness and came to a very small town, just a few buildings. When I asked what town it was, the MPs said, "None of your damn business!"

They took us into a small storefront which turned out to be city hall and the city jail. In there were four or five police officials of some type and a black man cleaning up. By then, it must have been 1:00 or 2:00 A.M., and why they were in there at that hour, I don't know. But they were, talking, socializing, passing around a jug of something, each taking a swig, including the black man. The MPs gave them the same story the conductor had given him: I'd been drunk and disorderly and cursed a porter. Then they left. And these "officials" decided they needed to search me. It was just an excuse for them to be obnoxious and offensive. I got patted all over. It had nothing to do with any real search for weapons because the gun the soldier on the train had given me was right there in my coat pocket and they never even looked in the coat. Nor did they search the young soldier with me—and anyone with sense would suspect a soldier might have a weapon. So this was no search for weapons at all. It was just their depravity.

Then they looked through my luggage. They put it up on a table, opened it and pulled out articles one by one. This was no real search either; it was just their curiosity. I had a silver fox jacket—they were very popular then—and one of them pulled it out asking, "What's this?" Another one answered, "That's possum." When they got to my mink coat, the same one who'd just identified my "possum" jacket said, "Oh, and this is rabbit!" These furs were entirely beyond their world. Then they went through my purse. They found the letter that all Red Cross people had been issued by the White House over President Truman's signature requesting all American citizens to extend this returning person every courtesy because of her service to the country. And they balled it up and threw it into their spittoon. Then they found a tampon. None of them had ever seen one before, and, as they tore the wrapper, they asked me what it was. I said it was "medicine," because I certainly wasn't going to discuss *that* with them. They pulled the cotton part out of the cardboard shaft and passed it between them, sniffing it, looking at it from every angle, and saying, "Oh, yah," as if they knew what it was. Thank goodness they were too bewildered to ask me any more about that.

After this "search" was over, they put me into a closet that was used as a cell. They allowed the soldier to stay outside with them, but, since I was the person under arrest, I was locked up. This was literally a closet, with no windows, one chair, and a bucket that served as toilet facilities. I knew right away that was its function because they hadn't cleaned out the fecal material of the previous occupant. Can you imagine what a small closet with no windows and exposed feces must have smelled like?

Fortunately, they put my luggage in there with me, and, as soon as they shut the door, I got writing paper out of my suitcase and began writing letters to people in New York asking for help. I wrote Al Deutsch on *PM*, a New York paper, Ted Poston, a black reporter on the *Post*, somebody on the *Amsterdam News*, Thurgood at the NAACP, anyone I could think of that might be able to get me out of this. I still didn't know where I was. I wrote that I was "somewhere beneath the Mason–Dixon line," and "Please find out where this is from the postmark. Please make as little fuss as possible and get me out of here!"

Now, how were these going to get mailed? I could hear the loud, foul conversation of the whites outside and I could hear the black man sweeping around near my door. I realized he was my only possibility. I didn't know if he'd mail them or take them directly to his boss, but I had to take that risk. I was sitting holding my letters, trying to figure out how I was going to get them to him, when he opened my door and asked how I was doing. I was so excited. I told him I was alright and asked him if he'd mail my letters. And he said, "Yes, Ma'am." When he took them, I panicked a little, wondering where this was going to lead. But he mailed them! Everyone who received those letters said they knew I must have been petrified when I wrote them because the handwriting was so bad and the tone so desperate. And people who knew me knew the charges had to be a lie because I had always been a teetotaler. Because of those letters, there were articles later in all the New York papers about the "Jailed Red Cross Worker."

But that night—and it must have been about 4:00 or 5:00 A.M. when I gave the letters to him—I had no idea if they'd even be mailed. After he left, closing me in again, I just sat there on the rickety chair, ramrod straight, trying to keep my uniform crisp and to keep my spirit strong, and praying to the powers that be that I keep my sanity in this stinking closet and get out of this situation alive. I was *so* frightened. I didn't know what to expect, but I knew how totally vulnerable I was. Honestly, I was more frightened that night than I had been during all the bombing in Italy.

After a couple more hours, one of the whites opened the door (the sun had come up, thank God!) and told me the judge would be there at 4:00 in the afternoon. I was exhausted but that news made me feel a little better. At least I knew when I'd get out of the closet. So I sat and I stood and I sat, never sleeping, never eating or drinking anything, all day long.

At about 3:45, they came and got me and walked me and the soldier over to what looked like a garage. Above the garage, there was a loft where court was held. And into this court walked the judge, a surprisingly young man who I later found out had just returned from the war overseas. They told him what my crimes were; that is, they gave him the conductor's story. Then he asked me my version of what had happened. And I told him. And, while I was talking, I could see some kind of little lights going on in his head. And he realized all of this was about southern racial attitudes. So then he asked, "Were there any witnesses?" And the men said, "Yes, sir, that boy," pointing to the soldier who'd gotten off the train with me. And the judge asked him, "Did you see any of this?" And this educated Westerner again spoke in a fake ignorant southern accent, "No, suh, Ah's sleep!" So there were no witnesses. They had no basis for anything. The judge said, "There's really no case here. Dismissed!" The soldier and I hugged and the local yokels looked thoroughly annoyed. They'd been waiting a long time for me to get my comeuppance. And when the judge ordered them to take us over to the train stop and put us on the first northbound train, they were even more disgruntled. But they did it. We got on the first train out of there (and "there," I'd finally found out in the courtroom, was Newport, Arkansas). We were put on the Jim Crow car, of course. But that was just fine; I welcomed being surrounded by black people. The soldier got off in St. Louis to make a connection to South Dakota and I continued on to New York, unable to sleep, as exhausted as I was, trembling a bit the whole way.

In New York, the incident got a lot of attention in the press. Reporters from all the newspapers—the *Post*, the *Amsterdam News*, the *Daily Mirror*, *PM*, *Journal America*—all came to our house in the Bronx to interview me. And Thurgood assigned the case to one of the NAACP lawyers to sue the Missouri–Pacific Railroad. He didn't take it himself because he thought the suit might entail a trip to Arkansas, and Thurgood, by that time, had a real aversion to going into the South. He had gone to Columbia, Tennessee, to try a case, and when he'd gotten off the train, the local sheriff—knowing who he was and why he was there—came up to him and poured liquor all over him. Then he arrested Thurgood for drunkenness and put him in jail. After that, Thurgood just didn't want to go South. But he worked with the lawyer assigned to my case and it was eventually settled out of court. The railroad paid me $1,500. They admitted the conductor was wrong and paid what was, at that time, a substantial settlement.

Back in New York, I applied to go to China with the Red Cross. Yes, I still wanted to marry Jimmy, but I'd always wanted to visit China, and since the Red Cross had operations there, servicing American troops, I thought I might do that before we were married. Jimmy had not yet been released from the army. He was still assigned to Camp Huachuca in Arizona and was saying he wanted to get his practice going in Alexandria and get his ducks together before we got married. I was to find out later he was also waiting for a divorce from a young Arizona school teacher he had married just weeks before going to Virginia. But, at that point, I didn't even know there was a wife. His claim that he wanted to be financially more secure when we married made sense to me; I had no reason not to accept that as a reason we should wait a bit. And I'd been curious about China since I was a little girl, when one of my distant cousins married a Chinese man and, because it was the custom, had to send her first son back to his village in China. That astounded and intrigued me as a child. I became fascinated by this country with such strange customs. While I waited for the assignment, I often went into the Bainbridge Avenue office where my friend Sybil Gowdy, another black Red Cross volunteer who remains a close friend today, worked. She did Red Cross kinds of activities: services to people burned out of their homes, that kind of thing.

As the weeks wore on, I became impatient with the reassignment to China not coming through. So I decided to resign from the Red Cross. Part of the termination procedure was a physical exam. And someone mixed up the results of my chest x-ray with that of a person with tuberculosis, and I got that frightening news. I'd already called Jimmy and told him we'd have to call off the marriage before they discovered the mix-up and told me I was quite healthy. It was a harrowing week. I thought I'd gotten the same disease my brother Jack had gone into a sanitarium for. But, even when Jimmy thought I had it, he wanted to look after me. Told me to come to Alexandria, that his mother would give me good care until he got out of the army. He was, I guess, really in love. But we were both so relieved when we found out it was all a mistake.

It was soon after that I first heard of his marriage. And in the most peculiar way. Jimmy called the house all the time from Camp Huachuca. They were happy calls, fun-filled and loving. Jimmy was and still is a very charming, playful person. Sometimes he'd talk to my parents, sometimes there'd be more than one of us on the extension phones. This call in late February—I remember I was upstairs in the library area and Mama was on the extension down in the kitchen—this call in late February was as pleasant and light as they all were. Out of nowhere, Jimmy said, "Now we can set a definite date for the wedding. My divorce came through today." I think I said, "What?" He repeated it. And I don't remember what happened after that. My mother heard a thud over her head and ran upstairs to find me on the floor. The news that Jimmy had a wife was so unexpected, so shocking, that I'd fainted! In all our talks, those piles of letters, in such apparent intimacy, there was never a mention of a wife. Even now, I still don't remember anything else about that day, after hearing his words about his divorce. Mama and I agreed not to tell

Daddy. He'd never approved of Jimmy, anyway, and he was not to be told Jimmy was divorced. Since then, I've wondered why I went ahead with the wedding plans after discovering he could be so dishonest. But I was very much in love, too. And a little stupid, I guess.

We set the date for March 16th. Jimmy would be discharged from the army by then, and we could have the wedding in New York. Everything went pretty much as planned. Jimmy flew in about a week before the wedding. (That flight was an adventure in itself. They were still giving military people priority, so, as a civilian, Jimmy was repeatedly bumped off of planes. The trip took much longer than expected.) Our time before the wedding was heavenly. Friends gave us parties almost nightly. We went to the theater almost daily. In fact, we kept neglecting to get the marriage license because we were having so much fun. We'd get up late because of all the evening entertainment, then set out for the License Bureau. But we'd see an advertisement for a matinee and we'd decide to go to that first. A couple of times we got to the License Bureau just after it closed. Then we'd come home for dinner, giddily happy, and having accomplished absolutely nothing for yet another day! What fun we had.

The marriage took place at the Church of the Master because I had worked with Reverend James Robinson at the NAACP, and he just loved marrying people. There were about two hundred people there. People from Abyssinian, from the NAACP, the Red Cross, all my leftist friends, and of course, all my relatives. My gown was ivory-colored with a high collar and long sleeves, fitted and full length. The veil was made of *point d'esprit* that I'd brought back from Europe. On the gown were lace inserts that also had the feeling of being *point d'esprit*. And that later became part of my first child's bassinet. Gretchen's bassinet was made with parts of my wedding gown, and also had a crocheted cover that had been made for my maternal grandmother's bassinet. Then it was on my mother's bassinet, then mine, and then Gretchen's.

The reception was held at Evelyn Vaughn's house in Sugar Hill. At that time, Sugar Hill was a northern extension of Harlem where better-to-do blacks lived. In Manhattan, blacks just kept moving north. The early black community of the eighteenth century was way down around Waverly Place at the bottom of the island. Then, in the nineteenth century, they moved to the area called the "Tenderloin District" around 40th Street. The Irish–black riots during the Civil War were in that area. These two groups were living in the same area and competing for the same jobs, so there was much tension. By the early twentieth century, blacks had begun to move up above 125th Street to Harlem. Harlem was originally a Dutch settlement, a farm area. In the latter part of the nineteenth century, the more successful elements in the Jewish population had been responsible for making it a community of apartment houses and one of the nicest parts of the city. These apartments were spacious, multiroomed, and with quarters for live-in servants. So better-off blacks moved into Harlem first, and then, as the area became predominantly black, they moved up to Sugar Hill just above Convent Avenue. Sugar Hill really was a hill, very serene and well kept. By the forties, this was were the "high-falutin' " folks dwelled. 409 Edgecomb Avenue was a famous address because so many outstanding black people lived there—Langston Hughes, Thurgood Marshall, Lester Granger, Walter White, and many other leaders of the community.

Evelyn lived on Sugar Hill, so that's where our reception was. Evelyn was the Red Cross buddy I'd roomed with on the trip over to Europe. Her house was *very* elaborate. Not a brownstone; it had a granite front and the upper part was English Tudor, a kind of bastard English Tudor. She'd recently been married, so we had a joint reception. There was a three-piece combo, endless food, dancing, and more dancing. It was just a very happy gathering.

After the reception, we went back to the house in the Bronx. Our honeymoon was just a couple of days at Godmother Ethelle's house in St. Albans because Jimmy had to get back to Louisiana to start his practice. Godmother Ethelle had converted her attic into an apartment, so we had privacy. And there were more parties given by some people on Long Island. Those few days were very happy, too. We then came to Louisiana by train. And I began my life here in the South. The South of 1946.[1]

EVERYTHING WAS SEGREGATED HERE THEN. Absolutely everything. Every restaurant, public building, school, water fountain, park, you name it. It was either for blacks or for whites. And the black facilities were always worse. The city buses were like those throughout the South: white people sat in the front and black people sat in the back, with the bad smells and bumpiness. It occurred to me this seating was just the opposite of the train seating. But that's because the noisy, smelly motors were at opposite ends, and we were always put next to the motors. In the front of the train and the back of the bus, as a friend of mine said. Always in the worst facilities. Stepping out of your home and your black community, at that time, meant stepping into ugliness, discomfort, oppressiveness. But I was determined this place wasn't going to oppress *me*.

My first big personal distress was when I went to register to vote. Now, I had been voting in New York since I was twenty-one, and I didn't intend to let these crackers stop me now. But it wasn't easy. They had two separate lines in the Registrar's Office — one for whites, one for blacks. They would have to finish the white line before they would deal with people in the black line. So, if you were black, you could spend the day there and the Registrar's Office could close without your ever getting to even fill out a form. That happened to me repeatedly. I had to go up to the Registrar's Office any number of times before I was able to get to the Registrar's counter.

When I did finally get to the counter, things became even more ridiculous: they put black people through a whole lot of foolishness that whites weren't subjected to. We had to read a part of the Constitution and interpret it to the Registrar, a somebody who couldn't even read all the words in it himself. And the interpretation had to meet with his approval. Then the Registrar might ask, "What's 'due process'? What's '*ex post facto*' ?" Only blacks had to deal with all that; it was entirely different for whites. For them, there was no reading of the Constitution, no questions, only filling out the form. But we had to go through so much. And, of course, most of the time, our interpretation of the Constitution and our explanation of *ex post facto* was considered incorrect. Very few of us — just a few professionals — were registered when I got here.

In that way, Rapides Parish (of which Alexandria is the seat) was better than many in Louisiana. There were some that wouldn't allow *any* black voters. West Feliciana, for example, southeast of here, allowed absolutely no blacks to register. The last black registrant had been in 1902, and, through intimidation and sheer wickedness, they'd prevented blacks from registering for decades. It wasn't until CORE became active in Louisiana that a black person, a Reverend Joseph Carter, was finally able to register in West Feliciana in 1963! And they didn't get any real numbers until after the 1965 Voting Rights Act. Alexandria was just a little better than that.[2]

Until the mid-forties, Rapides Parish had had only one black registered to vote since the 1920s. (I'm sure there were blacks registered during Reconstruction, but the Reign of Terror disenfranchised blacks here as everywhere else in the South.) In the twenties, a light-skinned insurance agent named

Howard Williams got himself registered. But he was in no way a threat. First, he was only one person. And, second, he didn't stand out as an irritant in the Registrar's Office because he looked like a white person. So the Registrar could be halfway civil to him, even knowing that he was black. The Registrar wasn't going to get fired for registering him because the white people in the office couldn't report that he'd registered a black person. They didn't know. And I understand Williams never voted. He registered Republican and Louisiana was overwhelmingly Democratic, so he took no part in the Democratic shenanigans. When I arrived here in 1946, there was just this handful of black registered voters. I heard that Spencer Bradley, Louis Berry, Teely Jones, and Linda Dorsey were the first group to register in the mid-forties. Then a few more followed. But, whenever the numbers got to what the whites considered too high, there'd be a purge, and black folks would have to start all over again.

Nevertheless, from the time I arrived here, I urged blacks to try to register to vote—because one of the NAACP mottoes was "A voteless people is a voiceless people." So everyone I talked to eventually ended up hearing about the importance of voting and the things that gave you rights as full citizens. I organized rides to the Registrar's Office and to the voting booths. I've never stopped working on this. Even today, I go and work at the registration tables set up at the shopping mall, still talking to our folks about the importance of their vote. But that kind of activity began almost as soon as I arrived here.

And so did my first pregnancy. Just after we moved into our apartment, I found out I was going to give birth in December. (This was about two months after I arrived in Alexandria. We'd stayed with Jimmy's parents while we looked for a place of our own.) I was absolutely ecstatic. Jimmy and my doctor had some concern because of my history of illnesses—which had never been definitively diagnosed but which, by that time, some medical folks were speculating might be sickle cell anemia. There was a question whether I could carry the fetus to term. In fact, the doctors expressed that same concern during all of my pregnancies, and after each of the births, recommended I not have any more children because it was so dangerous to my health. And here I am still, with four beautiful grown children and umpteen grandchildren. So much for medical wisdom. I always wanted children and I just knew I could have them. I did take the doctors' advice to slow down during the pregnancies. But I never doubted.

Anytime I see a pregnant person in the summertime in Louisiana, I say a little prayer for her and my heart goes out. Because it's really something to carry that extra load and live with the humidity and the heat. That first summer here, I was pregnant and the heat was very hard to adjust to. In 1946, there was no such thing as air conditioning in homes. We had a fan and I thought the fan was the most wonderful thing. I'd have it blowing right at me all the time. Despite all that, though, I stayed active in voter registration work, and I even got involved with the black YWCA. Until September, when I left to be pampered in New York.

Because of my supposed fragile condition, I went home to have the first baby because, as I've said, blacks didn't have access to any decent hospitals here in Rapides Parish. Jimmy drove me to New York in September and I stayed there until Gretchen was born on Christmas Day. Jimmy spent money like crazy flying to New York every three weeks or so for a weekend. I wasn't very active, and as I got bigger and bigger, Mama would laugh! My New York friends were always visiting. The house was always full. My Red Cross friend, Sybil, had just adopted my mother as hers after her own mother had died. Sybil was staying at our house then and so was another friend of mine, Carol Henderson. So, although I wasn't doing my usual running around, it was still a *very* nice time for me.

The birth itself was a long affair. The water bag broke on Sunday evening and Gretchen wasn't born until Wednesday. I was in Fordham Hospital and Jimmy flew up the day after she was born. It was all so special: the birth of your first child is such an extraordinary event in your life. I was a little disappointed that Gretchen could not be born at home in the same room in which I had been born. But I had to stay in the hospital for three days. Then we were back in that room. And if we'd still been sufficiently antediluvian, she'd have been born there too. It was still all so special.

We tried to come back to Louisiana right away, but there was a blizzard. We'd set out in a taxi but it was so bad, we couldn't distinguish street signs or sidewalks or anything. So we had to turn back and stay in New York for another week before we could fly out. The airlines said Gretchen was the youngest passenger they ever had. She was only ten days old.

Back in Louisiana, for a while most of my time went to taking care of Gretchen. But we did have help in the house. Jimmy always accused me of waiting on the maid. But that wasn't true, and our help—a woman to help with the baby and another for housework and cooking—they made it possible for me to resume my voter registration activities and to get more involved with the YWCA.

At that time, like everything else, there were two separately operating YWCAS in Alexandria—one white, one black. The white Y was housed in a beautiful old building and the black Y was in a room at the black community center. Now, this is how that had come about: during World War II, there were two segregated USOs in Alexandria—a white one on Bolton Avenue and a black one on Casson Street. The city had promised that, after the war, they'd become community centers. But, when the war ended, the city did create a white community center on Bolton but took back the facility that had housed the black USO and rented it to a pants factory. So black people protested and filed suit. Jimmy, Louis Berry (who had just gotten his law degree at Howard), Reverend J. M. Murphy, the president of the NAACP, Jim Hovell, Dan Anderson, some other black businessmen, they were at the forefront of that fight. And they won. So the black USO building became the Casson Street Community Center, and one room in the building was allocated for the YWCA.

Neither Y was a full member of the national organization. The white Y was called an "affiliate," and we, the black Y, had no official status at all in the eyes of the national Y. However, they were gracious enough to send us Y literature and respond to all our correspondence. The white Y could not get full membership because it refused to integrate its board and membership. We went along like that, operating completely independently, until 1954 when the United Fund and the national Y office demanded the two groups merge in some way or lose all funding and the right to use the YWCA name.

Prior to 'fifty-four, though, the black Y had excellent programs. Jo Lawson, the wife of a local black dentist, was the director, and I soon became president of the board. Jo ran an excellent program: there were classes in sewing, piano, nutrition, literacy, there was a Golden Age Club, Thanksgiving and Christmas dinners, all kinds of things. Most of our instructors were volunteers and did this as a way of helping the less fortunate in the black community. The white Y was much more middle-class in its focus, really largely a bridge club.

We were constantly writing the national office to come down and evaluate the situation in Alexandria. The white Y had better facilities, but we knew we had a better program, a program that was closer to the purpose of the national Y. I put a lot of time into the Y in the late forties and early fifties. It was very fulfilling to me. Anyway, it was up until 1954; after that, after "integration," it became something of a headache.

In 1954, the national office—very much influenced, I would say, by the Supreme Court *Brown vs. the Topeka Board of Education* decision—the national Y absolutely demanded that segregation here end. They told the white Y they'd have to incorporate us as a branch or they could no longer call themselves a YWCA. Right around that time, the United Fund came into existence, and it, too, told the white Y that no funds would be given to segregated organizations. So they had no choice.

(But let me say that Northerners should not be self-righteous about segregation in the southern Y's. In the forties and fifties, there was really not that much difference between the Y's operations in the North and in the South. The Y's in Manhattan were segregated. The YMCA on 135th Street and the YWCA on 136th Street were completely black, and the Y's downtown were white. There's no getting around that. If a black had tried to use the downtown Y's, he or she would have been told to go uptown to the Y. Segregation is segregation.)

In Alexandria, the change to integration was no real blessing for the black Y. We did start getting funds from the national office, but we had less autonomy, much more unpleasant paper work, and we had to be in contact with some very racist white women here. Some of us were required to be members of the board of the white Y, which became the main Y and we became the Bethune Branch. Just attending those board meetings was so aggravating.

The director of the main Y was a woman I just couldn't stand. She was a rabid segregationist and was now over us. Of course, she made life difficult for Jo Lawson in every possible way. She'd edit our reports to the national office in a way that would diminish Jo's accomplishments and exalt her own. Part of her motivation for doing this was just plain jealousy, because she knew our program was better than hers. But most of it was racism; she deeply resented having been forced to deal with black women. She'd make regular visits to our branch that were really to see that black folks were staying in their place. She'd always discourage us from contacting the national office directly, afraid we'd complain about how this supposed "integration" of the Y's was working. She'd snoop around at papers on desks and make remarks like, "You know that our being an affiliate is completely our responsibility. So please don't make confusion. You're not to make calls to the national office. We're all going to get along. We *love* you people!"

We were barely able to survive that love. In a sense, we didn't. All our courses now had to be approved by her and the white board. All our disposition of funds. That became a big issue because we'd been raising money for a new building before we became the branch of the white Y. And we felt we should continue to have control over that money. By the early sixties, we were able to purchase a newly renovated building on Broadway, between the homes of a black undertaker and a black school teacher. We operated in there extremely well for a few years. Then the main Alexandria Y said that two Y sites could not be maintained in a city this size. Alexandria was probably about 40,000 people then, and about half black. They used statistics to destroy what was a good program for the black community, saying it was economically unfeasible. Meanwhile—and maybe I'm paranoid, but I do believe that white folks plan such destruction way ahead—meanwhile, they were negotiating to buy a large piece of land beyond MacArthur Village, an area on the edge of the city where there are virtually no blacks. The argument was that they could build an even larger YWCA that could accommodate all the activities of both the main Y and the Bethune Branch. So they closed down our Y in 1972. And today, the only Y operating is so far out that poor people without cars—black and white—cannot possibly get to it. And that's who the Y is supposed to be for, isn't it? But the people who predominated on the white board were the wives of doctors and ministers and lawyers, upper-class people who didn't want "white trash" in their Y much more than they wanted black people. They liked the Y to be a place where they could meet for their bridge games. And that's pretty much what it's become.

A few upper-middle-class blacks go and use the swimming pool out there. But, because of its location, there's no danger of that Y being invaded by the people who would absolutely benefit by an association with the YWCA. For the longest time, some of the white board members were urging me, "Please come to the Y." But I don't want to go there. It's not doing what a YWCA should be doing. It's not servicing the people who most need it. That's my indictment of it.

When I was very active with the Y, though, back in the forties and early fifties, I felt it was very worthwhile. Besides being president of the board, I taught French and worked on fundraising for our new building. It was all *very* satisfying to me. Meddling has always been satisfying to me.

Ten months after Gretchen was born, I became pregnant again with a baby due in May 1948. There were many problems with my second pregnancy:

edema in the legs, pains that wouldn't let up. I was in and out of Flint Goodridge Hospital in New Orleans a number of times. But, when I could, I still worked on voter registration, with the YWCA, things like that. In southern cities at that time, there were so many kinds of racial injustices, you had to keep trying to correct things in some small way. But this pregnancy was tough. It did slow me down.

As before, I went to New York to have the baby. Jimmy drove me because I'd been having so many problems. And, although he hired Earl Gelden to help him with the driving, he did all the driving himself. We took Gretchen, and because this was his "precious family," he never let Earl get behind the wheel. He paid him chauffeur wages but didn't trust us with him. "This is *my* family," he'd say.

Because of all my physical problems, Jimmy took me up there in January, four months before the baby was due. Our trip up was in rough weather and it was difficult, without any tire chains or anything. It was good another man was there to help Jimmy. They left me and Gretchen in New York after hiring a woman, a follower of Father Divine, to help take care of Gretchen. For the next few months, Jimmy was again flying back and forth from Alexandria, looking in on his family while keeping up with his medical practice. On one of his visits, Gretchen told her father that the woman who was taking care of her would sometimes pinch her to discipline her. Jimmy took the woman to task on that, and her response was that she couldn't do a thing like that, she was part of Father Divine's church and she was "full of love." And Jimmy (who has always been "straightforward," shall we say, in his language) told her she was full of something else and he got rid of her. Miss Frances, whom Mama had hired to take care of the house when I was twelve, was still there and she volunteered to take care of Gretchen: "Let me look after that baby." She was just wonderful with Gretchen. We didn't need to hire anyone else.

The baby was born the second week in May in Fordham Hospital. He lived a number of hours but died. I was just devastated. Nothing could feel worse for a mother, because your attachment begins when you know you've got that baby inside you. And it deepens when it grows and moves and kicks inside you. The loss of a baby is a horrible experience. What made it worse was that people around me wouldn't let me share what I was feeling with them, wouldn't let me grieve. If I tried to talk about the baby—and for weeks, months after his death, that was all I really wanted to talk about—but if I tried to talk about it, they'd change the subject or say, "Don't worry about that. You'll have other children." I didn't want to hear about other children. What about this one?

While I was in labor in the hospital, Godmother Ethelle had created a nursery for me at our house. She used some yellow gingham I'd brought from Italy and created the prettiest nursery. Or so I heard. Because, by the time I got home from the hospital, it had all been dismantled. All the baby things were gone. They were going to forget the baby. They thought that was the best thing to do. But that wasn't very easy for the person who'd had the baby.

Jimmy decided I was still very weak and should just get bed rest. I wasn't allowed to go anywhere. Mama and Jimmy would go to the theater—they were good buddies—but I had to remain at home. When they came back, they wouldn't even tell me about the doggone play because they didn't want to upset me. I remember that one of the plays they saw was *Finian's Rainbow*. I remember that because my old friend, Carlton, had brought tickets to the house for me and my husband. But I couldn't go. I was being treated like an invalid, and, although I knew it grew out of their concern for me, I didn't think it was the right way to treat me. I was extremely frustrated.

One day during this confinement, when everyone had gone out to a matinee and I was just sitting in my bed crying, Earl, the chauffeur that was never allowed to drive, said, "Mrs. Hines, do you want to get out of here?" I said, "Oh, yes! I do!" So he offered to take me for a ride. I was so grateful to him. The car was there because they never drove into Manhattan; they always went by subway. So Earl helped me into the car and we drove around the Bronx. I showed him places I used to go—Poe's cottage, the Fordham Road shopping district—and we went past Fordham University, and then came home. What a treat that was for me! I had been a prisoner for days and days. They were lavishing all the love in the world on me, but it was a difficult and frustrating situation.

All this time, I was bound up too. For six weeks after the birth of all my babies, I was partially mummy. It was the custom then; this was the way to keep your figure. Jimmy and Mama were great for wrapping unbleached muslin around my middle which had to stay on all the time. It was *so* uncomfortable. Bathing was absolutely miserable. You couldn't take a bath; I'd have to take showers and I'd cover the muslin with a piece of shower curtain to keep it from getting wet. It would sometimes get damp but it wouldn't get saturated. I guess this wrapping made all the organs go back in place. When I emerged from this mummification, I did have the same outlines that I'd had before. But, because of those bindings, I hate tight-fitting clothes today. I can't stand being bound up.

I was still bound when we drove back to Alexandria. They had extended the back seat of the big Buick to make a bed in the back. Everything was made very comfortable, and I slept a lot. You get awfully tired delivering babies. Gretchen was held on Earl's lap. The two men never slept. We never stopped. This was one of Jimmy's insanities on long trips. Although, once we got below the Mason–Dixon line, it wasn't so insane; it was self-protective. Stopping could easily mean being insulted or worse. And Jimmy wasn't going to have us hassled by white folks on the road.

To avoid having to stop, we would pack enough food and water in the car for the entire trip. And we carried a vessel for urine. For other elimination, we'd stop on one of those long stretches of highway, wooded on either side, and that would be our bathroom. We'd pack food that would not perish. All the black people I knew who had to drive any distance through the South did this. Not grieving about it, though; it was like getting ready for a picnic. In preparing the food, you'd indulge in luxury items that you wouldn't necessarily have at home. All that was to compensate for the ugly aspect of the situation—which was that you were not wanted at any inns.

We'd stop only for gas. If you had a child with you, you might stop in a grocery store in a large city to get fresh milk and fruit. Not in any small towns, though. You tried not to stop in them even for gas. The gas attendants might be rude: "Looks like this car costs too much for you to be driving it." And then you'd have to be on the lookout that they didn't find some way to mutilate the car. The people in these gas stations were often very unhappy with their own economic situations, and to see a "nigger" in something they couldn't afford was troubling to them. We tried to always stop in big cities because cities had a higher level of living and less anger on the part of white people.

We plotted our trips carefully. We sat down with the road map and planned everything ahead. Usually the trip from New York to Alexandria took a day and a half. Lack of sleep was not a problem for Jimmy. That probably came from his thirty-six–hour shifts as a resident. He had been trained to function without sleep. Jimmy knew how much gas the tank held, how many miles per gallon the car did, what the mileage between each city was, all of that. He was firm he wasn't going to subject anybody to the things that could happen to black people on southern roads. And all that planning paid off: we never had an unpleasant encounter on any of those car trips through the South.

We arrived safely back in Alexandria. But for the next few months, I just wasn't myself. The loss of the baby had wiped me out. I neglected meetings I was supposed to go to. I just didn't really care. Most of the bounce had been taken out of me. My friends still visited me. Jo Lawson came often because her daughter was near Gretchen's age and the children would play together while we watched them. Actually, *she'd* be watching both hers and mine because I was just not really there. I don't have much memory of that summer, but people told me later I seemed profoundly sad.

But that was the last time I've gone through that kind of inertia. That period of doing nothing but feeling bad taught me something. You have to move. You have to get up and get involved when you're in pain. Doing something for other people, letting yourself feel others' love, that's what will keep you going. If you're alive, live. Don't sit down and wallow in your sadness. There have been blows since then; horrible, unspeakable things have happened to me. But I have never again become the kind of inert vegetable I was that summer after my son died. Never again.

By the fall, though, I was coming out of that depression. I resumed my activities, including a lot of entertaining. Part of being a doctor's wife in the South, at that time, was being a social worker. After Jimmy's patients told him all their medical problems, the next stop was to call on the doctor's wife and tell me what was really hurting them. And I would offer some kind of solace. I would say, "Oh, I'm sorry. Things are going to get better," and offer a kind of encouragement. I could not be aloof from the people, because they depended on me. Doc's wife was part of the service.

Not only did Jimmy's patients expect to be able to talk to me about their problems, but his colleagues, acquaintances, and sometimes even strangers expected to be able to stay at our house anytime they were traveling through Alexandria. Remember, they couldn't stay at white hotels, and, except in very large cities, there were no black hotels. So any long-lost fraternity brother or friend of a friend from school traveling from Tennessee to New Orleans or wherever would call—sometimes at 2:00 in the morning—and expect to be made comfortable. And he would be. No matter how inconvenient for us. Most of our guests were fairly interesting people. And I would act like they were even if they weren't. I knew that, too, was part of my job.

Our apartment was a small one-bedroom in a duplex on 3rd Street, owned by a black dentist, Jim Hovell. Guests slept on a sleep sofa in the living room, and it seemed to be occupied more than it was not. Some of our guests were total strangers who'd been given the name of the black minister and doctor in the city and just called needing a place to stay. And some were very notable people here to give a talk or receive an award or something. No matter how famous or rich, in those days, white hotels would not take them, and the black communities of the South made provisions.

That's how I met Jesse Owens.[3] He was traveling through the South promoting black films. Now, a white film promoter would certainly have access to a hotel. But Jesse Owens, as famous as he was, could not stay in any local hotel simply because he was not white. This was during the period he was ignored entirely by the country. He'd become famous at the 1936 Olympics, but when he came home, white America ignored him. The accolades came later. At this point, he was a has-been—at least in the eyes of white America. He'd gotten this little job promoting black films and he'd landed in Alexandria. He just went to the black neighborhood and asked for the name of the black doctor. (As I said, this wasn't unusual; black travelers often did this when in a town where they knew no one.) Folks gave him Jimmy's name and directed him to his office. And Jimmy brought him to our apartment. He stayed with us for the entire two weeks he was promoting these films here. And because he only had to appear on stage in the evening when the films were shown, he had lots of free time.

I enjoyed him immensely. He was just a wonderful person. He was a good storyteller, and I heard all about the Olympics in Germany. He was extremely bitter about how white America had treated him when he returned to the States, but I wouldn't say that he was a bitter person. No, he was a strong, positive, and very pleasant person.

Now, one of the things he wanted to do was try chitterlings. Apparently, his family had left the South and gone to Ohio before he became acquainted with some southern foods. He asked me if I'd ever had this stuff called "chitluns." And I said no, and I was really turning my nose up at them. Because once someone had explained to me exactly what they were, and after that, I had no interest in them. But Jimmy's Aunt Gert owned a little restaurant down the block where I knew they cooked them. "You think we could get some?" he asked. And I said we certainly could. So I called down there and Aunt Gert sent up a big kettle of chitterlings. I put some in a dish for him and he asked if I was going to have some. It would have been impolite for me to be feeding him what I thought was too poisonous for me to consume myself, so I said, "Yes, I'll try some." And very gingerly, I took just a tad on my plate. Meanwhile, he had plunged into his and was smacking his lips, saying "Oh, this is *good!*" So I took a big mouthful. And I *loved* them! And, pig that I am, between the two of us, we ate that whole big potful. What a discovery. After that, I ate them every chance I got. Now it's been forty years of loving chitterlings. Thanks to Jesse Owens.

THE 1948 ELECTION GENERATED A LOT OF INTEREST around Alexandria. We stepped up our registration efforts and people responded. I was excited that Henry Wallace was trying to get the nomination, and I was open about supporting him. That probably wasn't wise because, although he had been Truman's vice president and was running as a Democrat, he was being painted with a pink brush by States' Righters.

There was a funny incident with my parents during Wallace's campaign. They'd not yet come to visit me in Louisiana but we talked on the phone all the time. Now, remember, these poor folks had been through my NAACP escapades and my Red Cross escapades. They had survived all that and were grateful that I had too. Now, this day, they called just when I was going out to join a motorcade to hear Wallace speak. I told them I couldn't talk long because people were waiting for us outside to go hear Henry Wallace. And my parents wanted to know where he was speaking. I said, "Oh, it's a town up in Mississippi." And I heard Daddy gasp and say, "Did you hear that, Maude? Now she's someplace where Mississippi is *up!*"

Even though Wallace didn't get the nomination, I continued to organize car pools to take people to the Registrar's Office. We were too successful in our efforts: in 1948, the White Citizens Council—or whatever it was calling itself at that point—purged most blacks from the rolls. Our response was to encourage people to reregister. Even though, in the local elections, there was no one worth voting for, we had to exercise our rights as citizens, and I had to hope the time would come when we'd have candidates we really wanted in office.

Election day itself was very moving for me. This was the first time Jimmy had ever voted. That just broke my heart. He'd lived in Alexandria all of his life—and he was about thirty by then—and this was his first chance to vote. It wasn't that he didn't think he could pass their stupid test before—the Registrar's decision on your interpretation of the Constitution was so arbitrary, it was completely unpredictable. It was because to rock the boat in any way in Alexandria was to risk repercussions: maybe not for himself as a medical student or whatever, but for his parents and other family members. And Jimmy's family was very vulnerable. Both of his parents worked for whites; his father had been a meatpacker and his mother was a domestic all her life. Whites watched who registered and saw those who did as troublemakers. Not messing with voting was a way of protecting yourself and your family. So that's what Jimmy had done. But this year, with the national election, and, I suppose, because of my passion about the importance of blacks voting, he voted. We voted together in 1948.

I said that local candidates weren't worth voting for then, and that's certainly true. But that doesn't mean they were all equally bad. They all had to support segregation, of course, but some helped blacks more than others. The Longs, for example, as colorful and crazy as they were, pushed through a lot of populist legislation that helped poor folks generally, including poor blacks. And they even opened up some doors previously closed to blacks. But they had to do this in such a way that it was acceptable to their white racist constituencies because, since blacks could not vote in any numbers, blacks couldn't help them get reelected.

Earl Long integrated the nursing staff at all public hospitals in Louisiana. This was in the late forties, I believe. Very early for such a gesture. Do you know how he did it? Well, a group of black people from Alexandria had met with him requesting that black RNs be hired in our local Charity Hospital. They argued that since blacks made use of the public hospital, there really should be black nurses. Long said he could do it, but it would have to be done his way. So he took an assemblage of state officials on a supposed inspection of state hospital facilities. They visited a few, including Charity here in Alexandria. And he had rigged this scene: he got a small, pretty, and very blonde nurse and a patient who was a very large, very dark, black "buck," as they call our men. He instructed them that, as the inspection tour came through, the black man was to lean all over the white nurse and be in too close contact for these white inspecting people to stomach. They did this just as Long had instructed, and as this flower of white womanhood struggled to hold up this

black man, Long shouted, "My God, we can't have this! We've got to get some
nigger nurses in here!" Well, everyone in the inspection group heartily agreed,
of course. And that's how the public hospitals in Louisiana came to have black
nurses as early as the 1940s.

Jimmy had been saving to build a house for us. That one-bedroom apartment was far too small because of our constant houseguests. We were looking
for property that would appreciate in value over time, and we felt that ex-
cluded the black areas. The two black dentists had their houses there, and no
matter what kind of improvement they made on their property, it did not in-
crease in value because nobody who could afford what it was worth would
want to buy there. So we were looking for a piece of land uncontaminated by
this race thing.

The largest concentration of blacks live in the Samtown section. Yes, that's
really its name. Whites also call it "Niggerville" and "Niggertown," but the
name on the post office out there is "Samtown." And that's bad enough, isn't
it? Samtown is, by far, the worst part of Alexandria—although, technically, it
was outside the city limits. The houses were shacks, often with dirt floors. It
had open sewerage and flooded in heavy rains. Just an awful place. No one
who had a choice about it lived in Samtown.

So, finding a pleasant location in Alexandria wasn't easy. It's just not a very
attractive place. Pineville is. I thought the town of Pineville, just across the
river, was beautiful. It's hilly terrain and full of long-leaf pine trees. But to live
over there, we'd have had to live down in some basin part of the place that
flooded all the time, because that was the only property available to blacks.
The city of Alexandria, however, is plain; it's just absolutely flat. I found that
very ugly. All of southern Louisiana is flat. A few of the white residential areas
in Alexandria are very nice though, tree-lined and beautiful. In some places,
the trees have Spanish moss, and I've always found Spanish moss very ro-
mantic.

Back then, most of this area was also cluttered with trash. In Louisiana, they
just threw trash along the highways and streets and didn't put much energy
into cleaning it up. I guess, coming out of the Depression, all people wanted
to do was find something to eat. City governments didn't bother themselves
with beauty. It's better now; there's more of an effort to make the place beautiful. Ladybird's campaign against all the billboards helped some. This place
was peppered with them. And downtown, although it's just about deserted be-

cause of all the stores moving out to the malls, downtown now has trees planted along the sidewalks. They are making an effort. But, when I first came here, the public places were unkempt. And most residential areas were uninteresting or downright ugly.

We were so lucky to find a lovely location just off Highway 71 (the main north-south highway passing Alexandria) and owned by a black man, Sam Baker. We bought the land in 'forty-nine and started building this home, where I still live. At the time, no blacks were allowed to join the trade unions around here. Yet the most skilled folks—the best carpenters, bricklayers, pipefitters, electricians—were all black. Normally, in Alexandria, a white would be the contractor and he'd hire all the real craftsmen, who were black and who would be paid much less. Jimmy and I changed that: we made Mr. LaDuff, a fine black carpenter, our contractor. Absolutely everyone who worked on our house was black.

But we weren't able to move into our house until January 1951. We were the problem, not the workers. Our plans, our lives, our whole world was turned upside-down in the spring of 1949. My husband was indicted for murder.

VIII

The Trial

"... there's something dreamlike about that period."

IT ALL BEGAN WITH A DREAM. And there's something dreamlike about that period, that year and a half in my life, from May of 'forty-nine to December 1950. Or "nightmarish," maybe, is a better word.

The dream came to me in New York, in the spring of 1949 in New York. Jimmy and Gretchen and I were supposed to have gone to some kind of reunion in late March at one of the hospitals in St. Louis where he'd done his residence. But it had developed that Jimmy had some patients just about to deliver, and, at that time, just about all black babies were delivered at home. So Jimmy had to forego the reunion, and he said for Gretchen and me to go on to New York—which was to have been the second part of our trip, anyway—and he'd join us as soon as he could for a little vacation. So I went to New York, saw all the shows, had a lovely, lovely time. April came along; I was there through Easter and beyond that. And Jimmy still wasn't able to get away because, by then, he'd developed a tremendous practice. He was so likable and helpful to people. If he felt they needed food more than they needed medication, he'd get them groceries. So we were in New York and I'd gone to see all the plays I could see. And all my friends were there. You know, the house was a kind of hotel. When my friends would learn Odette was in town, they'd all come up there. And there was room for them to stay. We'd have a nice time.

One Saturday night in early May, after I'd come in from some play, I had a very normal, pleasant telephone conversation with Jimmy. He had to get up early the next morning. Jimmy always worked on Sunday because most of his women patients were domestics, and that was the only time they could really get to the doctor's. So he had practice on Sunday. After we talked, I went to bed, moving Gretchen from Mama's bed to mine. And I went on to sleep. Then I had this dreadful, dreadful nightmare that Jimmy had been accused of killing somebody. Oh, it was just awful. I woke up drenched and called to Mama, whose bedroom was right next to mine. I was so wet, at first I thought Gretchen had wet the bed. But she hadn't; it was my own perspiration, I told Mama about the dream and she said, "That's nonsense. You've been running around like a chicken with its head cut off and you are *tired!*" And she got fresh sheets and told me to go back to bed. "And I'm taking this baby with me," she said. Gretchen was about two and a half. So she took Gretchen and I tried to go back to sleep. But I couldn't, and I got up again. "What are you up for now?" Mama asked. "I'm going to call Jimmy." "That boy has to go to work in the morning," she said. "Are you crazy? You wait and you call him tomorrow."

So, the next day, we were going to visit Godmother Ethelle in St. Albans. I tried Jimmy's office number before we left, and there was no answer. Why wasn't he there seeing patients? I was so discombobulated from the dream and his not answering the phone that, on the way to Godmother Ethelle's, I gave the cab man a large bill I thought was small. And he didn't tell me I'd made a mistake; I didn't discover it until we were in Godmother Ethelle's house. I dialed Jimmy's office several more times that morning and there was still no answer. And I was really beside myself. I *knew* something was wrong.

When we arrived back from St. Albans, the phone was ringing. It was Jim Hovell, the dentist from whom we rented our apartment. And he informed Mama to tell me not to come home, to stay up there in New York. Because Jimmy had been arrested for killing his girlfriend.

I was stunned and not stunned. The dream, the feelings all night and day, as horrible as they were, they'd prepared me somewhat for this news. Of course, I was going to Jimmy right away. We all agreed Gretchen should stay in New York. And my cousin Lester flew with me to New Orleans that Monday morning. Jimmy's half-brother, Reverend Richard Bennett, drove down from Alexandria to get me; Lester took the next flight back to New York. And, on the drive from New Orleans to Alexandria, Reverend Bennett, who was just as nice as he could be, explained what had happened.

It seems a young woman, Jean Carr, who was a barmaid and one of Jimmy's patients (and, the prosecution would claim, also his girlfriend) had died of a beating that Saturday night. Her grandfather—who had raised her and with whom she lived—said she had staggered home bleeding from the head and collapsed, never saying anything, never regaining consciousness. But he saw a new bandage on her arm and thought she must have been treated by her doctor, Jim Hines. And, when he brought her to the hospital, he told them Jim Hines beat her. Soon after she died in the hospital, Jimmy was arrested. This was late Saturday night, the same night he'd talked to me, the same night I'd had that terrible nightmare about his being arrested for killing somebody. I can't explain that. All I can say is that we were very bonded to one another at that time. I had known that night and all day Sunday something terrible was happening to him.

Reverend Bennett and I went directly to the courthouse. We posted bond and they brought Jimmy down. (The jail is up in the top of the courthouse.) He went home with me that Monday. And I heard his version of the events that Saturday night. He said he had indeed treated Jean Carr for a cut arm that evening. Then, because she was intoxicated, he and two of his friends had driven her home. Actually, they'd only taken her to the end of her block, because it was pouring rain and she lived on an unpaved street. They were afraid of getting the car stuck in the mud. So they let her out at the end of the block and watched her walk home. All three said she made it into her house okay; they remembered seeing a light on her porch and they watched her go in. They also said she had no head injury when she left the car. (And the white doctors who examined her at the hospital that night would say at the trial that she couldn't have walked that distance with the kind of head injury she had.) So the evidence pointed to the grandfather. It was known in the community that he beat her regularly, and there was talk he'd sexually molested her, too. But he claimed his innocence, pointing the finger at Jimmy. And that was the version the police seemed to accept. The next month, the grand jury met and gave a "true bill," which means they felt there was enough evidence for an indictment. The trial was set for October.

I believed in Jimmy's innocence wholeheartedly. To show him and the world how much faith I had that he'd be exonerated, I suggested to Jimmy we go ahead and have another baby. The son he'd wanted had died, and I wanted to give him that. And I wanted to say to the world, we are a family with a future. He will be found innocent because he *is* innocent. And our life will continue to grow. This is how much I believed in him.

So Jimmy, Jr. was conceived. My doctor, Augustus Terrence, was horrified. On top of my record of poor health was this murder indictment. And Terrence was right when he said my emotional state would affect me physically: as it turned out, I retained no food, no nothing. It was not apparent for the longest time that I was even remotely pregnant. I have broad hips, and the baby was cradled well into the pelvis. It was only toward the end that I got big.

That summer, waiting for the trial, I was just crazy and pregnant and hot and vomiting and sick. Dr. Terrence was convinced that this would not be a healthy baby. His wife later told me he just worried himself to death: "Why did she do this?" I was far more ill during that pregnancy than any of the others. Sick and nervous and nutty.

Gretchen came back in July. Jimmy was missing her, so we arranged to meet my parents in St. Louis and bring her back here. From then, through the summer and on through the trial, I had the care of Gretchen and the care of the baby I was carrying.

What was immediately hurtful was that long before the trial began, many people—including some black people—had concluded Jimmy was guilty. Some blacks thought Jimmy was a disgrace as a doctor because of killing Jean Carr. Those who were of an element that thought Voodoo could help were doing incantations against him. Many others, some blacks and most whites I would say, resented a black man being a doctor and living comfortably, so were happy to see him brought down. That kind of resentment peaked during the trial itself, when we came to feel we were in danger in our own apartment.

The trial began, as I said, in October. Our lawyer, John R. Hunter—a white man who told "darky" jokes all the time and refused to let a police informant testify because "I don't fool with nigras who have no last name"—our lawyer did believe in Jimmy's innocence. There was no black lawyer in Alexandria then (Louis Berry had moved to California), so we had no choice. And I wouldn't say that Hunter disliked black people. No, he was fond of black people in a cracker way. Camille Gravel, who years later became my divorce lawyer, was the prosecuting lawyer then. I remember sitting in the courtroom looking daggers at Gravel; I just hated him for doing this to me and my family.

The trial lasted ten days. It ended on a Saturday night about 7:00 P.M. The judge told the jury they had to stay until they got a verdict. They deliberated seven hours. And found Jimmy guilty.

My God. I was ready to make an exit through the eighth floor window of the courthouse right then. But our friend Joe Sarpy kept telling me I had to live for Gretchen. No matter what happened to Jimmy, I had to take care of Gretchen and the new baby on the way. He convinced me. But the guilty verdict absolutely threw me. The evidence was so clear, I really didn't expect it. Nor did our attorney. Even the judge, Judge Alvin Hundley, was surprised. After the verdict was read, he said firmly, "There will be no outburst in this courtroom!" Because he knew some people would be shocked at the injustice of it and some people would be pleased at the guilty verdict. "And the doctor will go home with his wife!" Judge Hundley was devoted to Jimmy. And devoted to me. Later, when Daddy was visiting Alexandria, Hundley told Daddy that I was the kind of young woman any man would be proud to have as a daughter. (This same judge would also be later given an NAACP award for humane behavior on the bench.) So, having heard the evidence, he too was appalled at the verdict. And that's why he let Jimmy leave with me. But a guilty verdict is a guilty verdict. And there would have to be a sentencing.

We couldn't go to our apartment. People who were angry at Jimmy for supposedly killing Jean Carr or for being too uppity or for disgracing black people or for whatever it was they were thinking, these people had begun throwing rocks through our windows when the trial began. So, Ruth Orange took us to her home. And dear friends, Joe and Eloise Sarpy, stayed in our apartment to try to keep it from being further destroyed.

So we get to Ruth's, and Jimmy's skin is just ashen. Judge Hundley called and told me, "Now, I want to tell you what to do. Jimmy practices on Sundays. You get him up on time and send him on down there looking like a man going to church. And tell him to hold his head up and see his patients. And we're going to see what we can do to figure this thing out." The next morning— none of us got any sleep—I went with Jimmy to the office. Nobody came. He was devastated. But nobody came because they assumed he wouldn't be there. Hundley called the office and asked how Jimmy was doing. He advised Jimmy to stay the usual hours. In the afternoon, two patients did come. But mostly, we sat there alone. Jimmy was very depressed.

The next day, we went to our lawyer's office. He said he was absolutely nonplussed by the verdict because Jimmy was innocent and this shouldn't happen. "I don't know what to do," he continued. "But I'll try to work on an appeal as soon as I can. Now, do you know any lawyers in New York who might have an idea?" And I said, "Yes. I know a lawyer who's won twenty-three cases before the Supreme Court." Now this is long before Thurgood's name became a household word. And Hunter said in his southern drawl, "Mah Gawd, Ah wouldn't even know how to walk up the steps of the Supreme Court!" That made me smile a bit; he had no idea he was talking about a black man.

Hunter asked if I could get Thurgood on the phone and I did. I explained everything to Thurgood and his response was that the situation was bad. He said we couldn't complain about there being no blacks on the jury since it was our lawyer who'd kept them off. (I'd told him that a few blacks had gone through the jury selection process but had shown a bias against Jimmy and our lawyer rejected them.) Thurgood said the only thing that can happen now is for the judge to say that the verdict was not commensurate with the evidence. But he didn't want to get my hopes up about that tactic because, he said, no southern judge is going to say that twelve white jurors didn't know what the hell they were talking about. Maybe it could work somewhere else, but it was doubtful it could work in the South. "Harper, I really don't want to get your hopes up." Thurgood's so kind; he was pleading with me not to lean on this. I said, "Well, how can I help?" And he said, "You'd have to get a petition up and get 3,000 people to sign it saying they didn't think the verdict was commensurate."

Now, Thurgood didn't tell Hunter any of this; he already knew Hunter was a flaky cracker: "Don't you tell that bastard what I'm saying!" But Hunter wanted to get in on the conversation. "Would he speak with me?" he asked. And I told Thurgood that our lawyer would like to talk to him. Thurgood agreed. And Hunter was thrilled. Before taking the phone, he asked, "What did you say his name is?" And I said, "Marshall." Hunter gets on the phone and says, "Mr. Marshall, suh?" I got so tickled. Hunter just *knew* that any lawyer who'd won twenty-three cases before the Supreme Court had to be white. He had no idea he was being downright deferential to a black man. If he'd only known! This was the first time anything had amused me in months. All this, "Yes, suh; yes, suh; yes, Mr. Marshall, suh." I just grinned through the whole conversation.

Judge Hundley knew Marshall, and was all for this idea. He gave me the petition sheets. He said again he could not understand how the jury convicted

Jimmy based on the testimony given. So I had a whole corps of people—about twenty people—going around getting signatures on these mimeographed sheets. This began three days after the verdict. Even Jimmy's mother, Mama Mag, went out to get signatures. But the first house she went to, she got a negative response, and she couldn't continue. She went to a minister's house, a man who was one of Jimmy's patients. And he said no, he couldn't sign it because he thought the courts had dealt with Jimmy as they should. And Mama Mag fainted dead away on the man's front step. She just couldn't take hearing even black people say they thought her son was guilty. So she never went out again.

So this little corps, including pregnant me, went all over this town. People almost always signed when I asked. Because by then I was getting very large and they were afraid I was going to drop the baby on their doorstep. They'd say, "I think it was fair, Mrs. Hines. Oh, come on, child. Give me that thing. I'll sign it. Now, how're you feeling?" Folks who owned stores wanted him out because he spent money with them. And some people just wanted him out so he could continue to look after their health.

Judge Hundley called regularly to check on the number of names we'd gotten. And he'd tell me not to give up hope, we're going to work this thing out. Jimmy's patients began to come back in droves.

In the midst of all that, in desperation, I went to see Governor Earl Long in Baton Rouge. S. W. Jones, with the black teachers' union, suggested I go, and he drove me down. It turned out that it didn't help Jimmy any, but it was an interesting visit. Long was as courteous as he could be, putting a pillow behind my back, getting me something cool to drink. He listened with what seemed to be genuine concern, and he didn't talk any of that foolish talk. But he said he didn't think there was anything he could do. A very intelligent man. And well-informed. But you never would have known that when he was out campaigning. He knew what he had to say to get the cracker vote in Louisiana; he knew how to work a crowd. He was two different people.

So I went back to Alexandria and just kept collecting signatures. By early January, we had the 3,000 names, and I turned them over to Judge Hundley. He said he could now legally set the verdict aside and call for a new trial. We should just let this cool off, he said, forget about it, it's going to be alright. And he just never scheduled another trial. The second trial was to be in the future but that future never happened. I didn't realize he had no intention of scheduling another trial at the time, though. I remained apprehensive about the possibility of another trial for a long time. It was not an exoneration and I knew that. Jimmy was never exonerated. He just slid out of it. Justice, southern-style.

Class played such an important role in that whole thing. Jimmy's being middle class was, I think, why he was convicted *and* why he got out of it. You know, except for the first two nights after he was arrested, he never spent another minute in jail. It was supposedly so that he could take care of his patients, but the fact is that in the South the white aristocracy gives privileges to middle-class blacks who aren't troublemakers. It's still that way today. Because, I think, they're seen as a buffer. It's the working-class whites who have so much resentment toward blacks who have something. And that's who was on that jury. He was convicted for speaking standard English, for wearing nice clothes, for having too much. But he was let off by a man who had some respect for justice *and* was not threatened by Jimmy's achievements. This feudalism in the South works in strange ways. I'm not saying race wasn't important. If Jimmy had been accused of killing a white person, well, he could have just forgotten it, period. He might not have lived long enough to even come to trial. But he was a middle-class black man accused of killing a lower-class black woman, and that gave him an advantage with powerful whites even before the evidence was presented. I didn't really realize that at the time, either. If I had, I wouldn't have been so terrified.

Now, the worst of this—the trial, the conviction, running around for signatures—all happened when I was very pregnant. All of that was from October to February, really. And my son Jimmy was born in March. As I said, my doctor, Augustus Terrence, was unusually concerned about this pregnancy and birth because of all I'd been through. He was able to get me into a private, white hospital in Opelousas, about a forty-minute drive from Alexandria. But I couldn't be roomed with the white women; I was housed in a tin-roof shack in back of the hospital. For the birth itself, I was allowed in the delivery room. I remember nothing of that, though, because I was heavily sedated. Dr. Terrence had great fear the child was going to be some kind of monstrosity because my body had not been well nourished during the pregnancy, I was such a nervous wreck. He didn't want me to see it until he was sure the child was normal. So I was completely out during that birth. And afterwards, while my baby was allowed to stay in the nursery with the white babies, I was wheeled back to the shack. Dr. Terrence's concerns were unfounded. Jimmy was a beautiful baby and has grown up to be a brilliant, caring doctor. But, at the time, Terrence didn't know what to expect.

After that birth, again Dr. Terrence told me he didn't want me to have any more children. They'd found some percentage of my cells were definitely sickling, he said. And Terrence just thought it was too dangerous for me to have children. But Jimmy and I and Gretchen and then my son Jimmy all wanted more children. I remember one day, when Jimmy was still a toddler, all three of them came to me, when I was dressing, with this chant: "We want a baby! We want a baby!" And I wanted more, too. So we just didn't take Terrence's advice that time either. I would have two more beautiful children, Terry and Maggi.

When I was discharged from the hospital, Terrence insisted I stay with him and his wife, Ernestine, for a while so she could take good care of me. Ernie was wonderful; I was really beautifully petted. Jimmy would drive down each evening and spend a while with me, then come back here to Alexandria and work the next day. I stayed there for two weeks before returning to our apartment. During that period, Jimmy's mother had been taking care of Gretchen. When I returned, one of Jimmy's cousins, Mercedes, helped me with the two children.

Then, about four weeks after Jimmy was born, I said, "I want my parents to see that we're all okay, that we're a family again." So we put little Jimmy in a Carnation Canned Milk carton on the back seat of the car and took him to New York. This was before they had car seats for babies. We took him home so my parents could see everything was just fine. He was a little teeny baby. He and I were in the back seat and Gretchen was on Earl's lap in the front. Yes, Earl was hired again as a chauffeur, and no, he was never once allowed to drive on that trip either.

So that they wouldn't worry about the murder conviction hanging over Jimmy, I lied to my parents about the outcome of the trial. I told them the case had been thrown out of court. They'd never see an Alexandria newspaper, I figured, and, after all, here was Jimmy walking around free. In New York, people tried and convicted of murder didn't remain completely out of jail like Jimmy had. So my story was entirely believable to them. We stayed less than a week in New York. I think our visit did ease my parents' minds. I returned to Alexandria feeling good about that.

But, during that spring and summer, I see in retrospect, Jimmy was becoming less comfortable in the marriage. What was happening that was destructive was all these people continuously saying how much appreciation Jimmy needed to show me because of my getting him off with the petition. There was a steady stream of folks in and out of our house saying things like, "Jimmy, you ought to worship the ground this girl walks on!" And all of them were not really convinced he was innocent. They might've thought they were helping me, complimenting me, but they didn't do me one bit of good. I think he felt, if I'm innocent and my wife is loyal, that's what a wife is!

I remember one day, in particular, when a dean at Southern University brought some students by the house. The students, this dean, and I were all in my living room. I don't know where Jimmy was when the conversation began. They had just come from a Vesper Service at Southern where Martin Harvey had preached about sincerity. Harvey had said the word came from Latin and literally meant "without wax." In ancient Roman times, some of the pottery sold in the marketplace would crack when fluid was put into it and some would not. It was discovered that the pots that cracked easily were the ones that had already been mended with wax, wax that wouldn't show when it was sold. The buyer didn't know the wax was there until he put fluid into the pot. So a law was passed that pottery had to be labeled. Only those pots that had never been previously cracked and mended could be labeled "*sine cera,*" without wax. They would cost more but they were considered pure, dependable, and of the best quality. Harvey's sermon was about that. Then, he apparently concluded that we all have to strive to be sincere. And this was something you had to *be*, it wasn't something you could plaster on yourself, like wax. (Now, this is during the spring after the petition and all.) And, he continued, there was a woman in Alexandria who was "without wax." She had stuck by her husband when he went through all those trials. And the dean went on and on retelling the whole damn sermon Harvey had given using me as an example of true sincerity.

And I looked up and Jimmy was standing in the doorway of our living room, looking like someone had murdered him. I hadn't known he was within hearing distance. And when I saw his face, I felt just awful. Awful.

Those kinds of things kept happening. People talked about me like I was a goddess, someone he ought to be beholden to. And I think he began feeling then, I just can't be that beholden to her. So, in turn, he had to find somebody to look up to *him*, again.

That was, I think now, the beginning of the end of our marriage. That kind of talk never really stopped. There were other problems, yes, but that talk from so many people really began the dissolution. Few men can take being with someone others seem to think is bigger, better than they are. I couldn't see all of this then. And, if I had, I'm not sure what I could've done. Try to shut some folks up, I suppose.

What I was doing during that year was trying to recreate as normal a family life for us as possible. A lot of my time and energy went into the house, which was still under construction. Most of that work, *all* of mine, had stopped during the trial and the months we were getting signatures on the petition. I hoped our moving into as lovely and comfortable a place as possible, moving into a real home, would help ground us as a family again. So I gave that project my all. And I was delighted when my parents said they wanted to come for Thanksgiving and stay through Christmas. The more family around me, the better.

My parents wanted to see their new grandson again and the house, which was nearly completed. And I know they wanted to assure themselves again that I'd weathered the horrors of Jimmy's trial. Of course, I wanted to see them, too. But I was apprehensive about their visiting Alexandria because of the lie I'd told about the verdict. Jimmy and I were still hoping for some kind of reversal, some exoneration. At that point, the fall of 1950, we both thought there'd be another trial. But why worry my parents unnecessarily, I still thought. Both of them had heart conditions. And I was especially concerned about Mama because of the way her appearance had changed while I was in Europe. I felt she was somehow more fragile.

They came by train. And the visit started off well. I was determined to ease any concerns they might have by showing them our good spirits. We visited the new house and I showed them their room. It was at one of the tips of the U-shaped house, looking out onto the patio and the tree-lined backyard. I'd told them that eventually we'd put a swimming pool next to the patio and their room would overlook the pool. Mama said, "I don't know about getting in the pool but I'd like to watch the kids playing in it." That's the reason the windows are cornered in that room, so that Mama would be able to look out onto the pool.

My parents seemed to be really enjoying themselves. By then, Daddy and Jimmy had become real good drinking buddies, and Daddy's earlier reservations about Jimmy had completely disappeared. I kept thinking that I was really going to be able to pull this off successfully, that they'd return to New York thinking that Jimmy's case had been thrown out of court. And that their daughter was peaceful and happy. I should've known better.

By mistake, one of Jimmy's medical assistants told Mama the truth. She just didn't realize Mama didn't know. This is how it happened. In early December, Daddy decided that he was going to run up to Chicago to see his brother Harry. Because, you know, he was train crazy. For him, it was like riding a bike; it didn't cost him anything and he just liked riding them. So he went on up to Chicago. And Mama was worried about how he was going to make out. He did have a heart condition, too, and she was always worried he'd die in the next five minutes. The fact is, I was right that she was far worse off than he, because, as it turned out, he was to survive her by eleven years. (And he was also twelve years older than she was.) But Mama was worried about him and she said she wasn't feeling well. One day, she said something that let me know there'd definitely been a turn for the worse. Mama always wanted to look nice for me and she'd always put her makeup on. Then one morning, she said, "Baby, do you mind if I don't put any makeup on my skin today? Because I need to breath through all my pores." And I knew she was really feeling bad. I knew she was having trouble breathing. So I took her up to Jimmy's office for him to check her.

While we were sitting in the reception room, I left for a moment to go around to the drug store. And one of Jimmy's assistants, Thelma Metoyer, came out to sit and talk with Mama. And the conversation must have gone to Jimmy's verdict, because Thelma informed Mama that nothing was settled, that there'd been no exoneration, no case thrown out of court, that, in fact, there'd probably be another trial. Thelma was one of the people who had carried around the petition and she told Mama all the particulars. And Mama got sicker and sicker. She was assuming there'd be another trial. How can 'Dette go through that again? When Jimmy examined her, he became very concerned and took her to Baptist Hospital. This was a private hospital and had one floor for black people. Her cardiologist, Dr. Worley, said she'd had a heart attack. And, after a few days, said we should take her home, there was nothing more he could do. There was absolutely nothing to work with.

Mama couldn't lie down because she couldn't breathe in that position. So she spent most of her time sitting in my yellow chair in the living room. We had a nurse around the clock for her. She tried to hold on to life. I remember her asking if someone could do her nails for her. But she deteriorated quickly. In just a few days, she died. She died sitting in my yellow chair.

That was such a loss to me. It still is. Mama and I were always very close. We never had the kinds of mother–daughter frictions I've heard other people talk about. I always just enjoyed her and loved her. It's been forty years, hasn't it? And I still feel so sad when I think about her dying in my yellow chair.

And I still get goose bumps when I think about our trip back to New York. At that time, you couldn't send a body on the train without someone accompanying it. So I took a Pullman, using the usual subterfuge, while Jimmy and a number of his friends drove to New York. It was I who went on the train with her body. I was obviously disturbed, and the black porter was very solicitous: "Can I get you something, ma'am?" And I kept on saying no. Then, finally, he bedded down the Pullman and I tried to go to sleep. But I couldn't. And this same porter could see my curtain moving; he knew I was tossing and turning. He came and said, "Let me get you some hot milk. Maybe that will help you sleep." And I said okay. And I drank the hot milk. Then I would doze off for a few minutes at a time, but I couldn't really sleep. The road bed between here and Little Rock was so rough. The train rocked back and forth. And I was imagining Mama's casket slamming against the sides of the freight car. The images of her were bothering me so.

But I would doze, and when I would doze off just momentarily, I would dream Mama was beside me just like she used to be when I was a little girl and we traveled together in Pullman berths. And she would be there talking to me. Then I'd wake up and look around. And the pain would wash over me: my mother's dead in a casket back there. And I'd toss more. And if I had another little snitch of sleep, Mama was again right there beside me. But I always awoke quickly. I couldn't stay asleep for any length of time.

Again I dozed. And this time Mama sounded so concerned. I heard her say, " 'Dette, you are really worn out. You're so nervous and so tired. You need some rest. Tell you what I'm going to do: when we get to Little Rock, I'm getting off. And I'll meet you in New York." After she said that, I seemed to drift into a deeper sleep, and I slept and slept. I slept so heavily that even the noise of what they call the "break down" of the Pullman cars in St. Louis didn't awaken me. And the porter who was disturbed about me finally came and woke me up. He said he'd made up all his other berths but he'd just let me sleep because he knew I needed it: "I hope you don't mind, I peeked in on you. I was so glad you'd finally gone to sleep." Then he asked, "Now, you don't have to tell me anything. But, what's bothering you?" And I said, "Oh, I'm bringing my mother's body home for burial in New York." "Oh, well," he said, "that's the casket they took off in Little Rock. That casket will get to New York before you."

I felt engulfed and comfortable. I almost wanted to say, well, yes, she just told me that. But that would have sounded crazy. And I didn't feel crazy. I felt warm. There was no explanation for why the casket was transferred to another train. When I got to New York, my relatives were upset that the railroad company had done this for no apparent reason. Her body had indeed arrived before I did, but my family was baffled. "What is this?" my brother said, "Why did the casket get taken off your train?" I never told them why she'd left the train. Maybe because it was an explanation I knew other people would find hard to believe. But, mostly, I think, it was because I so cherished having learned that, even with her death, I hadn't lost her caring about me.

IX

The Fifties

"What color is cotton? Pick it yourself!"

MY MOTHER'S DEATH WAS THE LOWEST POINT in an extremely difficult period in my life. The following month, we moved into our new house. But what would have been a happy event was tarnished by my continuing sadness about Mama and the conviction still hanging over Jimmy. Nevertheless, I threw myself into fixing the house up to be as pleasant as possible. When I think about how I decorated this house, I realize that what I did mostly was repeat what I'd grown up with. There's the bay window on the front, with a drum table in front of it with two chairs on either side. That's exactly what was at home. I put a niche in the dining room just like the one in the front parlor at home. The mantelpiece over the fireplace and the mirror over the mantel are exactly like the fireplace in the New York house. At one time, I even had a similar brass clock. I was very much tied to the aesthetic images I'd grown up with.

A delightful, lifelong benefit of our choosing that particular property was the friendship that developed with the people we'd bought it from, our next-door neighbors, the Bakers. The Baker family had owned all of this land and much more since the nineteenth century. The property was called "Baker's Quarters," and it was acres and acres of choice farming land just off Route 71. Now, how would a black man get to own such property? Well, after the Civil War, a white Northerner had come South to farm. Samuel Baker, the son of slaves, was a sharecropper on this Northerner's land, and they became friends.

Sam was very hardworking and frugal, and, after some years, was looking for some land to buy to start his own farm. This Northerner, who was by then about to go back North, bought some prime property in an all-white area just to resell it to Sam. He fronted for Sam because he knew whites around here would not sell such desirable land to Sam directly. But, once it was sold to Sam, there was nothing anybody could do about it.

Sam Baker dairy farmed for years. He was, in fact, known to be one of the best farmers in the area. He began to win prizes for his farming and he engendered a whole lot of hatred from the white farmers. It was fine for blacks to be sharecroppers, but they resented blacks owning property. And don't be better at farming than they were. That was suicidal. Then one year, Sam had the largest potato crop in the parish and he won the title of "Potato King." That was just too much. One night in the 1890s—his wife, Frances, whom we all called "Mama Baker," would tell me this story—one night, they came to the house and took him out to lynch him. I can remember her saying to me, "They took my Sam away. They told me, 'You needn't expect to see this nigger again!'" "But miraculously, he was returned. They had taken him out somewhere and were beating him brutally. But somebody in the mob spoke up for him, said Sam didn't mean any harm, he was a "good nigger." Evidently, this man was very persuasive because they brought Sam back to Mama Baker. He was in terrible shape, but he was alive. And she nursed him back to health. He stayed on his land and he continued to farm, but he never entered any farming contests again.

Now, this story will show you the strange etiquette of the South: Sam Baker's property was surrounded, as I said, by white property. In the evening, he would sit on his porch smoking his pipe. Way into the late forties, the nights when there was a Klan meeting, his white neighbors would walk past fully hooded and call out cordially, "Evening, Uncle Sam." And Sam would call back, "Evening, Mr. Duhon," or the name of whichever one it was under the pointed hood. He knew these people so well, he'd recognize their shoes and their voices even with their faces totally concealed. He never told his wife who the men were who beat him. But he'd seen the men that night because, as they beat him, some of their hoods had fallen off. And he must have seen those same men off and on for the rest of his life. Sam knew he'd been lucky to come out of that alive, and he knew his continued survival was dependent upon his silence, his knowing his place, and his display of good southern manners. And survive, he did. Sent his daughter Plessy to Tuskeegee Institute, sold off parcels of his land for good prices as he aged and farmed less and less. Plessy was exactly my mother's age. And we became close, close friends. Actually, she and I and Mama Baker and my children all became family to one another. I'd met Plessy on that first Thanksgiving visit to Alexandria just after getting back from Europe. At that time, she was running a hot tamale stand on her property and Jimmy had driven me out for hot tamales. Plessy and I got to talking and I liked her immediately. So when I moved to Louisiana the following spring, she was one of the people who welcomed me. Two years later, when we were looking for land, I was delighted when we decided to buy some of hers.

Plessy and Mama Baker were the main reasons I was able to do so many things for all these years. They were like extended family, always willing to keep an eye on my children. I really had two full-time babysitters. It was an easy relationship. If I had something in my refrigerator Plessy needed, she'd knock, " 'Dette, you got a tomato?" "Yah, go get it." And the same thing over there. The only time I had words with the Bakers was one morning when my two rambunctious boys wanted to go over to the Bakers' house to visit, and I said no, "You can't go over there. You worry Mama Baker to death." So they somehow conspired to meet her out in the yard. She asked them why they hadn't come earlier and when they told her, she charged in here: " 'Dette, you and I have never had any words, but don't keep my children away from me!" She really went off on me. So after that, I let them go anytime they wanted to. And they wanted to visit Mama Baker and Plessy all the time.

When the whites of Alexandria realized we were building our house out on Lee Street Extension, there was a good deal of resentment. While the house was under construction, rocks were repeatedly thrown through the picture window in front. Jimmy put a stop to that in a very clever way. He had an announcement made on the radio, on a program called "Swap Shop," as I remember, that the window on Lee Street that was repeatedly being broken was being replaced and replaced by a white insurance company. That did it. I guess the whites who were doing it figured there was no point if it wasn't costing the black doctor anything.

It wasn't only the location of our house whites resented, it was also the size and the fact that it was the first brick house any black person had built in this town. It's a one-level house, but very wide. I deliberately designed it to accommodate our endless guests and create some kind of privacy for our family. Three guest bedrooms, a bath, and the kitchen are at one end of the house; in the middle is a dining room, the living room, and our large play room. Then our quarters are at the other end. It was considered very large back in the fifties, and in the South, as I've said, whites resent blacks having too much.

Right across the street was a white family named Brewer who tried to be pleasant, southern-style. Soon after we moved in, Mrs. Brewer came over with all kinds of plants and snips of plants to put in the yard. She was very warm: "Glad to have you as a neighbor." And she did seem to be reasonably glad. Although I found out later, she'd put her black maid in jail under the Work or Fight Ordinances of World War II when the maid left her employ after serving her for more than a dozen years. These were ordinances that cropped up all over the South during the war. They came into being because black maids whose husbands were drafted into the army were leaving their ridiculously low-paying servant jobs. A rumor got out among southern whites that there was something called Eleanor Clubs, supposedly organizations of black women inspired by Eleanor Roosevelt and encouraging black women to leave domestic service. Pure lie. But black women *were* leaving these jobs. The army had grabbed up their men, and as low as army pay was, it was higher than what most black men could make in the South. And certainly higher than any maid's pay. So these wives of soldiers were getting this little bit of army money to put food in their children's mouths without having to work twelve to fourteen hours a day, six days a week. So there was, indeed, a great exodus out of these domestic jobs in the South.

Southern cities reacted with the Work or Fight Ordinances, which stated that if your job contributed to the war effort, you couldn't leave it to be unemployed. These laws were specifically designed to keep the maids in the kitchens of white women and, as far as I know, were never applied to any other occupation. The rationale was—as if they needed one—that the business people (and Mrs. Brewer's husband ran a photography studio downtown) had to keep going as part of the war effort, and the business person was dependent on the work of his domestic. Thus, if you left your job, you weren't supporting the war effort. So, when Mrs. Brewer's maid, Maxie, left because her husband was able to support her with his army pay, Mrs. Brewer had slapped her in jail. She wasn't in for long because she immediately agreed to go back to work. She couldn't stay in jail and take care of her children. But the same woman who was bringing me plants did this. She was one of these southern whites who is very kind and even benevolent to black people as long as they know their place and stay in it.

So here she was when I first moved into this house, heavily laden with plants to put in the yard and saying she'd send her yard boy over to help me. And then she said, "And, by the way, what is your name?" I responded, "I thought you knew my name. My name is Hines." And she said, "Oh, I don't mean that. Of course, I know Dr. Hines' name. I mean *your* name." "Well, I guess Hines is my name now." "But I mean your first name." And then I realized what she was getting at and I said, "Oh, I don't feel that we know each other well enough to call one another by first names. What is your name?" And she said, "Mrs. Brewer. Now, come on, tell me what your first name is?" "I just said to you that we don't know each other well enough for first names, Mrs. Brewer." "Oh, you really feel that way? You want me to call you by your last name? I come from Georgia where we just wouldn't. It's not the way we talk to our colored." All this with sugary sweetness. And I said, "I just don't consider myself *your* colored. I'm *my* colored and, where I come from, people who don't know each other very well call each other 'Mr.' and 'Mrs.' " So she said, "Well, I just can't say that. I'm so sorry. I like you so much but I just couldn't say that." So I said, "In that case, I don't think I'd be able to say 'Mrs. Brewer'." "Well, we're neighbors," she responded, "and we've got to talk to each other. We just can't live out here and be alienated." So I suggested, "Well, I guess if we're neighbors, that's what we'll have to be. You are my neighbor and I am your neighbor. Thank you so much for the plants. And I think I have something to do right now." Then I escorted her out. She sent her black gardener over and he put in all the plants. And for years thereafter, the woman called me "neighbor." Very pleasantly: "Nice to see you, neighbor. How are you today, neighbor?" But she would not call me Mrs. Hines.

Names and labels on people are very powerful. Southern whites know this and have been reluctant to change the nomenclature that fortifies their superior position. Mrs. Brewer called her black gardener a "boy" throughout his life, long after he was bent over with old age. That was the southern custom: black men were "boys" or "uncles," if they were favored. The only respectable titles used were "doc," "rev," and "professor." No one was ever called "mister." Black women were "gals" or "aunties." You know what's curious to me? After we fought so hard to be called "Mrs.," the world now doesn't use that title.

Newspapers now just use a woman's last name. So we really didn't win anything.

But, back in the fifties, I was always being called "Odette" by whites who were perfect strangers. In the department stores, they'd call you "customer" or the condescending "dear" or "honey," never "Miss" or "Mrs." Not ever. I remember one incident at Whelan's Department Store. The saleswoman had just called me "Odette," and I said I didn't know her well enough for that: "I am Mrs. Hines." And her response was, "Oh, we don't say that." "Well, I insist you say that to me." "I'm very sorry, customer." (Now, this language was supposed to be more acceptable to "uppity nigras." They did want our trade, after all.) "I hope you understand," she continued, "I don't mean any offense. I really like the colored. I've always been close to them. Why, my grandfather owned slaves." "Oh, really," I said with some relish, "so did my great-grandfather. In fact, he owned my great-grandmother!" Her face turned beet red. And she ended that conversation quickly. Nothing made white Americans more uncomfortable, especially southern white women, I think, than reminding them of the pervasive use of black women by southern white men. And reminding them that just about all black Americans have European ancestry. Whites need to deny many truths about their history.

This disrespectful name-calling was something I battled daily when I came South. Racism assaults you every day. You're always irritated, always in a quiet rage in your interactions with whites. Your family and other black people are what keep you going. But everything outside the black community was designed to deny you, assault you, just destroy your human spirit.

The city newspaper, the *Town Talk*, had a policy that was typical of white newspapers across the country at the time: the only black news they would cover was crime. How's that for reinforcing negative stereotypes? Only the worst behavior in the black community existed in the local media. And that policy didn't change here in Alexandria until the very late sixties, until after the Civil Rights Movement. But we constantly objected to the policy during the fifties. One of those confrontations almost landed me in jail.

Clarence Forcia, another black physician here, had just died. He'd had a heart attack in the Catholic hospital while he was treating a patient. He knew he was very ill with pneumonia but he kept pushing himself; there were so few black doctors. He died taking care of a woman who was a maid. A wonderful man. After his death and at his wife's request, Vic Beaudoin and I went to the

Town Talk to report his death. Vic is a strong black man who has always demanded his rights and demanded he be treated with respect. When we entered the office, a number of their staff converged on us because blacks were
not expected to go in there. So, they get a little army to intimidate us, everybody comes forward to the counter. And when we explained why we were
there, we were informed that the paper didn't carry "nigger news," it only carried "nigger crime." But we could buy some space in the paper and make an
announcement, they said. They would even put a black border around it to
show their respect. But, no, they wouldn't carry it as news. We'd expected this
rejection, but we were still furious at the injustice of it. Then one of the white
men turned to Vic, who is a fair-skinned black man, and asked, "I can understand why she's in here but what the hell have you got to do with this?" And
that made Vic blow. He reached over the counter for the man saying, "Because I'm a goddam 'nigger,' that's why!" And Vic would have hurt that man
if I hadn't grabbed his arm. People in the crowd behind the counter were
shouting and very upset, and I heard somebody say they were going to call the
police. I urged Vic to leave: "Come on, Vic, let's get out of here before we end
up in jail." We did leave. And they did not print news of Dr. Forcia's death.
After that, I canceled my subscription to the paper and have never renewed it
since.

(I have read parts of it, though. As I said, the *Town Talk* became more reasonable in its coverage of black news in the late sixties and even hired some
black reporters in the seventies. One of them was Cleo Joffrion, an LSU grad-
uate that had been in my backyard preschool when she was a child. When she
got her own by-line of the *Town Talk*, she'd bring the paper out to me; she
knew I wanted to read anything she wrote. And she also knew about the vow
I'd made after Clarence Forcia's death that the *Town Talk* would never again
get one red cent from Odette. So she'd stop by after work and bring me the paper. I was so proud of her!)

Besides working on the house, and working with the YWCA and voter registration, I got very busy that first spring in the creation of the preschool program
in my backyard that Cleo would later take part in. This was not something I'd
planned to do, or ever envisioned doing. It just grew naturally out of a need I
saw around me. Maybe I was looking for something too, though. Jimmy's trial
and Mama's death had made the previous year a horrible time for me. I've
found that making myself useful to others has been a good way to cope with

pain. In any case, in the spring of 'fifty-one, I started this very informal daily gathering of kids.

There were lots of children in our neighborhood. On another parcel of the land Sam Baker had sold off was a little settlement of rental houses where many families of low-income blacks lived. And, in those houses were many kids on the verge of going to school. In most instances, the houses didn't have indoor plumbing, and the kids didn't even know how to flush a toilet. I knew this because they were the playmates of my children and when they made use of the toilets at our house, they would need a little instruction. So, we went from one thing to another. They got taught how to use a toilet. Then how to use a knife and fork. Then they got read to and taught rhymes. It began to be daily sessions with all kinds of instruction and activities.

The number of children coming here grew quickly. When the people in the settlement had children, they really had *children*. The families would have eight, nine kids in them. Before long, I had twenty or so kids coming here every weekday. It had to be structured around Jimmy's schedule; after dealing with a jam-packed office all day, he didn't want to come home to a houseful of children. So I talked to their parents and I had them arrive between 9:00 and 9:30—after Jimmy went to work. And they'd have to leave before 4:00 when he returned. He allowed me to have this program, but he never understood why I was doing it, "Haven't you got enough children of your own?" he'd ask. "What is all this?"

We did all kinds of things. We made little handcrafts, we did drawing and finger-painting, played games—"Little Sally Walker," "The Farmer in the Dell," and something called "Potsie" in New York, very much like hopscotch. We sang songs all the time. I taught them to jump rope. That was something they hadn't had before because you need a firm surface to jump. And around their houses was just dirt and grass. So we jumped on the patio out there.

Their parents were delighted to have a place to send their preschoolers. The kids would go home and talk about our activities, and the parents, who were often also Jimmy's patients, would come over and say, "Oh, that's so nice what you're doing for the children." They were truly grateful for the help. No tuition was charged; no money exchanged at all. I paid for the juice and graham crackers they'd have in the morning and a little lunch midday. And I supplied the crayons and paper and jump ropes and whatever they needed for their crafts. Their parents really couldn't afford anything. Alexandria was mainly agrarian. The work for men is seasonal, and there were many months when they could bring no funds into the house at all. The mothers filled in the gaps a bit working year-round as domestics in the houses of whites. But they were so poorly paid, then and now. It would have been ridiculous to expect anybody to pay for the kids to come and play some place.

It was actually a preschool child care center, but we didn't use those words. And it was more than child care, because I really wanted to prepare these kids for the first grade. Neither the black nor the white public schools had kindergarten in Rapides Parish. I wanted to stimulate and educate and make learning fun for them.

The stories and poetry I read to them were often about Africans or African–Americans. I told them Ananse the Spider stories, about Frederick Douglass and Nat Turner. We memorized some of Langston Hughes' children's poems. They especially loved the one about Baby Jesus, the one that ends:

> I'm just a shepherd boy,
> Very poor I am—
> But I know there is
> A King in Bethlehem.
> *What shall I bring*
> *As a present just for Him?*
> *What shall I bring to the Manger?*
> I will bring my heart
> And give my heart to Him
> I will bring my heart
> To the Manger.

And I always made sure they knew it was black people who wrote the poems we read. I wanted to help them feel good about themselves, feel good about being black. There was so much about Louisiana that told them they weren't much, they couldn't achieve much. I wanted to counteract that. So they got a heavy dose of stories and talk that would help them feel proud of being black.

We even started reading. Now, I'd never studied how to teach reading, but I found some things that worked. For instance, I found that if kids passed a billboard regularly and you told them what the words said, after a while they could identify those words wherever they saw them. Even the four- and five-year-olds. At that time, this area was peppered with billboards. (This was before Ladybird Johnson got a hold of the idea that America would really be more beautiful without so many.) The children would each have their favorite words from the billboards, and if you then opened a magazine and said, "Pick out your word," they'd recognize it. I also used flashcards to teach them letters and words. Many of them were reading before they went to school.

We'd put on little shows and the parents would come over and see them. The kids would have to learn lines and songs and a few dance steps. The parents would be so pleased. Folks in other areas heard about what I was doing and asked if their kids could join. That's how I met Harold Williams, a wonderful man from Pineville who would become one of the strongest, most dependable people in the sixties civil rights struggle here and then an absolute stalwart of our Headstart Program. He was a school bus driver and just volunteered to bring the Pineville children over to my program after he finished his regular route. Then, he'd pick them up in the afternoon. He received no pay for that, didn't expect it. I heard him say once, "It was just something that needed to be done and I did it." And that's how he's lived his life: not after money, not a "glory-grabber," as he would say, just doing what he thought was important and right to do for others. A wonderful man.

By the middle of the summer, the group had grown to about thirty children and I knew I had to stop there. I just couldn't handle any more, even with the help I was getting.

As more and more people heard about it, I got more and more help—mainly from high school kids, probably encouraged to volunteer by their parents. It was something useful and wholesome they could do with themselves. It became a regular summer thing at my house and, during all those years, many high schoolers and many, many preschoolers passed through here. In years since then, I've run into some of my volunteers and they recall, "Mrs. Hines, remember when we used to come down and help you out? Remember all the fun we had in your backyard with the kids?" I guess it was enjoyable for them.

We'd take the kids to the zoo. Now, that may not sound like a big deal, but in Alexandria it was. Because at that time, black people couldn't just walk into the zoo, although we paid for it with our tax dollars. But I would call the city and tell them I wanted to bring a group of children to the zoo and we'd get special permission to go at a designated time. We had to call every time. They didn't want us floating in and out of the zoo. We couldn't just walk in like whites.

And we'd take them to the black branch of the library. It was a small branch in the basement of the Masons' building. We'd take the kids to story hour there. Sometimes there'd be a film shown; we'd take the older children, who had enough concentration, to that.

Because I had children from three years to six years, I did have to plan different kinds of activities for the different age groups. In the mornings, the older children—the six-year-olds—would operate like little teacher aides for the three- and four-year-olds. And I'd say, "Oh, we're going to have our time together later." The toddlers always took a nap in the afternoon, whereas the older children did not. I'd lay mats on the patio or in the playroom, and the little ones would sleep for a couple of hours. And that was the time I'd have activities for the older children.

That backyard preschool program lasted for years. It started in the spring of our first year in the house, 1951, and it ended around 1963. I loved it—mainly because I've always loved children and I enjoy being with them. Beginning with that mother's helper job that I had when I was fifteen. No, actually it started when I taught Daily Bible School at Abyssinian Baptist Church when I was twelve. I've always been drawn to children, to talking with them, teaching them, just plain enjoying them.

Even today, I tutor a little boy whose father does odd jobs around the house for me. He's a bright little boy but he'd been doing poorly in school and his white teachers told his parents he was retarded. Integration has not been entirely helpful to us. Many black teachers and principals have lost their jobs in Rapides Parish and our children are often being taught by white people who believe we are intellectually inferior. Back in the segregated fifties, the black teachers were quite good. Some of them made only fifty or sixty dollars a month; they were there because they wanted to be there, not because of money. The black classrooms were always overcrowded, but the teachers really had the children's interest at heart. They tried to inspire them, wanted to make them good citizens, and they would spend time with slow learners. These black teachers were supportive and knowledgeable about black history and would really extend themselves for their pupils. Most of the white teachers our children have now don't seem to care about the black students. And there's a difference in language: around here, there's a white dialect and a black dialect. And there's a difference in the way people of different classes speak within both groups. But the white teachers are more acquainted with even the dialects of the poor white children from the rural areas than they are with our dialect. So they understand the white kids while they don't always understand what the little black child is talking about.

Well, this teacher had written off the son of the handyman. He'd received nothing but failing grades for the first nine weeks of the term. But I knew the boy was bright because I'd talked to him. So a few months ago, I asked his father if he could come by here every day after school for tutoring. And do you know he's getting nothing but A's and A minuses now? He's in a depression if he gets an A minus because he knows what he's capable of and he knows he can do better. Just because somebody believed he could do it and took the time.

The children who attended my backyard preschool left it, I hope, with a good feeling about school and learning and about themselves. And they were more ready to go into the first grade and a structured environment than they otherwise would have been. It went on that way for the next twelve years and brought me so much joy! It contributed to my getting over Jimmy's trial, then it helped me through an ugly divorce. My friend Sybil referred to it as the "mess" in my backyard, but that "mess"—with thirty or so vibrant preschoolers each summer, a few teenage volunteers, and so much fun and laughter and learning—that "mess" remains for me today a source of real pride and satisfaction.

In January 1953, my son Terry was born. Like his older brother, Terry was born in Opelousas. But, by that time, my doctor had hospital privileges. So I was in the hospital, not in a shack out back. Dr. Terrence was concerned about this pregnancy, too, just because of my illness, what they were still thinking was sickle cell anemia. I had had so many bouts that landed me in Flint Goodridge Hospital in New Orleans. But the birth went very smoothly, and after a couple of weeks at the Terrences' home, I was back in Alexandria and active again.

The following November, my brother Jack sent for me because my father was very ill in the hospital. He'd had a number of heart attacks since the early forties and this one was very serious. By the time I got to New York, Daddy had been through a "death" where he had been resuscitated. And he told me and

Uncle Willy (Godmother Mattie's husband who was visiting Daddy in the hospital with me), he told us this weird story. He said that when he "died," he realized how old and wrinkled he'd become because he was above his own body, looking down at himself and the nurse leaning over him. And, he said, it was such a lovely, lovely feeling. Daddy told me he no longer had any fear of death; he knew it was beautiful.

He turned to Uncle Willy and said, "Will, you just don't know how beautiful it was." And Uncle Willy, who always joked with Daddy, said, "Well then, why didn't you stay dead?" And Daddy answered seriously, "I would have, but 'Dette needs me and I thought I ought to come back. But, when I go, I'll go with a clear conscience 'cause everything is alright. I have a clear conscience!" And Uncle Willy mumbled, "Or a bad memory."

Now, this was long before they published anything on near-death experiences. Daddy described being whisked through a long tunnel that was light and beautiful. He got downright rhapsodic. And I was thinking, "Now, what is this?" It baffled me. But Daddy was just as serene as he could be. He said he saw these radiant people and they welcomed him. And he said they told him he could decide if he wanted to stay. And he decided to come back because I needed him. It was all very strange to me, but I was pleased he was recovering—whatever the reason.

He'd retired by then. But he kept drinking and playing *boccia* with his Italian friends in the saloon. He was to have more heart attacks before he died in his eighties in 1961, eleven years after Mama.

Back in Alexandria, I kept up with my activities—the YWCA, the Girl Scouts (because of Gretchen), and voter registration. In a few months, I found myself not only working for others' registration, I found myself fighting for my own.

The 1954 Supreme Court decision had many kinds of rippling effects. I mentioned that it was at that point the national YWCA demanded that their southern branches be integrated. Well, while some whites were prodded to try to remove injustices, others became even more recalcitrant in their racism. Shaken by the Supreme Court decision, the White Citizens Council of Rapides Parish, under the leadership of Brian Duke, became even more active. One of their efforts was the purge of all blacks from the voter registration rolls. As I recall, there was also an upcoming election in which some character no black person would ever vote for was running.

The law in Louisiana, at that time, allowed any person to challenge the registration of another person on the basis of an incorrect application. I, as well as every other black registrant I knew, received a notice that I was no longer on the roll. Because I knew how hard they were on blacks, I'd taken great care to fill out my application perfectly, crossing all "t"s and dotting all "i"s. So what could they have found wrong?

I went to the Registrar's Office immediately and questioned my removal from the roll. The Registrar got out my records, looked them over, and asked, "How do you say your first name?" And I said, "It's Odette." And he said—now this is very strange in an area that has many Cajun people who speak a French patois—he said, "If it's 'Odette,' then you don't need this extra 't' and 'e' that you have at the end. That would make it 'Oddity.' You've spelled your name incorrectly on your application. And if you're too dumb to know how to spell your own name, you're not qualified to vote! "

I was so angry. He and I both knew this had nothing to do with the correct spelling of my name. It had everything to do with controlling black people in every possible way. I'd heard stories all my life of places in the South where blacks had lost their jobs or been beaten and even killed for trying to register to vote. By comparison, Rapides Parish was mild, I guess. Nevertheless, I was furious. And even more determined to get myself and as many other black people as possible back on the roll.

The next day, I returned to the Registrar's Office with my birth certificate. I showed him the spelling of my name on the certificate: "Now, this is my legal name of my birth certificate. It is a French name and this is the correct spelling! " He hemmed and hawed and said he would check into the matter. It took months before I was restored to the roll. Other blacks experienced the same delay in the resolution of their challenge to the purge. And, not surprisingly, an election took place in the interim. The obnoxious white candidate we were all against was elected.

These periodic purges were disheartening, but they never stopped the group of us who were committed to gaining citizens' rights for all black people from continuing our voter registration efforts. Today, since the 1965 Voting Rights Act, anyone can register here and there are no requirements at all. You can vote in this state if you can just make an "X." (And that includes a lot of people. Louisiana has the highest illiteracy rate in the nation!) But I think every year there's a kind of shaky feeling that they're going to take away voting rights legislation.

Yes, I have to admit that I do have a kind of underlying wariness, because those of us who were here in the fifties, before the Civil Rights Movement, know just how outrageous these white folks can be. Another incident that took place around this time illustrates their outrageousness well. One August, the all-white school board announced that the black schools would not open that fall. Why? So that the children could all go pick cotton! That year, they'd had an unusually big crop, so they needed more pickers than usual. And decided to take the black kids out of school and put them into the cotton fields. Do you know the truck came by here to pick up the Hines children? A number of us quickly organized a picket line. We went to the school board building with signs saying: "What color is cotton? Pick it yourself!" The whites were aghast. But it worked. They changed their minds and opened the black schools on schedule.

This wasn't an original idea with that school board. It was just the first time it'd happened since I'd been in Alexandria. Now, years before I'd arrived here, the entire schedule of the black schools was set by the needs of the cotton growers. They'd have three months of school in session in the hottest part of the summer. Then, they'd close the schools at the end of the summer so the kids could tend to the cotton. School would remain closed until the next summer. The black kids only got three months of schooling a year!

So, when they pulled this in the fifties, trying to close the black schools in the fall, there was plenty of precedent in Alexandria's wicked history. Maybe they even thought they were being reasonable by closing the schools only for a couple of months rather than the full year. But the atmosphere in the nation, if not Alexandria, had changed enough by then that we were able to stop them. And they've never tried to pull that again since.

It was also in the fifties that I encountered one of the most horrible scenes I've had to witness in Alexandria. And I'm so sorry my children were with me. I was driving them to school one morning and, in the middle of the city, right in front of Casson Street Community Center, there was a black man's body hanging. Hanging from a magnolia tree. I stopped the car and just stared. And the lyrics of Abel Meeropol's song "Strange Fruit" washed over me: "Black body swinging in the southern breeze, strange fruit hanging from the poplar trees. . . ." I was shocked and repulsed. A part of me wanted to go and help get him down. But I remembered the children, and I started the car up again. Somewhere (I don't remember now where), I made a telephone call to the police. They already knew about it. And did nothing for the longest time. He stayed up there for hours before he was cut down. Many, many black people saw the hanging body that morning. People taking their kids to school, people going to work. I guess that was the point, wasn't it? They hanged him on a main street right downtown so people could see yet another time what happens to black people who step out of line.

Jimmy was called to look at the body and arrived long before the police. He said the man hadn't died from the hanging; he'd been murdered, then hanged from the tree. The police and the FBI (and the head of the FBI here at that time was real Klan material, if not a member), they ruled it a suicide! He had hanged himself, they said. And, of course, no one was ever brought to trial. The rumor was that the man had struck up a friendship with a white woman. But that kind of rumor was almost always circulated in the South to justify lynching. Certainly, he'd stepped out of line in some way. Like Emmett Till. Like scores of others in the fifties who never hit the headlines. He'd stepped out of line and became an example for other blacks. Ghastly. It was a ghastly scene and an obscene ruling. But that was Alexandria in the fifties.

Three years after Terry was born, my second daughter Maggi came into the world. She was a healthy, delightful baby. But the circumstances in my life at the time of her birth were difficult. Very, very difficult. As I said, the trial created cracks in my bond with Jimmy. Not because I loved him any less. I didn't; I continued to adore him. If anything, his having to go through all that and having the conviction hanging over him and being subjected to the doubts of so many people in Alexandria, if anything, that made me care even more. But *he* began changing after the petition thing, becoming more critical of me, being argumentative, spending more time away from home. As I said, I'd become too much of the heroine in the eyes of others, too much the star of the show. I really think he needed to be in a situation where he could be the star. And, in his mind, that was no longer possible with me.

But, at the time, I thought the problem was me. When he criticized something, I'd resolve to fix it. I could be better. I don't think I had low self-esteem. No, I liked me and thought I was pretty competent. My family in New York had given me a good feeling about myself. But I knew there's always room for improvement, so, I thought, I'll take this perfect man's advice and try to become better.

By the mid-fifties, though, it was clear the marriage was in trouble. There was talk of divorce, and I went to Camille Gravel for advice. Yes, the same Camille Gravel who'd prosecuted Jimmy for murder. Even when I was hating him back then, I could still appreciate his skill as a lawyer. (Later he told me he really admired me too: any woman who could undo his successful conviction, he said, was a better lawyer than he was.) Gravel also had a reputation for being decent on issues of race. So, I respected him and I thought it would be good to have him on my side. He and some tax lawyer concluded that Jimmy would never go through a divorce—for financial reasons. And I accepted that and tried to work on the marriage.

In the spring of 'fifty-six, Jimmy suggested that I go home to have the baby that was due. It would give us some space he thought we needed; he too wanted to work on the marriage, he said. It would be better for me if the baby could be born up there because certainly the circumstances of the birth in New York were better than here. Things would be fine, he said. So we were all deposited on an airplane, me and my three children, with Terry still in diapers. It was June when we went; and Maggi came into the world in August.

She was born in the same hospital where Gretchen had been born, Fordham Hospital. We were back in the house in the Bronx two days after her birth. Jimmy called me from Louisiana that same day. And said I should go to New Jersey and file for divorce.

It wasn't a shock. It was as painful as it could be, but it wasn't a complete shock. Jimmy's behavior in the last couple of years had made me somewhat cynical, and I hadn't completely swallowed his "things will be fine" line. I called Gravel and asked him what to do, things weren't working out the way he thought they would. He told me to get back to Alexandria immediately and occupy my house. If I didn't, Jimmy could declare I'd deserted him, gone off with the children. And he could get an immediate release from the marriage with little financial responsibility. So we got on a plane—my friend Sybil, me and the kids—just four days after Maggi was born. We put cotton in her little ears and carried her in a blue canvas baby carrier. And flew back—into an abyss of pain.

The marriage ending was the worst thing I'd ever gone through. It was far worse than Jimmy's trial for murder because, throughout the trial, we had our love for one another. And I had my belief in him. He was under a horrible threat, but I knew he was innocent and I loved him totally and I knew he loved me. But the ugliness between us that led up to the divorce, the loss of his love, the revelations about his unfaithfulness, these were stunning blows. When you're left, you feel like trash thrown by the side of the road. Valueless. Useless. Undesirable. It is a horrible thing. My marriage and my family were everything to me. I remember saying a little prayer in the early years of our marriage that I would die before he did, because I didn't think I could live without him. And the Lord had to tell me, you're a darn fool. You *can* live without him! And I've learned that lesson very well. But, back then, he was my base, my foundation. And, even during the divorce, I was still thinking he was perfect and I must have done some things wrong. I know better than that now. And I've tried to raise my daughters so that they will never have so much of their identity tied up with a man's. But that's how I was then.

When Jimmy exited, for the first time, I lost some of my spiritual strength. Throughout my life, I'd had a religious thing inside me that made me feel I was getting some help from above. But the devastation of the divorce left me wondering. Now, there was a flowerbed in our backyard. And some little plant had shot up very early in the spring. Usually, that would make me feel good. Springtime had always made me feel good. But not that year. I saw this little plant and something in me was saying, so what? And I kind of moped over to the wooden fence and was leaning on it. And a little lizard, one of those salamanders, appeared on the fence right in front of me. It just sat there without moving. And I looked and was struck by how exquisite it was. That little thing was so beautifully formed. And, all of a sudden, in my head was this lovely old hymn, "How Great Thou Art"—which, I think, is one of the best. I *knew* somebody had cooked up this universe. And I knew that I, in my little sorrows, was not as important as trying to do whatever I ought to be doing instead of "poor Odette-ing." That experience was a turning point. Since then, I have never again doubted the existence of a higher power or my own human worth as a part of His creation.

My spirituality and my friends and my family are what got me through the divorce. My two surrogate mothers next door, Plessy and Mama Baker, were so important. (Many people that I'd thought were friends disappeared. These were Jack and Jill and Links people. They'd been friends of the doctor's wife and I no longer had value to them because I wasn't a doctor's wife anymore. But when they deserted me, I didn't feel diminished; I just recognized that they were not truly my friends.)

And I stayed *very* busy. To make a little money, I started selling insurance.

Uncle Lester gave me a station wagon—he knew the divorce had changed my financial situation drastically—and I used the wagon to drive all over this parish selling insurance and collecting premiums. But that was part-time. What I did to fill up my days was teach. I started teaching first grade at St. James Catholic School—with infant Maggi in a doll bed in a corner of the room.

I'd come to believe that the only way you cope with heartbreak in your life is to work like the dickens. I'd learned that during that summer after my baby died and I just did nothing. All I accomplished was to lose a whole block of time. That was pointless. If you're alive, live. So I taught at the black parochial school my three older children were attending. This was good in another way, too: the school was around the corner from Jimmy's office and the children were able to spend some time with him every afternoon while I prepared my lessons for the next day. And, afterwards, we'd all pile into the station wagon. I'd have a snack for the children ready in the car. Then we'd go on the insurance tour. They'd do their homework back in the flat part of the station wagon while I drove to Cheneyville and Bunkie, LeCompte and Boyce, all over. Maggi would be in the doll's bed on the seat next to me. I sold insurance because I needed the money. But I taught school mainly to stay sane. I had to teach after the dissolution of the marriage or go nuts. You have to have some reason for getting up in the morning when you don't feel like you're alive anymore.

After that year teaching first grade, the school instituted French for their third-graders and asked me if I'd teach the class. This was an experiment, really; they'd never before offered a language in such a low grade. No public school—white or black—offered a foreign language, not even in high school. And it turned out to be a delight for me. Youngsters at that age will imitate any crazy sound that comes out of your mouth. Whereas, at high school age, they anglicize a foreign language. But not the little kids. They did *very* well and the diocese was extremely pleased. The kids could say "Hail, Mary" in French faster than you could spit. We even got some prize from the diocese that year.

Generally, the Catholic schools here were better than the public schools. That's why I'd enrolled my kids in one. They had a kindergarten; the public schools did not. The Catholic schools taught things like art and music while the public schools didn't. (Now, their art classes weren't great. They were small, tight classes. It was mostly making little wreaths to go around the Virgin Mary's neck or something. And, very often, the nuns would outline exactly what the children were to draw. There was no freedom of expression at all. But the classes did give an idea of composition and a notion of color. Things could be gained from the classes. And nothing like this was in the public schools.)

The black Catholic schools also taught civics, which was illegal to teach in the black public schools. Our teachers were not even allowed to give their students information on the structure of government. That sounds crazy, but it's true. No civics classes because whites thought they could create dissatisfaction and unrest. Civics classes *were* in the white public schools. But prohibiting them from the black schools was another part of their efforts to keep blacks under control.

The following year, I was asked to teach French to the high schoolers. But I still taught third grade too. The high school kids were much more difficult to teach. I couldn't get them to pronounce the words correctly. But all this activity did fill up my life and help me heal. And I continued teaching until 1963. After a while, it was less for the survival of my sanity and more so that Gretchen and my son Jimmy could have at least a small acquaintance with a second language.

Gretchen had always been good academically. Because I had enrolled her in the first grade when she was only five, and then she later skipped a grade, she went into her senior year at St. James when she was only fifteen. She did well on all her college entrance exams and received a scholarship and loan to attend Dillard. So, in the summer of 'sixty-one, when she was only fifteen, she left for college. I was proud but sad about her leaving. And very grateful Dillard was less than four hours away.

Every summer, I still had the preschool program in my backyard. It became more and more difficult, though, because, after the divorce, the funds just weren't there anymore. I was no longer affluent. The teaching I was doing was entirely volunteer. I couldn't be put on the payroll because it would have interfered with my alimony, and, I'd discovered after the divorce, I was held jointly responsible for income taxes Jimmy hadn't paid during our marriage—a debt I had no knowledge of during the marriage. The alimony payments (when they came, and that wasn't dependable) couldn't provide for anything near the standard of living I'd enjoyed during the marriage. So providing food and supplies for the preschoolers became more and more of a problem. There were times, during those years, when I was barely able to provide food and supplies for my own children!

I did get some help, though. Mama Baker would often fix the children snacks. She'd say, "I'm going to whip you up a batch of tea cakes." And make enough for thirty preschoolers and the volunteers. And Miss Cooper, who'd been household help here during the marriage, still came by regularly, often bringing food for the kids. She'd bring a pot of spaghetti or something, and those little folks would have a hot meal. But the expenses of running this program became a constant concern in a way they hadn't been before the divorce.

The final blow to the program came when one of my volunteer helpers, a woman who had two boys coming here, asked to be paid. She was unemployed, living with her grandmother, her husband had left her, and she needed money. "Mrs. Hines, if I could earn a little money over here, we could hold things together." I had no money to pay her. But I wanted to help. The only thing I could think of was to ask parents to pay a little. But I should have known better. Although I asked for only one dollar a week, it was a hardship for them. Some were able to keep paying a dollar a week for a month, some for two months, but before long we were down to five or six kids. And there was no way I could pay her, feed those little preschoolers, transport them, and buy supplies on the income from those few parents. It didn't even cover the gas I used bringing them to and from my house in the station wagon. So, trying to give her a job ended the program completely. That was in the summer of 'sixty-three. It was painful to have to admit I just could no longer afford to do it. I knew how needed it was. And I couldn't have imagined that two summers later I'd be running a similar program for *hundreds* of children throughout the entire parish, with all the supplies and food and staff we needed: the Rapides Parish Headstart Program.

My son Jimmy left for prep school in New England during the summer of 'sixty-three. He was thirteen and had been accepted into something called the Dartmouth Program, in which a number of New England prep schools participated. They recruited and financed gifted black kids to attend schools like Choate and Mt. Herman. Jimmy was accepted at Portsmouth Priory, a Catholic school in Rhode Island. So, in the summer of 'sixty-three, he left to go into the ninth grade in New England. Once he left St. James, I stopped teaching there.

Terry and Maggi, my two younger children, felt the diminished family we now had. I was still selling insurance and "meddling" in various community activities, but I knew I had room in my heart and my home for more people, and I, of course, thought of children first. Through discussions with Violet

Leger, who was the head of Child Welfare and on the YWCA Board with me, I
became aware of a new phenomenon in the black community: babies being
given up for adoption.

This was something encouraged by white social workers. They'd succeeded
in persuading young black girls to put their children born out of wedlock up
for adoption, which was white folks' notion of how best to handle this difficult
situation. Before this, unmarried black girls who had babies usually had the
support of their families. There might be ire too. They might be temporarily
sent to another town to hide the disgrace. But, typically, some family member
or family friend would take the child in, maybe pretending it was their child.
There was no such thing as putting black babies out for any kind of adoption
by strangers. The child would be informally adopted by someone in the girl's
extended family. But, in the early sixties, welfare got into it. They would pressure the girls to put the baby up for adoption. The problem was that, because
there was no tradition in the black community of adopting totally unknown
babies, and certainly no tradition of going through a white agency to do so,
these babies were very difficult to place. In one conversation with Mrs. Leger
about the problem, she asked if I would be willing to be a foster parent to one
of these babies until it was adopted. She knew of one that was just about to be
born.

I asked Terry and Maggi—who were then ten and seven—how they felt
about it. Terry said, "Oh, we'd love to have a baby here, Mama. Even if it's retarded, we'll take care of it." I wondered why Terry thought about retardation
right away, but I was pleasantly amazed at their openness and welcoming
spirit. Maybe my "Christian charity" talks had really sunk in. Anyway, they
were very receptive. So I told Mrs. Leger yes.

Henry Harris' arrival in my life was very dramatic. I had been invited down
to Southern University to speak on newspaper work at a career day event. I
knew the birth of the baby I'd agreed to take was imminent, so I'd left the
phone number at Southern with Mrs. Leger. Whitney Young was speaking at
this career day, and I was looking forward to hearing him speak. I'd seen him
at house parties in Texas and I'd enjoyed listening to him because his mind
worked very nicely. And I knew he'd been groomed by Lester to take over the
Urban League. So that was an additional reason for going to Southern. Anyway, it was right in the middle of my talk that the call came from the Alexandria Child Welfare people. And someone came into the room where I was

talking and said, "I'm sorry to interrupt you, Mrs. Hines, but your baby has just been born." I was delighted to hear the news. The students in the audience looked bewildered about how my baby was just born when I was standing in front of them.

The child welfare people brought Henry to my house when he was three days old. He was in a box on the back seat of the white social worker's car. And she delivered him as she would deliver groceries. No, not even groceries. Because she would have picked up a bag of groceries and carried it to my door. But Henry's brown flesh was far more distasteful than that to her. She knocked at my door and I had to go out to the car and get him.

Henry was a darling little boy who, even as an infant that young, looked like a prizefighter. My own children delighted in him, too. And they were just great about taking care of him, feeding and cuddling him, changing his diapers and powdering his little backside. He brought us real joy. So when Mrs. Leger called over here about two months later and said she had another baby that needed a foster home, we said yes without hesitation.

This baby had a health problem, a skin disorder. The same social worker who'd delivered Henry knocked on my door again and told me "Billy Bell" was in her car. I knew where to look for him: on the back seat, away from her. Billy was a fair-skinned child, but he was still black and thus, to her, untouchable. All of this reminded me of the physical exam I went through for the Red Cross where the female physician wouldn't touch me. Even parting my toes with a pencil so she wouldn't come into direct contact with my flesh. Billy was about three weeks old, and her behavior made me wonder how much love he'd received in his short life. If all the social workers behaved like this one, cuddling is something he'd probably never experienced.

Billy's problem was inactive sweat glands, which caused his skin to blister. We couldn't fasten him up with anything too tightly because the blisters would break and an infection could set in. So we had to take great care with him. But, as with Henry, my children were just great with Billy.

Do you know how they got those names "Henry Harris" and "Billy Bell?" Child Welfare assigned names alphabetically and always with alliteration. So Henry must have arrived right after a child they'd assigned a name beginning with "G," and "Harris" was just added arbitrarily. It wasn't his mother's last name. And "Henry" hadn't been his mother's choice. They didn't allow either the birth mother or the foster mother to give the child a name. But the adopting parents had the legal right to change the child's first name, if they chose.

These babies became my children. They both stayed with me for over two years. I took them everywhere with me, each in a well-padded oval wicker laundry basket. Because they were forever with me, everywhere I went, they were with me when I met the man who would become Henry's adoptive father.

I'd gone to a meeting being held in the auditorium of the community center. The meeting hadn't begun yet and people were still out in the lobby. Everybody was playing with Henry and Billy, who were, by then, absolutely adorable, active, friendly two-year-olds. A man I didn't know was playing with Henry, especially. (I found out later he was visiting Alexandria from Arkansas.) As I said, Henry was built like a miniature prizefighter, a very husky little fellow. And exceptionally strong. This little bouncy boy would succeed in taking all the pickets out of the playpen we had for him at home. He demolished it daily, and we'd have to reconstruct it every night. He was a strong fellow and always had a big smile. So this man really fell in love with him and said, "I just wish I could take this little fella home with me." And I said, "You can!" Now, up to that point, he'd thought this was my child, and he was frankly horrified when I seemed willing to give him away. He looked at me like I was the most despicable somebody he'd ever seen. So I had to explain to him that the children were state wards and that the Child Welfare people were actually looking for homes for them. And I gave him the address of the agency and directed him how to get there. The very next day he went over and negotiated with them to get Henry. Ended up taking Henry back to Arkansas.

Then a professional couple here in Alexandria took Billy. Because they lived right here, I thought I'd be able to keep tabs on his well-being. But I was told by the agency that, after he was adopted, I was to stay away from him because the child actually regarded me as his mother and seeing me would confuse him. The social worker said children are like little animals: they can even smell their mothers. "And we're not telling you that you need a deodorant, Mrs. Hines. We're just saying that children know the person who first nurtured them, and being around you would be bad for him." So I kept my distance. I never saw Billy until he was graduating from high school. The principal down there invited a number of us "community leaders" to lunch. And someone who knew he'd been my child pointed him out to me. He was a fine-looking young man! Then he went to college and I hear he's doing quite well. He doesn't know anything about me. He's never been told anything.

I know nothing of Henry. He was taken to Arkansas when he was only two, and I have no way of knowing how he's doing. The babies' leaving was so difficult. I can remember getting Henry's little duds ready to pack and my daughter Gretchen, who was home from Dillard, saying, "Mama, you really don't need to sprinkle those things you're ironing." I hadn't sprinkled them. I was ironing and weeping. It's a very wrenching thing to have a child—whether you've given birth to it or it's under your care—to have it and then to give it up. When you take in a foster child, they ask if you understand there'll be a time when you'll have to be separated from your child. No matter how you think you'll manage it, if you cared enough to take them and regard them as your children, they *become* your children, and their leaving is a deep hurting thing.

As I said, the babies were with me for over two years. Together, we went through one of the most fearful periods of my life: the time of the Civil Rights Movement here in Alexandria. The foster babies were here when I allowed three CORE workers to stay at my house while they really shook things up in Rapides Parish.

I can't say I wanted that kind of danger. My concern for my own two children and the foster babies made me petrified all the time the workers lived here. But, at the same time, my concern for them was a large part of the reason I housed the workers in the first place. Because what kind of a world would they grow up in without drastic changes in the South? What would it be like for Henry and Billy and Terry and Maggi, for all those hundreds of bright little preschoolers who came to my backyard program, if the goals of the Civil Rights Movement weren't at least partially realized in Rapides Parish?

No, I despised the danger; I hated living in fear. But the alternative was worse. The alternative was for Alexandria to remain the same. Degrading black people in every way, hanging black men who got out of line, not educating our children, not even letting us register to vote. I couldn't bear the thought of all these beautiful black children having to live their lives in Alexandria as it was. No, things had to change. Alexandria needed CORE.

X

The Civil Rights Movement

"It was a real community effort."

I DON'T REMEMBER ALL THE DETAILS of how I came to house the CORE workers who came to Alexandria. I believe the state office of CORE—which was then in the town of Plaquemine—contacted some folks at the black community center about wanting to start a project here. This would have been during the summer of 1964. In the early sixties, CORE had been very active in Louisiana. I remember hearing about confrontations in New Orleans, in Tangipahoa Parish, in West Feliciana. There'd been a big to-do in Plaquemine during the summer of 'sixty-three that got national press coverage because James Farmer had almost gotten himself killed by state troopers determined to remove the national director of CORE from the face of this earth.[1] So I was already aware that CORE was active in the state, and it didn't surprise me when Popeye, the director of the community center, paid me a visit and said CORE wanted to start a project here in Rapides Parish. And that I should not even think about housing them.

Popeye had been installed in that position by Mayor W. George Bowden, the same person who'd perpetuated himself as mayor for eleven years without an election. Bowden said there was no need for an election, he had no opposition and he'd be wasting the taxpayers' money going through that process. Whites accepted that, and blacks, of course, had no say. Mayor Bowden placed people who would do his bidding in key positions. Popeye was one of those people. He'd been a disc jockey before that and I believe he's a disc jockey today. But, at this point, because he would follow the mayor's dictum, he was the director of our community center. So when Popeye came out here and said, "Everybody thinks you're going to let them live here. I know you've got better sense than to do that, Mrs. Hines. Don't let those people in your house. You know we're doing good here," well, that was my signal to do it. When he made it even clearer why he'd come by saying, "The mayor doesn't want them here," I responded that this was *my* house and I'd let anyone in here that I wanted.

Why did Popeye come here? I guess, by that time, everyone knew I'd be the most likely person to welcome civil rights workers. I was still seen as an outsider, a Northerner, and everyone knew what I was capable of doing to help black people get their rights. After that conversation with Popeye, I knew I wanted to help. Things *were* awful here. And even the black people, like Popeye, who said otherwise, knew better; they just wanted to preserve the little bit they had. When I heard the workers needed housing, I was glad I had the space to give them. I remembered that night I spent locked in a filthy toilet in the bus station in Quitman, Mississippi. Because black people were afraid to house someone asking about the atrocity of a lynching. What could have affronted them more? But fear stopped them from doing anything to help a person who was there to help them. In 'sixty-four, I was afraid too. The Klan and the White Citizens Council were active in central Louisiana. And I had four children in the house—my own two younger children and the two foster babies. But I couldn't let fear stop me from doing what was right. And I knew giving the CORE workers a place to live was the right thing to do.

Ronnie Moore, the state director of CORE, drove the three young workers to my house in September. The project leader was Judy Rollins, a black college student from Boston who'd volunteered for the 'sixty-four CORE Summer Project, and then, like many others, decided to stay through the winter. The other two workers were both male: Henry Brown was a black man from Clinton, Louisiana who'd been involved in the Louisiana movement for a couple of years, and Bob something was a northern white college student who'd also just come to Louisiana that summer. (I can't remember Bob's last name partly because he didn't stay very long.)

It's hard to describe the atmosphere in this town at that time. Some of what we were feeling came from what was happening all over the South then. Those three boys—Chaney and Schwerner and Goodman—had been killed that summer in Mississippi. Their bodies had been found just weeks before the three CORE workers came to live at my house. Those boys weren't the only ones killed, though. They just got national publicity because two of them were white. Blacks in the South had been disappearing and turning up dead for years. During that six-week period when the FBI was searching for the three boys, they kept finding bodies of black men. They found them in the Mississippi River, they found them by the side of the roads, they even found the body of a fourteen-year-old with a CORE T-shirt on floating in the Big Black River! And they didn't investigate any of those deaths. They didn't care who they were or how they were killed. They were just black men. They wouldn't have cared about James Chaney either if he hadn't been with Goodman and Schwerner.

In Louisiana, churches had been burned all over the state, civil rights workers shot at, people beaten for trying to register to vote in some parishes. These events were constant. We'd hear about them through the black press, sometimes through the white media, or from people in other towns. Once the CORE workers were here, we'd hear about them from them. It was their colleagues going through these things, so that brought it all very close to home.

Not that we didn't have enough going on right here. As soon as the workers moved in, the telephone calls began. Threats about bombing the house, burning it down. Threats to the children. Some of the most frightening voices knew the specifics of my family situation, and would say they were going to get "those nigger kids." And I'd think, oh, my children are in danger. They usually called the workers "northern agitators" or "outside agitators" and the white worker a "nigger lover." But it wasn't the name-calling that bothered me. It was when they'd say something like, "You'd better be ready for us tonight," or, "The sun doesn't shine all night and you'd better watch out," or, "If you want to live, nigger, you'll get those northern sons of bitches out of your house." I'd hang up on them as soon as possible, but I'd always have heard enough to be frightened by the call. Sometimes the people would identify themselves as someone in authority: "This is the Police Department. We understand that you have white people living in your house. You know better than that, girl." I'd hang up on those calls too. It may have been the Police Department. I don't know. But there's nothing to say to that, anyway. There was only the deep terror because you'd never know when they were going to show up and do whatever they thought they could do.

The whites of Alexandria clearly knew the workers were here as soon as they arrived. And the only way they could have known was through Mrs. Brewer, my neighbor across the street who couldn't bring herself to call me "Mrs. Hines." At that time, there were laws in Louisiana against interracial socializing and cohabitation. The only exception was a black servant living in a white house. So I was not only challenging all the mores of the town, I was breaking the law.

The workers were out all day every day and into the evening—canvassing, going to meetings, picketing and, on Sundays, speaking in churches. So, for a long time, only I heard those calls. And I didn't tell the CORE workers about the threats. I thought they were facing enough, getting chased down the highway, getting shot at, always in danger. And I would keep praying that the calls were only talk, only a scare tactic.

Most of the callers were white men, but there were also some calls from blacks, both men and women. Some blacks were undoubtedly acting on their own, fearing the upheaval of civil rights activities. But most, I think, had been prodded to call me by their white employers. The maids would be told at work to try to get that crazy woman to run those folks out of her house so our town could go back to where it was supposed to be. I was still the Yankee import: anyone who'd put up civil rights workers would have to be opposed to the lovely way we get along in the South, they'd be told. So, on the heels of that, the maid would phone over here. Sometimes they'd identify themselves and say something like, "Mrs, Hines, it ain't the time. We ain't ready for this. Now, we've been living here and getting along. Stirring up all this trouble. No telling what those folks will do." It was not that they were really opposed. They were afraid, afraid of losing their jobs, afraid of the unknown. It wasn't that they didn't want to be liberated, but they didn't want to go through the agony of getting liberated. After calling me, they could go back to their employers and say, "I talked to that woman last night. I don't know what she's going to do but I surely talked to her. And, Miss So and So, you're so right." Appearing to be totally against me and the movement protected their jobs.

Those calls are one of the first things that come to mind when I think of that period. They were constant for the entire ten months the civil rights workers stayed at my house. Those calls and the fear. There was just an atmosphere of violence. I was afraid all the time. Afraid for my children, afraid for the CORE workers, afraid for myself.

CORE immediately started working in cooperation with other activist groups in Alexandria. The NAACP, under Reverend Joseph Rax, was somewhat active. And the group that included the Torreys, Zora Banks, Louis Berry, Harold Williams, A. C. Dubriel, myself, and a few others was already doing some things. CORE formed an umbrella group called Total Community Action which included all of us, and that arrangement worked very well. It meant that those of us who did want change were working together, coordinating our efforts, not competing with one another.

Louis Berry gave the CORE workers office space above his law offices downtown on 9th Street. He owned this small wooden office building and gave CORE the space rent free. (That was not only generous, it was courageous of him, too, because he immediately started getting phone calls about his building being blown up if he didn't get CORE out of there.) The Masons paid CORE's telephone bill. And Total Community Action raised money to pay for their office supplies. It was a real community effort. Well, why not? They were here to help our community, weren't they? They were working to make this place a better place for us. So we were all involved together. And I think that's why, even after CORE left, our activism never stopped.

I had tried to arrange a place for the CORE workers to eat lunch cheaply near Berry's office. They didn't have time to be coming all the way out here for lunch every day. And it had to be inexpensive food; their so-called "subsistence wages" were only about twenty-two dollars a week, as I recall. So I called Virgie Collier, who owned a place called the Chicken Shack on lower 3rd Street. We were very fond of each other. I liked her and she liked me. So I called her and tried to make a blanket arrangement. I'd eaten there and I think it was fifty or seventy-five cents for a lovely meal. She was a good cook. But when I asked her about feeding the CORE workers, she went crazy. Vivian Bassett was in the restaurant when I called and later told me that Virgie was shaking while she was on the phone. The police would arrest her, she said, she'd lose her business, her husband was an invalid, and didn't I have better sense? When I said the CORE workers were very nice people but a racially mixed group, she went totally to pieces. And just about hung up on me. Vivian said she couldn't stop trembling even after she hung up. That's how terrified people were. So I wasn't able to arrange any regular place for the workers to have lunch.

I remember a humorous conversation that took place another time I was trying to help CORE. (Anyway, it's humorous now. Then, it was saddening.)

The woman CORE worker wore her hair natural, in what's called an "Afro" today. This was something very unusual in the Alexandria of 1964. I knew it was
becoming popular in other parts of the country, but we're always behind. Anyway, I was talking to a schoolteacher friend of mine who was somewhat supportive of CORE's activities. I asked her if she'd like to make a donation. She
said, "No, I won't give anything for CORE. But I will give you some money for
that girl to go to the hairdresser and have her hair straightened out!" She was
missing entirely the point that black women wearing their hair natural were
trying to say, we are beautiful people as we are. And we don't have to change
our appearance and get to look as much like whites as we can in order to be
acceptable on the face of the earth. When she offered the money, I tried to explain to her that this hairstyle was part of the movement, that it was an important political statement. And that I was certain the money would not be
used to go the hairdresser. But this was very hard for many people in Alexandria to accept because, up to then, the only standard of beauty that blacks operated on was how white you could be. You were higher on the aesthetic scale
the more white-looking you were, even if your features were objectively not
harmonious or pleasant. Both blacks and whites found whiter-looking blacks
more acceptable. It was a sorry state of affairs.

So this energetic group of people got the civil rights movement really going
here in Alexandria. First and foremost, they worked on voter registration. And
that continued throughout CORE's stay in Alexandria. No matter what else they
were involved with, voter registration efforts were the basic element of their
program. As I remember, CORE received funds from the Voter Education Project in Atlanta to help with that part of their work. But, even if they hadn't, it
was a high priority of all of us who'd been active in Alexandria, so we'd have
wanted them to work on it.

They set up classes all over the parish to teach people how to fill out the registration form. The classes were held mainly in churches (in this area, Lone
Star Baptist, True Vine, Good Hope Baptist, Bright Morning Star, and Reverend Bennett's Zion Hill), in people's homes, occasionally at the Casson
Street Community Center. Not too often there, though; remember, the director, Popeye, was very close to the mayor and the mayor was dead set against
"outside agitators." So usually when CORE called the community center to try
to schedule a voter registration class, it was "already booked" for whatever
dates CORE was requesting. I taught in some of the classes held in Alexandria;

I'd been doing that kind of thing for years anyway. Most of the people in Total Community Action volunteered for those classes. Henry and Judy and Bob would also have to be at the classes in other parts of the parish. Those classes kept them on the road most evenings. Between the voter registration classes and their continual meetings, they were somewhere out there in the parish almost every night of the week.

Then they'd carry people up to the Registrar's Office on the days it was open. They'd stay with them to give moral support because getting registered was still a headache here. The Registrar manipulated people. If he heard a group of blacks were on the way, he might take his lunch hour right then. When he did see them, he'd hold each person in his office for an hour or more, chatting about the weather, having them recopy the form, doing anything so that he'd see only a few people that day. By then, we no longer had to interpret the Constitution; we just had to fill out the registration form perfectly. And I mean perfectly: if you didn't dot an "i," that was enough to disqualify you. But, because of the classes, the Registrar was having a harder time finding mistakes on the forms. So his only recourse was to let as few people in as possible. Another tactic the parish used was to change the day the Registrar's Office would be open without notice. The office had never been open every day of the week. In most parishes, the Registrar's position was a part-time job, and the office opened irregularly. So sometimes there'd be the frustration of picking up four or five people in different locations, driving them to the Registrar's Office downtown, only to find the office closed for that day. Working on voter registration took incredible patience. At best, we could get seven or eight people registered in a day. But even that was unusual.

In addition to teaching in the voter registration classes, I always went to the Monday night meetings of Total Community Action, where decisions would be made on projects to be undertaken. Those meetings were usually held in Louis Berry's office or at the Masons' or one of the churches. Sometimes I'd just carry the foster babies with me, but usually I left them with Plessy and Mama Baker. My own two children were no problem: Terry was eleven by then and Maggie was eight. This was a good experience for them, living with civil rights workers. Today, they are both very aware and concerned about the plight of black folks in the world. Terry, especially, has remained actively committed throughout his adulthood to helping his people. He still says the civil rights workers were models for him.

There were many small triumphs that winter. CORE definitely accelerated our activism, and whatever we undertook seemed to generate more activity and more interest in change. By mid-November, only Judy was here. Bob was sent back north and Henry was assigned to another CORE project. But that didn't slow us down a bit. I think the reason Ronnie Moore, the state director, didn't replace either of them was because he recognized that the community was giving CORE so much support, only one CORE staffer was needed here. And he was right. With only Judy from November to March, we accomplished so much!

Bob's leaving was actually helpful. He'd become more of a liability than an asset. He'd done a number of small things that none of us—including the other two CORE people—appreciated. He was disrespectful: he'd go into black church services in scrubby jeans and shirts after being told that black church-goers would take offense to that. He smelled bad and just wouldn't take a bath. And, I was told by the other workers, he'd put them in danger unnecessarily because of his immaturity. The last straw was when he put me and my family in danger.

Bob was always taking pictures. I'd told him not to go into a particular photography store because the owner was the head of the local White Citizens Council. After Bob had been here about six weeks, he not only took film into that very store, but when they were filling out the envelope for development, he gave them his correct address, *my* address! When he came home and told me what he'd done, I felt more frightened than I ever had before. This was like flaunting a red flag in front of an organized, racist group. And I was furious: why had he gone into that store after I told him not to? And why come home and tell me about it? Viciousness? Self-destructiveness? I still don't understand it. When I told Judy, she was furious too. And the next day, she drove Bob to the CORE state office—which was, by that time, in Baton Rouge—and came back in the afternoon without him. We heard a few days later that he'd been sent back north.

So, yes, there were a few civil rights workers who had problems, but most of them were just marvelous. I met a lot of the Louisiana CORE staff because they'd stop in Alexandria to confer with Judy or sometimes just for a short social visit. Alexandria is right in the middle of the state and CORE had projects all over Louisiana—in Jonesboro and Monroe to the north, and in Clinton, Bogalusa, Greensburg, many places south of us. So Alexandria was a comfortable pit stop for staffers traveling from one project to another. They were all lively, interesting, and committed people—Ronnie Moore, the state director, Richard Haley, the director of the regional office in New Orleans, Oretha Castle, Kenny Johnson, Sharon Burger, Dave Dennis, Mike Lesser, many others. And there was Mike Jones, a quiet young black man from the North who would later be run off Route 20 as he drove from the CORE project in Jonesboro to their project in Monroe. He was alone and was immediately killed when his car hit a tree. No one was ever charged with his murder. And the all-white police department ruled it an accident. We all knew what happened that Sunday morning on Route 20 was no accident. Attempts to run civil rights workers off the road were commonplace. It happened right here in Rapides Parish. This time they succeeded. But we'll never know who. Or just what happened. A very nice young man. They were all impressive—welcomed guests at my house.

All of the CORE people worked too hard. Seven days a week. Week after week after week. I wasn't surprised when Judy told me that the Medical Committee on Human Rights, some northern doctors who volunteered to come south and treat civil rights workers, found ulcers rampant among the CORE and SNCC staff. I remember admonishing Judy and some of the others to relax more, play more. But they were all idealistic, passionate, young people. I could understand their dedication. They'd seen their coworkers beaten, jailed, even killed. I understood their sense of urgency. But I also knew the importance of balance if you're not going to burn yourself out.

One of the biggest breakthroughs that winter was in the area of school desegregation. Yes, the voter registration classes were continual, but until Johnson signed the Voting Rights Act in August of 'sixty-five, the numbers of blacks able to register always remained low, no matter how hard we worked. Those classes were not a waste of time, though, not by any means: they got people involved, they created a setting for discussing all kinds of problems, and they got folks to think about their rights as citizens. Throughout that year, many more people would come to our voter registration classes than would take part in some of our riskier efforts. Like being part of the first group to integrate the Rapides Parish schools.

For most parents, agreeing to let their child go to a white school was just too dangerous. But Total Community Action had decided to tackle school desegregation. I mean, it *was* ten years since the Supreme Court had outlawed segregated schools! And absolutely nothing had changed here in Alexandria. The schools, including the catholic schools, were totally segregated. And, of course, they were not equal: the black schools had lower budgets, poorer facilities, everything about them was poorer than the white schools. Except the dedication of the teachers. As I said, the black teachers were wonderful. Many of them had had second-rate educations themselves. Southern University never received the kind of financial support from the state that LSU did, for example. With a few exceptions—like Howard and Lincoln and Fisk—the black colleges were just not as good as the white schools. And the white colleges in the South were generally not as good as those in the North. So many of the people teaching in black schools had really not been well equipped by their formal education. But they cared and they equipped themselves. They often bought material out of their own pockets for the kids. Books on black history. They visited homes and stayed in touch with the parents of the children they were teaching. Still, limited supplies and poor facilities were always a problem for them. And, like most black Americans of that period, we all really believed that integrating the schools would improve the quality of education for our kids. So, in the fall of 'sixty-four, we set that as one of our goals.

We decided to try to integrate the twelfth grade first. Having seen what happened in Little Rock and New Orleans and other places, we decided we didn't want to expose our younger children to the possibility of that kind of violence.[2] We would let the strongest and more mature take the first step. Finding the children was not difficult. The young people were ready to challenge the system. The problem, as I said, was getting their parents to agree. Judy spent so many evenings in their homes trying to convince them this should be done. She began these discussions in November with an eye on the February school registration date. Parents would agree and then change their minds. And Judy would go back and talk with them more about the importance of desegregating the schools.

Their reluctance was understandable, though. It's hard to put your child's life in jeopardy, even for something you believe in. Your own life, yes. But your child's? I understood how they felt because I often wondered if I had the right to jeopardize my children and the foster babies by letting CORE workers live with us. I knew it was the right thing to do. But if the house had been blown up and one of them hurt or killed, would I have felt so morally "right?" So I knew why the parents were so hard to convince and why it took months,

literally, to get twelve sets of parents to agree to let their children register for
the white school.

Total Community Action made the decision to integrate the schools at the
suggestion of CORE. And CORE really did all the leg-work, at that point. The effort was fully supported by the NAACP but Reverend Rax, the president, was an
older man—maybe in his late sixties—and not very well. So it was Judy who
did the traveling around, talking to parents, instructing the students, everything. On the day of the registration, however, Judy invited Reverend Rax to
join her escorting the twelve high school students. The press was there. A large
number of people from the community—black and white—were outside. No
one knew quite what to expect. But, the registration went smoothly. Even the
Alexandria *Town Talk*, the same newspaper that would carry no black news
except crime, came to cover that story. And they did—but in a very peculiar
way: CORE was never mentioned. I personally think it was part of a deliberate
blackout of CORE because it was the organization that was shaking this town
up. But some thought it was because Judy blended in with the high schoolers
in appearance and the reporters really thought Reverend Rax was the only
adult. In any case, the *Town Talk* reported that Reverend Rax of the NAACP had
escorted *thirteen* black high school students down to the Board of Education
to register for the white school. We were all annoyed CORE didn't get the credit
it deserved. And I heard that the state and national offices of CORE were more
than just annoyed.

What's important, though, is that the registration went through and the
twelve students attended Bolton High the next year and were graduated in the
spring. Sounds too easy to be true, doesn't it? And it was. The next year, the
Board of Education—apparently more prepared than they'd been the previous year—would not let blacks register for any other grades or for any other
white schools in the parish. So we had to sue to desegregate all other schools.
In the mid-sixties, mind you. A decade after *Brown vs. the Board of Education*!

In the spring of 'sixty-six, we had Louis Berry go into federal court to seek
an injunction; we needed a judgment that outlawed segregation all over the
parish. Reverend Valley was the plaintiff for the class action suit on behalf of
his minor daughter and seven other families. The school board still resisted,
saying they had the police power to keep schools segregated in spite of *Brown
vs. the Board of Education*. Judge Edmund Hunter heard the suit here in
Alexandria. He had a pretrial conference, and Berry and the lawyer for the

school board read their statements. Hunter signed the judgment outlawing segregated schools in Rapides Parish, stating that segregation violated the 14th Amendment. And that should have been it, right? No. Hunter said he'd desegregate the schools one grade each year, beginning with the first grade. That's what "all deliberate speed" meant to him. And since only the senior year at one school was already desegregated, that would have meant another twelve years before there was complete desegregation in the parish. So Berry filed a motion for a new trial on the theory that, since the Court of Appeals had said three grades a year, Hunter should have said three grades a year. And, finally, in the fall of 1966, school desegregation really took off in Rapides Parish.

Even after that, though, there were resistant school boards. Three more suits had to be filed. In the late sixties, PACE—that was Parents for Action in Community Endeavors, a group we created to run the Headstart program— we did a survey in the Pineville schools and found that some of the textbooks in the black schools were ten years behind those in the white schools. And we documented what we knew had always been the case: that certain courses, like Civics, were still not taught in the black schools. That survey became part of one of our suits. Inferior books, missing courses. Our kids *had* to be behind! Those school desegregation battles went on for many years. But they started that first fall when the CORE people were living with me.

That winter, CORE also started testing restaurant integration in the parish. We started the testing in January. Usually once a week, the CORE worker and a local person—interestingly, it always turned out to be a woman at the beginning—would spend half a day going to six or seven restaurants. By then, whites knew about Title 2 of the Civil Rights Act of 1964, and knew they were breaking the law if they didn't serve blacks. So most of them did, begrudgingly. The testers would come to our meetings and report on restaurants serving them with paper cups and paper plates while the white customers had glasses and china. One restaurant turned off the TV and the lights and all the white customers turned their backs while the two black people ate. It was clear they'd planned this ahead. They found ways to make us very uncomfortable while not breaking the law.

But there were some restaurants that refused service. The Southside Cafe, Louie's Bar B Q, Lazarone's Drive-In. And Herbie K's, a restaurant right down the street from my house, ushered Judy and Barbara White into a small back room dimly lit and separated from the main room with beaded curtains, claiming all the tables in the main room were reserved. We'd file complaints with the Justice Department. Nicholas Katzenbach and John Doar were the folks we filed complaints with.[3]

The very first day of testing it was Judy and Betty Chenevert, a young Pineville woman, very active and very strong. (Pineville is just across the river from Alexandria.) The two of them planned to eat at a number of restaurants on Highway 71. But they hadn't learned that there's a technique to "testing": because you're going to eat at so many places, at each of them, you have to limit yourself to very small amounts of things that go together. Well, Betty and Judy just jumped out there gung-ho, ordering meals at every restaurant. They ate Chinese food, chili dogs, po-boys (submarine sandwiches), crabcakes, and goodness knows what else. And there's no telling what those angry crackers might have put in their food. At one restaurant, they saw the man spit into their Cokes and they didn't drink them. But what might have been put in their food at other restaurants that they *didn't* see? Spit or worse.

By the fourth or fifth restaurant, they were uncomfortable, but they had planned to test a certain number that day and they kept on going. By the time Judy got back here, she was complaining of a stomach ache. And before I could even bring the Alka Seltzer, she was over the toilet, bringing it all back up. That was really the best thing that could have happened. We found out the same thing had happened to Betty. So the next time they went "testing," they paced themselves and coordinated their food much more wisely. More spit was forthcoming, I understand. But no more upchucking.

Today, it's not even noticed when black people go into white-owned restaurants around here. There may be some small hole-in-the-walls in the rural parts of this parish where they'd still look at you hard. But around Alexandria, integration in public facilities is a way of life.

WHILE WE WERE STRUGGLING HERE IN ALEXANDRIA, we were always, of course, hearing about outrages in other parts of the South. In early March, we watched that horrible scene on TV when civil rights marchers in Selma got tear-gassed and clubbed and rundown with horses on the Edmund Pettus Bridge. Men, women, and children. Just awful. It was SCLC that led that march, I think, and some SNCC people were involved. They were pushing for voting rights. Just the right to vote. But the beatings some of those people took that day! I still remember seeing John Lewis being clubbed by an officer on a horse. It was either one of Jim Clark's deputies or an Alabama state trooper. They were absolutely vicious. But, really, George Wallace had set the tone for this. The working-class whites in the sheriff's department or the state troopers were just doing the dirty work for those with real power. And what they did that day was definitely dirty. Women and children, mind you, clubbed and tear-gassed. It was just awful.

Another march a few days later voluntarily turned around when they met the state troopers at the bridge. I don't know why they turned back. But when we heard a third one was planned for March 21st, and this one would try to make it across that bridge and all the way to Montgomery, a group of us here in Alexandria decided we had to go and support it. Robert and Phyllis Torrey, Zora Banks, Judy, and myself. We were all so busy with activities here, though, we couldn't afford to stay any real length of time in Selma. But we wanted to be there at its beginning, we wanted to see it cross that bridge, where it had been stopped so violently before.

We learned that the marchers would be gathering at Brown's Chapel A.M.E. Church around 8:00 A.M., I think it was. So we decided to leave Alexandria at a time that would bring us into Selma around 8:00. That meant leaving at midnight. And since we were all busy that previous day, none of us had time to nap; we had to drive all night with no sleep. But we did it. Robert Torrey did the driving—it was his car—and because we wanted to keep him company, we all stayed awake and we talked for the whole ride. About Alexandria. About Selma. About the desperate need for federal legislation on voting rights. The southern states were clearly not going to become reasonable on this issue. The large number of potential black voters were just too much of a threat.

We arrived in Selma a little early and found Brown's Chapel. We knew when we were getting close because crowds of people were already there. Hundreds, I thought at the time. But I was to find out later that when we set out from Brown's Chapel and crossed the bridge, there were actually over three thousand people. From everywhere. I talked to people from New York and Wisconsin, even California. Such excitement in the crowd, but apprehension too. We all knew what had happened here just two weeks earlier. The crowd itself was full of well-meaning, decent people, but we knew we were surrounded by irrational, frightened rednecks, even more agitated than usual because Johnson had federalized the Alabama National Guard and sent in some other military people—army people, I think—to insure there'd be no violence this time.

Those troops are one of the things I remember clearly about that morning. As we moved toward the bridge, they were lined up on either side of the street. Faces placid, rifles at "port arms," held diagonally in front of them at an eighty-degree angle, each man about ten feet from the next man. I looked at their faces, trying to discern what they were thinking. I wondered how the white Alabama boys felt about guarding civil rights marchers. Were they more afraid of the potential for redneck violence or more afraid of us—uppity blacks, white liberals, New York Jews—everything they'd been raised to despise? And the black soldiers. Were they proud of us? If they'd not been in uniform, would they be marching with us? Or were they, like so many in Alexandria, frightened by our activism and wishing we'd just stop it? We walked by them quietly, as I remember—in our part of this huge crowd there was no singing—and their faces revealed nothing to me. They were just doing their job. And, this time, it was without incident.

This march had no violence at all. Thank God. We left the march after about two hours, as I recall. By then, the marchers were well on their way to Montgomery on Route 80. The march had successfully gotten across the Edmund Pettus Bridge this time and it looked like it would be completed. That's what we'd come for.

We walked back to the car and headed right back to Alexandria. I don't remember even being tired on the way back. I remember feeling exhilarated and having a sense of real satisfaction. So relieved there'd been no violence. And so glad, grateful really, to have been a part of this.

Three hundred marchers made it all the way to Montgomery in a few days. There, they held a huge rally where all the celebrities appeared. We watched that on TV with the rest of the nation. There are those who feel today that the Selma marches are what pushed through the Voting Rights Act that was passed the following August. Perhaps so. Perhaps we actually should thank Jim Clark and the state of Alabama for actions that were so outrageous they received international press coverage. And created that kind of pressure on our government. I don't know. I do know it was wonderful being there that day, feeling that camaraderie, that sense of community, being a part of what we knew was an important gesture toward black equality in this country.

But the threat of violence was an ever-present reality for black people in the

South. And everyone believed it was the lower-class and working-class whites who were the most dangerous, and, ostensibly, the most resistant to black progress. But I didn't for a minute hold them mainly responsible for the threatening atmosphere in which black folks down here had to live. I saw them as tools of upper-class whites — manipulated, unconscious tools used to maintain a very unequal economic system. Even more unequal than in the North. I vividly remember a dinner Judy and I went to in Pineville that really made that all very real for me.

I had a friendship with a professor over at the white Baptist College in Pineville. One of her closest friends was a woman named Beth, who worked at the Baptist Conference Building here. They turn out literature and administer this loose confederation of white churches. Beth met Judy and invited both of us to her house for dinner. She lived in the gatehouse of a large estate owned by a minister very high in the Baptist Conference hierarchy. He and his wife were invited to dinner too.

He was an affable man, educated at Princeton, as I recall, with all the gracious charm and good manners of the southern aristocracy. But with all the sickness, too. First, he started telling us about the venison we were being served. He'd given it to Beth, in fact. He was a hunter and had lots of venison in his freezer. Then we heard every detail of how he'd stalked the deer, shot it, slaughtered it, and hung it up to let the blood drip out. And, as he was describing every gory detail, Judy and Beth and I could eat less and less. But, as he talked, he seemed to relish the venison all the more.

Then he proudly described the underground bomb shelter that he'd built near his house. Now, this was at a period when America was teaching school children to crouch under their desks at school because the Russians were coming. And those who were sufficiently affluent were supposed to prepare a place for themselves so they could survive this Russian invasion. So this very wealthy man had built him a bomb shelter, equipped with everything he needed to maintain his family, his wife and children. At one point, Judy asked what would happen if someone else sought refuge there. And he calmly responded that he would not let them in, he would exclude them. He had to, he said; there was just enough food and supplies for his family. And she asked how he'd keep people out. And he said by any means necessary. Any means. After all that hunting talk, we were certain those means would include using his hunting rifles. Then Beth asked him why he thought it was important to survive.

Because, he said, we have to preserve the American way of life, the Christian way of life, the *southern* way of life.

And he didn't stop there. Maybe he'd become uncomfortable with our questions, our growing discomfort with him. And he knew Judy worked for CORE. So here it came, the "nigra" talk. He really didn't condone what some of his parishioners in West Feliciana Parish had boasted about doing, he said. They'd not only hunted animals, but they'd hunted down "nigras" and killed them—for sport. No, he didn't condone that. (Yet, we heard no feeling of remorse from him about pastoring people like that.) There were, after all, certainly many "good nigras." He just couldn't understand what all this civil rights hullabaloo was all about. Because, as long as folks were willing to go along with the accepted way of life in the South, a way of life which wasn't bad at all for "nigras," then things were really very pleasant here. And the rest of us knew that this was a man who felt blacks were people who had to be contained and kept in their place. He accepted that. And he accepted that what his West Feliciana parishioners had done was sometimes necessary. The southern way of life had to be protected.

I think he was typical of the southern white upper class. I hold them more responsible for the violence that the white lower class has visited upon black people than the lower class itself. It was to the advantage of the upper class to promote separation of the races, so they could exploit the poor whites and the poor blacks. But they could only do that if they made the poor whites think they were better than the blacks, encouraged them to see blacks as a threat, and allowed them to be violent against that threat with impunity. They gave poor whites the wonderful luxury of being white, of being respected for their skin color, if nothing else. The poor white man was made to feel he had some mobility, he could get to be the boss man. But in order to hold onto that opportunity, the poor white was told he had to keep his heel in the neck of the blacks.

This well-educated, well-mannered southern gentleman represented that powerful class for me. He'd probably never be one of the people shooting into a black voter registration class or burning down a church. But it was men like him that created the mindset, the *ideas* which led the lower-class whites to beat women and children demonstrators, to blow up churches, to hunt "nigras" for sport. And these upper-class men knew exactly what they were doing when they promoted those ideas. They were protecting themselves, their own

wealth, their power. He was unabashedly one of that class. That was so clear
to me that evening. Maybe that's why I remember the details of it so vividly.

IN MANY WAYS, CORE'S ARRIVAL HERE WAS PERFECT TIMING. Those
of us who'd always been pushing for black equality had laid the groundwork
for CORE's aggressive tactics without knowing that's what we were doing. Just
that summer, after Johnson signed the Civil Rights Act in July of 'sixty-four, a
group of us had decided to push for black employment in all-white businesses.
We'd sent letters—drafted by me and signed by Louis Berry as our attorney—
to all of the businesses, stores, and banks we could think of, telling them they
were violating the law with their discriminatory hiring practices, but we'd be
happy to talk this matter over with them before we filed a lawsuit. The only
immediate response we got was from Sears and Roebuck. One of their managers called Louis Berry and said he was glad we'd sent the letter because he'd
been talking to management about this. And he asked to meet with us right
away. As I recall, it was Berry, Reverend Rax, and Reverend Valley who went
to talk with him, carrying a list of black people qualified for white-collar jobs
at Sears. After that, this man called a meeting of his employees to tell them
about the change in hiring practices. He interviewed a number of the people
we'd suggested and immediately hired an accountant and some sales people.
Sears has continued to hire blacks since then. Of all the white businesses in
Alexandria, at that point they were the most cooperative. Actually, you could
say they were the *only* cooperative white business. We didn't get any other re-
sponses to our letters. Until CORE came.

At one of those Monday night meetings of Total Community Action, this
employment issue came up. CORE's forté was nonviolent direct action, so none
of us were surprised when Judy suggested a picket line. But where? A vulnerable target, she suggested, a place where success was probable, like at a retail
store in a black neighborhood. The A&P on Lee Street! This store was a particular affront because it was right in the middle of an all-black area and would
only hire blacks to sweep up. We also thought that it being part of a national
chain could be helpful to us if we ended up needing support in other areas.
And our success could affect the policies of A&Ps all over the South. That store
was our unanimous choice. But, now, the details of the picket had to be
worked out.

The number of people who could or would picket was limited. Some people who worked for whites just couldn't be seen on the picket line. Some people were not available during the day. (Domestics in Alexandria, for example, usually worked from Monday through Saturday.) And some, we sensed even at that meeting, were just too frightened to picket and could not be counted on to show up. So rather than set up a daily picket that we might not be able to sustain, we decided to picket Saturdays only, since Saturday was A&P's busiest day. We'd be out there all day—from the time the store opened at 9:00 until it closed at 5:00. People signed up at that meeting for the first two Saturdays. And we contacted some others after the meeting that we knew would be willing to picket.

Preparing for the picket was exciting. We made posters using magic markers: "Don't Shop Where You Can't Work," "A&P Discriminates in Hiring," things like that. As I made some of these posters, I couldn't help but think, well, here I am in 1964 doing exactly what I'd done in New York in the thirties and forties: pressuring white-owned retail stores dependent on black business to hire black employees. The battle had long been won on 125th Street, but not without bloodshed and violence. Would there be violence on Lee Street too?

The first Saturday, we were all apprehensive. We'd made no public announcement of the picket. The picketers—about fourteen or so—just arrived near the store about 8:50, chose the spots on the sidewalk where they would turn (careful not to obstruct access), decided who would hand out flyers and who would talk to the press, if it arrived. When the store opened, there they were. Dorothy Hobdy, Bernice Spears, Ella Compton, Nettie Wells, Edith Benson, some more people from Rigolette and Samtown, and, of course, Judy. Yes, it was mainly women on the picket line. That Saturday and every Saturday, mainly women.

The whites inside just looked bewildered. Apparently, word hadn't gotten to them ahead of time. There was the manager, three cashiers, and a butcher, I believe. And they just didn't know what to make of this. Right away, the picket line affected their business. Blacks would come down the street to shop and just stop in their tracks, read the signs, take a flyer and then walk away. Some would stand around looking and a few even joined the picket line. "Yah, you all are right. You got another poster?" As the morning wore on, more and more were standing around just looking, and that made the picket seem larger than it actually was.

A few whites came to shop. Probably many more came in their cars to shop, but when they saw the crowd of black people out in front and the picket signs, just kept on driving. But some did park and walked right through the picket line and shopped. The picketers didn't say anything to them. We'd discussed this possibility at our meeting. Our objective was not confrontation with anybody. Our objective was to hurt A&P's business.

By 11:00 or so, it became clear that "officialdom" in Alexandria knew we were there and had sent their emissaries to check on us. Reporters from the *Town Talk* appeared. And three or four white photographers. Some were newspaper photographers. Some were police photographers. And some were not known by any of us. They'd be out there taking pictures every time we picketed. They might have been FBI men. (Everyone knew the FBI kept close tabs on civil rights activity.) And they may have been working for the White Citizens Council. Not that any of those categories were mutually exclusive, mind you. We'd expected that kind of thing. That's why many people whose jobs were dependent on whites didn't picket. We knew everyone in the city would know exactly who was on the picket line.

Robert and Phyllis Torrey, for example, couldn't be seen picketing. They were school teachers, and, at that time, the school board of Rapides Parish was entirely white. So every black teacher was dependent on whites for their employment. But the Torreys still helped so much. They fed the entire picket line and managed to do it without being seen. They brought sandwiches, donuts, and a large coffee urn in the back of their station wagon. And parked it around the corner from the A&P. We arranged all this ahead of time. Beginning at 11:30, two picketers left the line and walked around to the station wagon for lunch. When they came back, two more would go. This lunch was such a treat. After walking slowly in a circle in thirty-degree weather for a couple of hours, being able to sit down someplace warm and get hot coffee and food was most welcome. And the Torreys paid for it all. They did that every Saturday there was a picket. Altogether, it turned out to be about eight or nine Saturdays.

Others who couldn't be seen on the picket line donated money or gave rides to community people who wanted to shop somewhere else but didn't have a car. People could call the CORE office if they needed a ride and it would be arranged for them. The picket, too, turned out to be a real community effort.

We were to find out later that on that first Saturday, we cut A&P's business by 40 percent, and every Saturday after that their business decreased more and more. Even whites stopped shopping there—not because they supported us but because they were afraid of the possibility of violence. Despite the fact that we were immediately effective, though, the manager would not negotiate. He'd talk to Louis Berry over the phone but refused to set up a meeting. Nobody was going to tell him how to run his store, he said. Nobody was going to force him to "hire the colored." He gave all kinds of reasons why the picketing should be called off. But he would not meet with us. Maybe he thought the picketers would get tired and disappear. But they didn't. Saturday after Saturday, they were out there when the store opened.

Now, what was great was that a few weeks into the picketing, we heard that two other markets in predominantly black neighborhoods—Food Mart and F&F—went ahead and hired their first black cashiers. I guess they felt they could be next. But that made us know our efforts had already gained something. And it helped us continue the A&P picket.

By the sixth week, there was only a trickle of customers going into A&P on Saturdays and a big decrease in the number shopping on other days of the week. Finally, the call came. The A&P district office in New Orleans called Berry and requested a meeting. Finally, they were ready to negotiate.

Total Community Action met with two A&P representatives from New Orleans and the local manager at Berry's office. Just getting them there was a victory. And we all knew that. The New Orleans men were cordial and respectful and ready to talk specifics. But we could tell the manager of the store we'd been picketing had been forced to come to this meeting. He was clearly angry. At one point, he glared at Harold Williams and said, "You all are cutting off my bread!" And Harold Williams responded, "Well, I'm glad to know that, because now you know how we feel when you cut off our bread." The manager looked surprised and annoyed at that response. Did he expect an apology? Didn't he know that was exactly what we wanted? The New Orleans people told us something we hadn't realized: that business at the A&P in Pineville had also been affected by our picketing. I remember him saying, "You know, you all are really doing some damage." More good news. So they had to negotiate. The local manager remained uncooperative and sullen, claiming he couldn't bring in any more employees because he couldn't "displace" the current ones. But the men from the district office knew it had to be done if A&P was to survive in Alexandria, and they agreed to bring in a black cashier immediately and to bring in management trainees and butcher trainees and bag-boys within months. When they asked us for the name of someone qualified for the cashier's position, we knew just who we wanted to recommend: Dorothy Hobdy.

Miss Hobdy had been one of the few blacks working for whites who'd been willing to picket. She'd been active with the Pineville Help Planners and Po-litical Association, a black organization in Pineville that was part of Total Community Action. When her group decided to support the picket, she said she was determined to see it through. A very courageous woman, small, slight but unusually strong in spirit. The Monday after that first picket, her boss at Rapides Baptist Hospital called her into his office. Apparently, another em-ployee had seen her on the picket line and reported it to the hospital. She was never able to find out who reported her. Her boss told her that they couldn't have employees walking picket lines. And he fired her on the spot. She re-ported this at the Total Community Action meeting that same night. We all felt so bad. Miss Hobdy wasn't rich and she needed that job. But, you know, as difficult as the next two months must have been for her, she never missed a picket line. Such a committed woman. So, when the A&P people asked for a recommendation for the cashier's job, we all knew we wanted to recommend Dorothy Hobdy.

She passed the math test A&P gave her with ease, and she was working within two weeks of our meeting. And you know what happened? Now this is heart-warming and funny. The black people in the area were so proud of her—you have to realize that many had never seen a black cashier in a white-owned store—they were so proud, they wanted to support her in any way they could. So they would line up for her register and just wait for her. No matter how short the other register lines were. Even when the other cashiers had nobody. They thought she worked on some kind of commission and they wanted to help her. And they were willing to wait as long as necessary to do that. The other cashiers would tell them to come over to them but the blacks would just say politely they wanted to wait for Miss Hobdy. When she herself would en-courage them to go to the other cashiers, they'd say, "No, we want to help you make some money." And she'd explain to them that she was paid by the hour, that what they were going to do was kill her with work. When Miss Hobdy told us this at the meeting, we laughed! But we were touched by how much black people were behind her. And we knew that these little victories—getting jobs for a few blacks here and there—had great spiritual effect on our community.

After the success of A&P, there was an acceleration of activity around discrimination in employment. Some businesses were frightened enough by that success to contact us and ask to meet with us. Rapides Bank hired a black teller that spring. The sheriff's office, which had never had any black officers, hired two.

But other businesses remained intractable. In April, we had to put up another picket line at D'Amico's Supermarket at 3rd and Broadway. But they'd learned from A&P's experience, and they contacted us requesting we send blacks in quick to interview for cashiers' jobs. That picket line didn't last long at all. And we had brief pickets at Whelan's Department Store and Pigly Wigly Market. They too quickly hired some blacks. We met with the managers of Grants, Kress, Walgreen's and J. C. Penney's. All of them agreed to start hiring blacks without our having to picket them. But, don't forget, all of these places had received letters from us the previous summer and had done nothing. It was the other picketing that got them going, not any genuine good will.

There are a number of black women who are nurses today because of the activities of Total Community Action back then. There was a nursing school in Avoyelles Parish whose constitution stated only whites could attend. So Berry filed suit and won. In no time, Dolores Croal, Beulah Harper, and Daisy Dempsey were out there studying nursing. And they're all still practicing at the VA Hospital today.

Today, blacks are employed in all the stores and banks and restaurants. Maybe we're still not in top management very much, but certainly in all other levels of white-collar jobs. And we can eat just about anywhere, as I said. There's no question that, for the black middle class, for people with some education and money, there is definitely an access that just didn't exist before the sixties. But whether the situation of our community as a whole has improved, I'm not so sure. Our economic situation certainly isn't better.

What the Civil Rights Movement did was eliminate superficial racial barriers. I'm no longer stopped from going into places just because I'm black. For people like me, life is easier. I have much more freedom of movement than I did. Alexandria itself has improved a bit. We have a museum now with good exhibits coming through. We have a nicer zoo and a little theater movement. And black folks with a little money have access to those cultural things that they wouldn't have had in the fifties.

But for people on very low incomes and without education, there's not really much difference in the way they live now compared to how they lived in the fifties. There are people who don't even know what's out there on that highway. Because they certainly don't have the thirty-five-cent bus fare. And, if they got it, they would buy some malt liquor that would dull their thinking so that they wouldn't worry about the fact that they can't buy shoes for their children. And then they are further exploited by not even being able to enjoy the smaller cost of food in the supermarkets because they can only get to the little store in their community that charges three times the price of what an item is worth. So their diets remain ridiculously inadequate because they're trying to find the food that fills you up, not the kind that "bills" you up. And their health is very, very poor. No one goes to that public hospital over in Pineville until they're ready to die.

In one way, our community is even worse than the fifties—because of drugs. Drugs and the crimes that drugs inevitably bring. Drugs destroy people, destroy families; they have destroyed a communalism which was very much a part of poor black life in the past. And it seems to me, the proportion of our community that's just not making it, not getting any real education, not even eating enough, it seems to me that portion of us is getting larger and larger.

Unemployment is rife here. Big industry won't come into Rapides Parish. For a long time, the large farm owners and the lumber companies didn't want them in here, because that would raise the cost of labor. Now, industries refuse to come because of our uneducated labor force. So the growing economic sector here is the retail sector, retail and service. Because we're in the middle of the state, we attract consumers. But those jobs don't pay well. And they're precarious. Because there's such a pool of labor, the least thing you do out of line is cause for dismissal. But there aren't enough of even them to put a dent in our unemployment problem.

I'm sorry to say that today I question the value of school desegregation. The attitude of some of the white teachers toward the black children often destroys any possibility of our kids learning. (And many good black teachers lost their jobs when schools were merged.) Our kids are bussed to mixed schools where many of the teachers are white and absolutely ignorant of black culture, don't know what the children are talking about because they don't understand the language. And the children don't know what the teachers are talking about because they don't understand the white dialect. Too many of our children are put in "special education," which means no education: you can't learn, so we won't bother. And that happens to our children who arrive at school with black skins and don't express themselves as white teachers think they should. They are separated from the regular classes and they are not allowed to learn.

And I think about David Duke. His popularity. The unbelievable amount of support he's gotten in this state! It makes me wonder if everything we did in the sixties means anything. He represents the thinking of white Louisiana in the fifties. And, here he is, one of the most popular politicians in the state today.

I'm proud of what we did, though. I have so much respect for people like A. C. Dubriel, Vic Beaudoin, Harold Williams, H. P. Williams, and Georgia Johnson. All the CORE workers. Giving, courageous people. I am proud to have been a part of all that. But when I look around Rapides Parish, at our communities in this parish, I sometimes wonder what it all really meant. I wonder.

XI

Headstart

"I simply could not have
not done it."

IN THE SPRING OF 'SIXTY-FIVE, in the midst of all this Civil Rights activity, I received a letter from my friend, Sybil, in New York. She wrote me that Ladybird Johnson was starting something I'd probably be interested in because it sounded very much like "that mess" I'd had in my backyard. Maybe I should check it out, Sybil said. It was called "Headstart."

I sent for information, and when it arrived, I got so excited! What Ladybird Johnson envisioned was exactly what I had been thinking for years was needed. It was indeed what I had been trying to do with the preschool "mess" in my backyard: prepare youngsters for school — in their skills and in their love of learning and in their confidence in themselves. I shared the information with Total Community Action, the same group that was active in civil rights, and they were wholeheartedly in favor of our bringing Headstart to Rapides Parish. We agreed that Total Community Action would oversee Headstart. Louis Berry, the attorney who'd given CORE space in his building, also gave us office space. And the group told me to go ahead and write the proposal; they would support me in any way possible.

That was the go-ahead I wanted. But I didn't have a clue how to write a federal proposal. And no one else did either. But, somehow I did it. The CORE workers helped. (In March, Judy had moved to the CORE state office in Baton Rouge to take over public relations, and was replaced here in Alexandria by three other CORE workers.) We gathered together the statistics requested, wrote in the language that we thought would be acceptable to the people who reviewed such proposals. It was an intense task because we were working against a tight deadline: we'd received the forms just four days before they were due in. I worked day and night in our space in Berry's office, writing, revising, sometimes typing myself. Berry had offered us some of his secretary's time, but she was only available at certain hours during the day and this proposal had to be completed fast.

Harold Williams, the same bus driver who'd brought Pineville children to my backyard program and who'd been so involved in civil rights, he did all he could to help me get that proposal written. When I was working in the office at night, he'd be in and out checking on me, giving me moral support. "Look," he'd say, "can I get you a Coke? Do you need something to eat?" Vic Beaudoin and some others stopped by during the day but they all had their own businesses to run and couldn't spend much time at our office. It was Harold Williams who gave the most time and support. The actual writing of the proposal was my responsibility. (That year and every year for the next eight years, my responsibility.) And, somehow, I did get that first proposal in on time.

Then the problems really began. One of the requirements was that the board overseeing Headstart had to be an integrated one. Total Community Action was all black. So we had to find whites willing to be a part of this, which was certainly not easy to do.

We asked Minnie Bass to be on the board. She was an elderly white Alexandria woman who'd moved away from the prevalent attitude toward blacks because Jimmy had been able to help her medically when she'd been languishing for years under a white doctor's care. She'd fought the Welfare Department to stay with Jimmy because Welfare at first had refused to pay a black doctor for treating a white patient. When Jimmy successfully treated her after years of her not improving with the other doctor, Minnie Bass changed her ideas about blacks. She began publicly saying that black people should be able to vote, black people were fine people, statements that caused her to be ostracized by Alexandria whites. But she never wavered. And when I asked her if she would be on our board, she accepted immediately.

We also got Terry Easterling, the liberal wife of a local psychiatrist; another man who turned out to be a snitch for the white social service agencies; and

Alvin Moore, a long-time NAACP member. It was Moore who suggested we ask for $100,000 that first year.

The initial proposal I'd written was for $50,000. But Moore happened to come into Louis Berry's office one day because he said he was concerned about blacks being excluded from the pipefitters union. As soon as he revealed this attitude, I immediately nabbed him to be one of the members of the Headstart board. He agreed and was looking over the proposal I'd prepared. He thought that I was asking for too small an amount of money because he thought in large figures. So the amount got doubled. And, as it turned out, we needed every cent of that $100,000.

The next problem was finding places for the Headstart classes to be held. We wanted to be able to include all children who were going into the first grade. This would be an especially useful program in Rapides because, as I said, the parish public schools had no kindergarten. Any kids could come into Headstart; we did no economic screening. In the beginning, the Headstart Program was not just for low-income children. The only requirement was that it be racially mixed. But, in the South, you'd expect just a small number of whites because only those parents relatively free of racial prejudice would take part. And those would tend to be of the upper middle class because lower-class whites had no other luxury except that of whiteness, and they were not going to hobnob with blacks.

Because we wanted to include as many kids as possible, we went to the school board for space. Morgan Walker was the head of the school board then. They said absolutely not. And the reason they gave was that, if we used school facilities, we'd have to use their janitors. And the janitors in all the schools were black and were receiving a wage that was below the minimum wage the federal government required for Headstart janitors. The school board was not going to "ruin" the situation by letting them receive higher wages during the summer than they could make during the school year. They actually said that to us!

So, then we went to black and white churches for space. The white churches all said no, "We wouldn't think of doing anything like that!" But the black churches came through. And some of the white officers from England Air Force Base who had large homes allowed us to use them. You know, there's no way in the world you can say all white folks are impossible—because there are gems among them. Perfectly sane human beings. There were some of those folks out at the base. And not all of them were Northerners, either. They were willing to let us use their homes all summer, move around furniture, put up partitions, everything. It was these military people and the black churches that enabled us to get underway here in Rapides Parish that first summer.

But our biggest problem in the beginning was a competing white group that wanted to run Headstart in Rapides Parish. Whites too heard about federal funds being available for a preschool program. (In fact, they may have heard about it from me. Some of the people in the group overseeing Headstart were also on the United Way board with me.) Now, I don't think for a minute these whites cared about the progress of the poorest children in the parish. But they were certainly interested in controlling any substantial amount of money coming into the parish. So they wanted to control Headstart. After we'd done all the work of getting the proposal together, Al Kurtz and some other United Way whites organized themselves into a group to oversee the Rapides Parish Headstart Program. They contacted our group requesting we turn our proposal over to them! They said, "We do want you people to benefit from this, but we're the only ones who have the know-how and the contacts. If you want to make sure it's funded, turn the proposal over to us. We'll see that it's handled just the way you want." They got very fraternal: "We're all going to stand together." Can you imagine? They wanted that money and because *they* truly believed that for anything to work, it had to be engineered by whites, they thought we should believe that too. But they were right that they had the contacts in Washington and political representation from the state that we didn't have. We took the position that we were not going to turn our proposal over to them. But how were we going to stop them from blocking our funding in Washington?

We decided to call Adam Clayton Powell's office. He was Chairman of the House Education and Labor Committee, so he had access to information about the Headstart proposals. But we probably would have called him even if he were not on any relevant committee. For a long period in this country, Powell was *the* representative of black America. Not just his constituents in Harlem, but all of us. Whites were very uncomfortable with his style and when he became too powerful—sixth in line to the presidency, I think—they found a way to get rid of him. But for years and years before his decline, Powell cared and worked and spoke out passionately for black America. So when we called his office, I wasn't surprised that the response was immediately supportive.

He remembered me from New York, and, when I explained our problem with the white group trying to take over our work, he said this kind of thing was happening in many places and he would do everything he could to help. He said he had good cards in his hand, and he'd tell the white outfit that there'd be no funding if they continued their attempted takeover of something they hadn't developed. Powell wrote them directly. I saw the letter; he said if they wanted cooperation from him in the future, they'd have to stop interfering with our efforts because what they were trying to do was unfair. He had to write and call them a number of times. It wasn't easy, but, ultimately, he got our proposal through and it was funded. Adam's assistant, Chuck Stone, was very involved in all of this. There were so many phone calls back and forth! Every time we met with the white group, Adam or Chuck Stone would call and ask what had happened. They really cared. They gave a lot of time and effort to seeing that Headstart money—in many locations in the country, apparently—reached the people it was supposed to reach. They were so supportive. It's improbable we'd have had our proposal funded without their help.

During the period when they were deciding on our proposal, Sargent Shriver requested more documentation of the level of poverty in the parish. Mayor Bowden was telling Washington that there was no poverty here, just "lazy niggers" that didn't want to work. He was trying to stop Headstart from being funded by claiming there was no need for the program. So Shriver asked us to document the extent of the poverty. In addition to getting together unemployment figures, income figures, all that, Plessy and I went out to take some pictures. The closest area of extreme poverty was Samtown, so we went there and took pictures of the open sewers, the shacks, the outhouses. Actually, conditions were even worse out in the country, but we had a deadline, so we didn't have time to get to out-of-the-way places.

We did get lots of good shots, but we encountered some anger, too. At one house, we'd just climbed out of the car and were getting ready to take a picture when a man came out with his shotgun aimed at us and said, "If you shoot that, then I'll shoot this! 'Cause you're not going to take a picture of my house!" And we realized we were invading his sense of dignity. He wasn't going to have pictures of how bad things were for him. We tried to tell him we were getting pictures to send to the federal government so that things would be better here for us. But he didn't care: "This is *my* house. And you're not taking pictures of it!" He was adamant; so we left. There were a few others like him, people who didn't want the revelation of how bad things were for them because they had their own shame about it. They were right that we were invading their privacy. It was a touchy situation. We needed the photos to let Washington know just how bad poverty was here. But we didn't want to exploit in order to explain.

We did get enough to send off, though. From Shriver's office, we heard that they understood the degree of poverty. We also let them know that this mayor, who was claiming there was none, had perpetuated himself in office since 1953 without an election and had ordered that civil rights workers not be allowed to alight in this town. So they seemed to understand that his claims were based in southern resistance to change, not in reality.

We also had to justify our numbers. The Superintendent of Schools, E. A. Atkins, challenged our plan to service 1,500 children. He said there weren't that many four- and five-year-olds in the parish. I asked all our volunteer bus drivers (and Harold Williams had gotten together a great crew of volunteer drivers) to scour the parish that spring. And they were wonderful. They combed the rural areas, went down country roads, all out in the woods. And they'd stop at houses and get names of children from families that had never been included on any listing because none, *none* of the people in the house had ever been to school. The parish never cared about educating black kids, so there was never a truant officer or anything to get these rural children into school. We ended up with a list of over 1,700 eligible children, far more than Superintendent Atkins claimed existed. So we easily filled the 1,500 slots we'd requested funding for—with a waiting list of 250 more!

Yes, we were finally funded. Then came intense preparation for the July–August program. The private homes that were going to be used had to be altered. Black carpenters and electricians volunteered their work and the black churches raised money for the building materials we needed. We purchased plasterboard to create separate classrooms. People with trucks (especially the husbands of teachers hoping to be hired) would volunteer to pick up material. We didn't have to have first-rate material—if a corner of a plasterboard was chipped, we'd be able to purchase it for just about nothing. We salvaged stuff. And at each location—in the churches and the homes—we'd create classrooms. That first year, the federal requirements were minimal. We just had to have so many feet of space for each child, and preferably more than one bathroom. State law required that children in a day-care situation be on one floor; and we had to comply with that because they were anxious to shut us down, anyway.

The staff of teachers and teacher aides had to be trained, especially the teacher aides who were not professionals in the field of education. It was very important that they receive training because there were two to each classroom and they had to know what to do with the children. They were women and men from the community, often parents who benefited greatly by this. The teacher aides didn't need a degree; they didn't need anything but a concern with children. If they'd been through high school or nearly, they were adequate.

There was an insistence on making as wide a use as possible of men in the program because so many of the children had come out of situations where they didn't have a male role model. That worked well; we had a good number of male teachers and teacher aides.

The few white teachers and teacher aides we had were mainly from England Airbase, because most local whites just wouldn't take part at any level. The few white children enrolled were, as I'd anticipated, the children of the more enlightened upper middle class. And there were more white children in Alexandria than in the small towns and rural parts of the parish. The small towns were and are even more backward than Alexandria on issues of race. For example, that first spring, a white hairdresser in LeCompte who had agreed to be a teacher aide and to enroll her daughter in Headstart was asked to leave town by other whites. Just because she was planning to be involved with us. So we integrated the program as much as we could, but it really wasn't much.

As I said, Harold Williams organized the school bus drivers and they worked out their routes for picking up the children. That first summer, they drove completely on a volunteer basis; they didn't start getting paid until the second summer. And they were all so reliable. Williams also became treasurer of the Headstart board during our second year. And could he handle money! The federal auditors said he did very well, every year. I was Executive Director of the program for the entire eight years of Summer Headstart, although I never accepted pay because that would have interfered with the alimony and I'd have had to give a big chunk to the government for Jimmy's taxes. I think it was good for Headstart that I wasn't paid; no one could claim I was doing anything for money.

When we got underway, it was truly what Sybil had said it would be, a greatly enhanced version of what I'd done in my backyard for so many years. We had to follow federal guidelines, but the guidelines were exactly what I would have written myself. The essence of the program was to acquaint children with normally equipped homes and schools, to let them experience the fun of learning and books, and—just like in my preschool—to help them feel real good about themselves.

When setting up a Headstart room, we equipped it with sections representing the normal rooms in a house. There would be a child-size kitchen area, all constructed out of salvaged packing boxes. The refrigerator was one packing box. You could insert a disposable aluminum roasting pan that you got at the supermarket into a packing box and that became a sink. And there'd be a kitchen table and chairs. Then, in another part of the classroom, there was a bed and all the things that would properly go on a bed—sheets, pillows, blankets. Some children in this parish slept on pallets and had never seen a properly made bed. And we'd always have a full-length mirror. Many little kids know what their friends look like and can describe them in great detail, but they don't know what they themselves look like. The mirror was important so that the children could meet themselves and begin to approve of themselves and like what they saw. The teachers were expected to stand by them and point out nice things about them, admire their pretty eyes and such. Self-esteem. So much of what we did was about building self-worth and self-esteem.

Each room would also have plants that the children would care for. There was just time enough in the summer—the climate here is helpful—to see a shoot coming up. We had goldfish in each room and the children were responsible for taking care of the goldfish, seeing that they were fed. At the end of the summer, we'd draw numbers and give the plants and the goldfish away.

At every center, we had pet corrals so that the kids could have the pleasure of playing with cats, dogs, turtles, all kinds of animals. Each locale also had a portable, plastic swimming pool and a hose so they could have water play. Most of the kids didn't own bathing suits, so we collected extra panties so they could put on the panties and run through the water coming out of the hose and yell and scream and have a good time the way kids do.

Food was a *very* important issue because we discovered that, if we asked these kids what they had to eat before leaving home, many would tell us, "We had some sweetnin' water." Sweetening water is just water with some sugar in it to give the child a charge of energy in the morning. So we set up a breakfast program for them and fed them when they first arrived at the Headstart center. We realized that, if we didn't, many were going to fall asleep in the middle of the morning because of lack of nourishment. So, in addition to the hot lunch that the federal guidelines recommended, we also had breakfast. And also, since nutrition was such a problem, there would be a fruit juice interval mid-morning, after they'd done some playing outside.

All the children had a physical exam and their parents were given whatever medicine the child needed. (We had a social service person attached to each center and she would take the medicine to the home and explain to the parents how it was to be given to the child. We did that because four- and five-year-olds are not necessarily reliable about delivering packages and notes. And also, since the illiteracy rate is so high in Louisiana, we couldn't assume parents could read our instructions.) Every child was tested for TB and went to the dentist. During that first summer, we discovered what was to be the most common medical problem of the children in our program, year after year: intestinal parasites.

During the first few weeks that summer, the tests for parasites were just part of a whole litany of routine testing. Until we got back the results. At some of our centers, half of the children had pinworms! Intestinal parasites were absolutely pervasive. There was one shocking and terribly sad situation in LeCompte, a town about fourteen miles south of Alexandria.

We treated two black children who lived on a dairy farm, one of many contracted by the head of the school board, who also owned a milk company and the nation-wide Trailways Bus Company. These children were two of eleven children of parents who took care of the animals on this farm. Of course, workers who take care of animals are supposed to be free of worms, but these two children who'd come to Headstart were not. So we had them treated at Charity Hospital, along with many other children. And, by the end of that first summer program, they were parasite-free.

But we should have guessed they'd become reinfected. The Headstart social worker who'd visited their shack had reported that the living conditions were just awful. Many of the farms around here are like that: the owner and his family live in nice, sometimes opulent homes while his workers live on the same property in squalid conditions. Living in the shack rent-free or at very low cost is part of the compensation for working for him. (Does it sound like nineteenth-century sharecropping? It's *very* similar.) So the head of our school board contracted with this kind of farm because it was profitable to him. And these fully employed, hard-working dairy workers lived in what can only be described as deplorable conditions, extreme poverty. I saw it for myself when these same two children came back to Headstart the following summer and were visibly ill. Because of what'd happened to them the previous summer, I guessed it was pinworms and I carried them to Charity Hospital myself. I didn't wait for their scheduled parasite test; they were sick and I knew it. So I took them to the hospital. But the diagnosis was worse than I'd expected. Much larger worms, called ascaris parasites, had invaded their bodies and had been consuming the little nourishment the children received for so long the kids were severely malnourished. They were immediately hospitalized and treated. Fed like crazy. But it was too late. Both children eventually died.

We sent a nurse and social worker to the home and we examined everyone in the family. They all had worms. We took photographs of how bad things were to try to get help from the Health Department. When we showed the Health Department the photographs and told them about the children, they agreed to go out to the shack and investigate. They discovered the whole place was permeated with worms. And they announced to me that the only thing to do was to burn the house, all the clothes, the outhouse, everything. Particularly the soil where the worms were concentrated. But where would these people live, I asked. So they burnt just the clothing and the outhouse; and they brought several tons of dirt and covered over the land around the house.

We were able to get a washing machine and dryer donated to the family. Our social worker went in and instructed the mother on how to use it. And we had to get the farm owner to extend the electrical wires from his house down to the shack. Before that, these people had existed on kerosene lamps. It was just absolutely primitive.

And here's the irony of that situation. The place was so infested with worms that they had reached the children of the farm owner. The Department of Health had insisted on testing his family too, telling him worms didn't know the color of skin. All of his children had pinworms, and one of them had ascaris. But it was caught early enough to treat him. At that point, there was a big to-do in the parish about getting the whole place cleaned up. But it had to reach one of *them* before it became important to parish officials.

Every single summer — and I ran Headstart for eight summers — intestinal parasites were the most prevalent medical problem among the children. Many, many people in this parish, black and white, live in just awful conditions. It's a poor parish, a parish with chronically high unemployment. And things like malnutrition and worms are natural outgrowths of squalid living conditions.

What is disgusting is that the unemployment and very low wage scale are deliberately maintained by those who benefit. As I said, this parish stayed agrarian because the elite wouldn't let any new industries come in. This means that, for most black men, the work was seasonal and there were no alternatives. This available and cheap labor force benefited the folks who had parcels of land that have lumber or cotton. And the owners of the land didn't want anything else to come in here because salary scales would be affected. They wanted to keep the level of employment where it was so that there'd be no disturbance of their income. The result has been a parish with large numbers of poor people living in deplorable, just the worst imaginable conditions.

The second summer we were able to use the schools. That made our program so much better. But getting the use of the schools was not easy. It took a little "creative subterfuge," shall we say, on my part. Remember, Morgan Walker and the rest of the board had said no the first summer because the federal minimum wage we were required to pay the janitors was higher than their school-year salary. Now, this was true. But the more basic reason they'd refused us was because this all-white school board simply did not want to help a predominantly black program. Knowing that, I nevertheless tried again the next spring because the school buildings were obviously the best possible places for us to conduct our programs. I told them it was ridiculous for these buildings to be sitting there empty all summer when the children could make use of them. I argued as calmly and logically as I could. And got turned down again.

In the midst of all this, I was talking to Camille Gravel, who'd been my divorce lawyer and who'd become something of a friend. He was a decent man who'd stood up in the Louisiana legislature after the 1954 Supreme Court Decision and said that segregation was morally wrong. Of course, he was attacked by everyone there. They said he had those notions because he was a Catholic. (In Louisiana, the Catholics tend to be more liberal than the Protestants. That's why southern Louisiana—where Catholics are concentrated—is much more liberal than northern Louisiana. There's a saying here, "Northern

Louisiana is really western Mississippi," and, culturally, there's a lot of truth to that.) Anyway, they dismissed Gravel's position as the ranting of a Catholic. So he submitted a report to them that I helped him prepare on the positions of the Protestant denominations. All of the national organizations of these denominations had passed resolutions saying that segregation was morally wrong. They all gave lip service, at least, to that position. He threw that back at those folks. Who changed their position not one iota.

Gravel and I discussed racial issues regularly, and I told him about the school board turning us down again. He said, "Well, you know what to do about that." And I asked, "What?," because I didn't have a clue. Gravel said, "Didn't you tell me that A. Philip Randolph's threat of a march on Washington in 1941 was the reason Roosevelt issued Executive Order 8802 for the employment of blacks in the war industries?"[1] Yes, I remembered having that conversation with Gravel years before, telling him that it was actually a bluff on Randolph's part, but Roosevelt had no way of knowing how much unity there was among blacks. And because Roosevelt didn't want to deal with that as well as the war, he issued the Executive Order. Gravel went on: "You only have to pick up the phone this evening and tell Morgan Walker that you feel he needed to be forewarned that the colored people in the community are going to march and demonstrate at the school board office tomorrow morning. The tactic worked with the President of the United States, didn't it? It'll work with the President of the Rapides Parish School Board."

So I did exactly what he said. That night, very late, I called Walker and told him I thought he ought to know what was happening in the black community. And, personally, I said, I didn't want to see it happen because I didn't see what was the point of all of this confusion. I'd done what I could to quell it— to keep the march from occurring—but hadn't been successful. And I thought it was only fair that he be alerted. "Whatever your decisions are, they are your decisions. But I don't think you need to be surprised by this demonstration tomorrow morning because I know you have the good of the community at heart." I was choking on the words. This to a man who wouldn't pay his black janitors the minimum wage and who contracted with a farmer who housed workers in such deplorable conditions that two children would die. But I said what I had to. And it worked. The next morning, first thing, we got a call at our office from the school board and we were told to select any schools we wanted in the area, white or black.

We were all excited. I didn't tell the Headstart board or anybody else what I'd done. I didn't want it to get back to the school board or to anyone who was against us. But I was secretly delighted to have successfully tricked that awful man into doing exactly what he did not want to do—help poor black kids in Rapides Parish. And I knew this meant that our program would be even better the second year than it was the first.

We got schools throughout the parish. We chose schools in areas with high concentrations of disadvantaged kids. That was our concern, after all. We chose some schools that were black and some that were white. Now, folks weren't happy about our using the white school buildings, though, because our program was always predominantly black children and that meant that all these blacks were going into schools they normally couldn't attend. Here in Alexandria, we got the school behind K-Mart and the school at Arcadian Village. There were whole colonies of poor whites there and we hoped to include those children in our program.

Some of the black facilities were newer because they'd been built since 'fifty-four. In hopes of circumventing integration after the 'fifty-four Supreme Court decision, the Rapides Parish School Board had constructed some decent buildings for black schools. They were hoping that if they could show that separate *was* equal, they could maintain segregation. As a result of that, some of the black schools were better physical facilities than the white schools, and we chose them for that reason.

We even got a school in Samtown. Remember, Samtown was the absolute worst section of Alexandria. Open sewerage. Dirt floors in houses. Poor sanitation. All reasons for people being sick and not living very long. The one good thing about Samtown was that people could build a little house and pay no taxes on it. Rapides Parish had something called "homestead exemption" which exempted property under a certain value if inhabited by the owner. And *all* the property in Samtown was below the specified value. But, even with that little break, the extremely poor black people who lived in Samtown— and it was all black—were barely able to survive.

The children who came to our Samtown Headstart Center were wonderfully bright and lively. But they were desperately in need of the meals, the exposure to books, and our medical services. We discovered that over 60 percent of them had pinworms. And we almost didn't find that out in time. It seems the white Visiting Nurse who was assigned to that center just didn't want to go there. She kept canceling her appointments, not showing up. Apparently, she just couldn't bring herself to do physical exams on fifty little black kids from the very worst part of the city. She'd been not showing up for her appointments for three weeks when the black social worker at the Samtown Center realized that if the exams were put off any longer, Headstart would not have enough time to visit the homes with medical information on the children before the program was over. Knowing parasites had been the most common problem the previous summer, she went to one of our doctors and asked to be taught how to do the intestinal parasite test. She tested all fifty kids herself, and, as I said, over 60 percent had pinworms. Fortunately, there were no cases of ascaris. The social worker had taken most of the pinworm medicine into the homes before that Visiting Nurse finally appeared at the Samtown Center. Relieved, no doubt, she didn't have to do the pinworm test herself. So, we did have some problems of racism even within our program. But it was always outweighed, as in this case, by a tremendous dedication on the part of most of our staff.

In addition to getting the use of the schools that second summer, we got pay for the bus drivers (who not only brought the kids to and from our centers but took them on field trips, too). And we expanded the program to include three-year-olds. More children and more diverse activities.

Walker required that the regular principal of the school be on the premises whenever we were there. To protect the white-owned buildings from the black barbarians, no doubt. And he insisted we use their teachers. But we continued training teacher aides from the community. That second year, they went for training at the University of Texas at Austin. White teachers were, for the most part, still wary of the program. So our teaching staff remained predominantly black, even in the white areas. Whites here, generally, were not persuaded that any black folks could do anything for them. For example, according to a friend who worked at the Alexandria TV station, the reason "Sesame Street" was canceled in Alexandria very soon after it began was because there were too many black adults on the show and whites at the station felt, "what can a nigger teach?" This was part of their fear of integrating schools here. In addition to not wanting black children in class with their children, black instructors were also something they didn't want.

But our teachers and teacher aides were just great. They all seemed to appreciate how important this program was, how good it was for the children.

They worked hard and gave so much of themselves. The "early childhood development" training in Texas covered not only teaching skills, it also dealt with issues of poverty and race. Our teachers had to be sensitive to children coming to Headstart not knowing what a bed was, for example, much less a pillow and sheets. Their homes simply did not have some of the basic items most Americans take for granted.

And, since most of the children in our program were black, we talked a lot about how to address the self-image of black children. We deliberately used black professionals—doctors, dentists, social workers—to show them you *could* be a doctor, you *could* be a social worker. We'd let them play with stethoscopes and microscopes. Every classroom had pictures of black scientists, like George Washington Carver. And when we read about the nation's capital, we'd be sure to tell them that one of the two main designers of Washington was Benjamin Banneker, a black man. And we'd show them the D.C. map with the streets so finely laid out. Black people can be engineers. Black people can be anything. We were always trying to say that.

We'd go through *Ebony* magazine and find photographs of people in various professions, and we'd talk about what they did. We really had to do that kind of thing because, when we asked these kids what they wanted to be when they grew up, we'd get such a narrow range of jobs. So we'd ask, "What other things can black people do? Can you be a policeman?" And there'd be blank faces because, at that time, Rapides Parish would not hire blacks as policemen. Or firemen. So the kids had never seen such a thing. We'd have to find photographs of even these nonprofessional jobs so that the children could have an image of a black policeman and fireman. Their own fathers were agricultural workers, most likely; and their mothers were maids. *If* they had jobs.

Of course, we used Countee Cullen's poems and Langston Hughes'. And stories all the time. We *read* stories. A main goal was to teach them to love books. So, instead of storytelling, verbal storytelling, we emphasized books as the sources of wonderful stories by always reading to them. We'd find books that had lots of pictures. And the book was passed around or the children would cluster around the teacher. And they got acquainted with printed words and they came to associate books with pleasurable experiences. As in my backyard program, these kids learned colors and numbers and shapes and the rudiments of reading. In one short summer, children can absorb so much!

Headstart was only a summer program, but it took up most of my year. In the fall, there was the follow-up medical program. After the first year, we got funds for the nurses to be paid in the fall. They'd visit homes to make sure the kids were taking whatever medicine they'd been prescribed and check their progress. And they saw to it that any child that'd been in our program saw a doctor if he or she needed it. In the fall, I'd also write an assessment of the summer program for the government. And follow up with some parents myself, especially those with children who had special problems.

We also kept the parents involved all year. People here usually have large families. So many of our families had another little fella coming into the program the next summer. Sometimes, we'd have three kids from one family all at the same time, a three-, four-, and five-year-old. So we'd have parents' meetings all during the year. And they were really gung-ho, really great. They became parents' organizations. What we were trying to do was make parents participate in their children's education. And most of our parents were very receptive, very involved.

The rest of the staff wasn't funded for the fall and spring, only the nurses. But we had so many people doing volunteer work! They'd go to the parents' meetings. The board members, the bus drivers, the social workers, everybody would be there. And certainly, those teachers who knew what the program meant to them monetarily in the summer would show a special interest in what was going on and would encourage parents, too. After a while, the teachers who taught the first and second grades, say, would have established good relations with the parents of kids coming to them—because of that earlier Headstart contact.

After the first year, Total Community Action was no longer overseeing Headstart. But I, and most of the people originally involved, we were still running it. What happened was that there was a dispute within the organization about how funds should be spent. Some folks wanted to raise teachers' salaries, and I wanted to use that money to expand our breakfast program for the kids. So, a number of us left Total Community Action and formed PACE, Parents for Action in Community Endeavors. Vic Beaudoin became chairman of our new board, and, as I said, Harold Williams became treasurer. Both groups wrote proposals that year; and ours got funded. PACE was given office space in the Bricklayers' Union building at 4th and Fulton. That's where we'd have our parents' meetings, too. We'd get chairs from the undertaker's and just pile in there. The bricklayers are mainly black here, descendants of Creoles who were able to become artisans. The union is integrated now, but it's still predominantly black. So we ran Headstart for the last seven of the eight years from that building.

In January and February of each year, we really had to get going. We had to decide what schools we were going to use, arrange for teacher and teacher aide training, figure out what children were eligible, how many children to write into the proposal. Every year we'd be on the lookout for kids in families way out in the country who'd never heard about the program. And every year, we'd find more of those families that had never been exposed to any kind of formal education. Our numbers kept increasing, and so did our budget. The first year, as I said, we had a budget of $100,000; by my last year in 1972, our budget was $240,000.

Yes, I had to write out a proposal every spring. You couldn't simply say, we want it refunded. You had to have all your statistics together and do all that paperwork, write out what you were anticipating. And every year, there'd be battles. You were always working between two factions: there were some blacks who could, at times, be a pain in the backside, and there were whites who were permanently a pain in the backside. We never got support from powerful whites in this parish. They remained angry that so much money was going to a black-run program that helped mainly black kids. And, year after year, they would create whatever obstacles they could to interfere with us. But we ran a good program. We knew it and the federal government agreed. So they just couldn't stop us, try as they may.

Headstart was a year-round job for me for eight years. I stopped doing it when the government ended the summer program. We'd been saying all along it shouldn't be just summers. So, in 1971, they began a September to June program, separately funded, separately administered. The government even constructed buildings for that program, buildings that sat empty during the summer because we continued to use the schools. So, of course, it didn't make sense to have two Headstart programs. They ended ours and told the other one to operate year-round, which it still does. 'Seventy-two was our last year.

And that worked out well for me. My cousin, Lester Granger, by then elderly and not well, came to live with me in the fall of 'seventy-two. He would slowly deteriorate, physically and mentally, over the next five years. And my elderly Godmother Ethelle came to stay with me in 1974. If summer Headstart had continued, eventually I would have had to resign anyway, because taking care of them took up more and more of my time.

But for the eight years I was involved with Headstart, it was a very large part of my life. Headstart and my own children really filled my life. (The foster babies had left right around the time Headstart began.) And I feel good about those years. Anybody who experienced the program will say that it was a great time and a good thing to do. I was glad to be doing it. It was so worthwhile. There are some things that you do in life that you think, well, that was really a waste of time. But I don't feel that way about Headstart. Or my civil rights activities. Both were desperately needed. They still are needed. The year-round Headstart they have in Alexandria now could be better; it could reach way more of the population. And if more children were included, I don't think we'd have the high drop-out rate we have today. But the tenets of Headstart are excellent. I think they're the best thing in the educational system that we have today. The rest of it—the kindergarten to twelfth grade—that's really badly messed up here.

Yes, I gave a lot of my time to it. But anything I do, I put myself into fully. I just figure, if you're in it, *do* it. I don't know any other way to do something. I give all of me to the things I care about. Whether I'm spinning my wheels or not. If I'm spinning my wheels, I spin 'em hard. But Headstart, no, that was time well spent. There were so many benefits to so many people; I still see them today. Kids who went through the program and are now college graduates. People who come up to me and remind me what a good time we had those summers. I enjoyed it all. Once I heard about the program, I had no choice but to do it. As I said, I've loved working with children since I was a teenager. Headstart was like my civil rights efforts: I simply could not have *not* done it.

XII

Taking Care

"If you're alive, live."

WHEN I LEFT HEADSTART, I WAS ALMOST SIXTY. And one would have thought my life might slow down somewhat after that. But it didn't. Things haven't slowed down one bit. And, you know, I've learned some of the most important lessons about living just in the last twenty years.

In fact, it wasn't until I was well into my seventies that I experienced the greatest psychic destruction of my life. But, somehow, going through that gave me a small opportunity to help other folks survive similar situations. And out of that hideous experience, I learned this: if you've faced death and your life is somehow spared, no matter what your age or circumstances, you are left with one tremendous obligation. And that is to continue your life. In other words, if you're allowed to be alive, you must *live*.

But I'm getting way ahead of my story. When I left Headstart, as I said, I was less active in community work than I had been. I still went to NAACP meetings and other community organization meetings, but because of responsibilities at home—which began with the arrival of my cousin Lester Granger—I just couldn't do as much out in the community. After Lester came, I took in two retarded girls. And then, unexpectedly, my elderly Godmother Ethelle came to stay with me. So I became very housebound, really. Much more so even than when I had small children.

But this was what I wanted to do. I've always been glad when I've been able to be there for people in need. I was taught by my family that this is a large part of why we're put on earth. My family had set that example. Not only did Grandmother feed every hobo who came to our door, but she'd give money to every beggar on the street. And when her friends chided her, saying the beggars would just use the money for wine, Grandmother would say, "Well, that's between them and their God." She knew that, for her, the right thing was to give to those in need of help. And I've always believed I should give, too. Especially if those people have given me so much more than I could ever return, like Godmother Ethelle and Uncle Lester.

I called him "Uncle Lester" because he was my parents' generation. Actually, his mother and my grandmother were first cousins, both of them the grandchildren of that Virginia planter and his African wife. And Lester called me his "illegitimate goddaughter" because he was asked to step in at the last minute when Daddy's brother, Uncle Harry, who'd agreed to be my godfather, didn't show up for the service. Uncle Lester had been wonderful to me. All my life. He'd brought love and gifts and fun to me as a child. Intellectual stimulation and loving support to me as an adult. In a way, he was the odd one in his family. His five brothers had followed their physician father into medicine; but he had chosen social work. He was the only one of my relatives who would sneak up with me to visit Uncle Durock after he'd been banned from the Bronx house for "living in sin." And when I was working with the Writers Project and the NAACP, he'd often invite me to lunch at the Harlem YWCA. There'd be the most interesting people at his lunches. Uncle Lester was more understanding of my leftist leanings than others in the family. In fact, he had some leftist leanings himself back then. There was a group called the Abraham Lincoln Brigade, American men who were willing to go to Spain to the aid of those who opposed Franco. Lester's sympathies were definitely with this group. In those years, he was already deeply involved with the Urban League, and in 1941 would become its Executive Director. But Uncle Lester was always a joy to be around, charming and bright and just a wonderful person.

It was Lester who'd flown with me from New York to New Orleans when I first heard of my husband's arrest for murder, because he felt I was too upset to make the trip alone. And, when he realized my divorce had left me financially hurting, Lester saw to it I had transportation: he gave me a station wagon. (It was that station wagon that enabled me to make a little extra money selling insurance all over the parish.) He even kept up the taxes on the Bronx house when I was having so many financial difficulties. Extraordinarily caring and generous. I had three godmothers and one godfather, but he was the equivalent of three godfathers. Just a very special person. All of the people in my generation in the family just adored him. He never had children of his own, but he became a wonderful extra father to many of us in the family. It seemed to me that there was nothing I could do that would ever match Lester's kindnesses to me.

After retiring from the Urban League in 1961, Lester was elected president of the International Conference of Social Workers at the time of the organization's annual meeting held that year in Rome. He was the first American—black or white—to hold that office. In addition to being such a good person, he was also quite a capable person.

In the late sixties, he'd taken a teaching position at Dillard, then at Tulane and Loyola. I'd seen him often during that period because New Orleans is only a three-and-a-half hour drive from here. Then, in 1970, his life changed dramatically. On a trip to Brazil, where he was presiding over an International Conference of Social Workers convention, his wife got some infection that attacked the heart, and she died. He became very bereft and, I would say, never fully pulled out of that shock.

His own physical health became fragile. He had surgery for prostate cancer and then for hemorrhaging intestinal ulcers. Some cousins in New Jersey, Leo and Edith Granger, had brought him to their home to nurse him back to health. They loved him dearly, too—Leo was his nephew who'd also become one of his surrogate children—but they were finding him more and more difficult to deal with. As he became physically stronger, he became untypically crotchety. And Leo and Edith were concerned that they couldn't give him the care and protection that he seemed to need. (Because of their jobs, they had to be absent from their home from 8:00 in the morning until 6:00 at night.) So they sent for me.

I flew to New Jersey and stayed there about six weeks, and, when I got ready to leave, Lester said he'd drive me back. We all objected, telling him he wasn't strong enough. But he was so determined that he just took off in his car one morning before the family was awake and drove back to New Orleans, to Loyola University, where he'd been teaching. The people at the school realized he wasn't well enough to teach and told him to take more time before returning. Meanwhile, I'd flown back to Alexandria. Lester called me, very distressed about not being able to resume his teaching responsibilities, and asked if he could come up here and stay with me until he'd fully recuperated.

I suspected, even when he first arrived, that this stay might not be as brief as he expected. In the beginning, he kept saying he was here temporarily, but this is where he was to live for the final five years of his life. He tried to return to teaching once. There were telephone conversations with Loyola. He told them he was feeling great. And, on the phone, he sounded great. But, when he went down there, they realized he wasn't able to teach. There were times — and these spells became more frequent and more extended as time went on — there were times when he was very confused. So Loyola ended up giving him another honorary degree but not letting him teach. He was more than disappointed. He was despondent about that. But he settled into Alexandria, I think, and eventually began to think of it as his home.

Shortly before Lester's arrival, there was an incident in the parish that reminded all of us that the civil rights legislation of the sixties barely changed things culturally in this part of Louisiana. My son Jimmy was then married and in school at Southern in Baton Rouge. One day, he called me and said he and his wife, Elise, and two college friends had a day off and would like to drive up and have a backyard barbecue on the patio. I said, "Come on."

Now, this is the period when young people were wearing their hair in long Afros, and all four of them had these Afro hairstyles, styles that some whites took to mean militancy and anger. They headed out from Baton Rouge with a boy named Larry driving, Jimmy's wife in the front passenger seat, and Jimmy and another male student in the back seat. When they got to Meeker, a small town outside of LeCompte, they stopped at a truck stop to use the bathroom. Just Jimmy and the other boy in the back (whose name I can't remember) got out and went to the back of the building where the toilets were. These truck stops are gas stations and diners combined. So, like other gas stations, the toilets were around back. This left Larry and Elise in the car.

Just as Jimmy and this boy were coming back along the side of the building, a white man with a shotgun came running out of the front door. Larry saw him first and yelled, "That man has a gun!" And Jimmy, by then able to see the man also, called to the man, "Mister, we only wanted to use the bathroom!" And, as he was saying that, Larry jumped out of the car. And the man aims at Larry's guts and shoots. After he shot, he just turned and walked back into the diner, locking the door behind him so that no one could come in after him, and so that the only phones on the place were inaccessible.

This shot had blown Larry's lower torso apart; his intestines were on the outside. And Jimmy started yelling about a telephone. A white man, who'd been standing outside the diner and who'd seen the whole thing, told Jimmy the nearest phones were down the highway. He also said no black people were allowed to use those bathrooms behind the diner, and that the black woman who worked in the diner had to walk down the highway to use a bathroom. And he told Jimmy he'd take him to a telephone.

Meanwhile, Minnie Bass—the same white woman who'd been on our Headstart board—happened to be going by in a truck with her nephew. She stopped and, when she found out what had happened, she commandeered a passing car to carry Larry to the hospital. (There wasn't room for him in her truck.) She told the driver to take him to Cabrini Hospital, and she and her nephew would follow in their truck. Jimmy's now off somewhere trying to find a phone so he can get his father to meet him at the hospital.

When they reached Alexandria on their way to Cabrini, Minnie Bass and her nephew turned off into my driveway and she came into my house yelling: "They shot him, Mrs. Hines! They shot that boy! He's going to Cabrini. Come on, Mrs. Hines. Come on!" She was so hysterical, I didn't know who'd gotten shot. If it was Jimmy or what. I just picked up my purse and ran out of the house with them.

When we arrived at the hospital, my son Jimmy was still en route but his father was already there. They'd taken Larry into surgery. The bullet had shattered all of his intestines. I got the names and location of Larry's parents and called them from the hospital. His father, Dr. A. H. Chatman, was a psychiatrist in Louisville. They said they were coming immediately, they were taking the next flight out. While they were en route, I stayed at the boy's bedside in intensive care, talking to him, holding his hand, trying to give him a parent's love as best I could.

The day after the shooting, a group of us went to Sheriff Marshall Capelle's office—Larry's parents, A. C. Dubriel as president of the NAACP, my ex-husband, and I. The sheriff was trying to placate us; we shouldn't worry, everything would be taken care of, he said. He gave all kinds of assurances that this was a very tranquil community, that everybody got along. And Dubriel said: "We sure do. We sure do. Just like a horse and its rider. But I'll tell you one thing. We're damn tired of being the horse!" Sheriff Capelle said, "Oh, that's not exactly true, Dubriel. Odette, do you think that's the way this community operates?" I'd been on various boards with Capelle, so I guess he thought I was "reasonable." But I said, "No, Marshall, I don't believe that. There is not any real harmony in this community. The quiet that appears to be there is because some people have power and others have none." Then he became very anxious to protect the name of the parish and said, "Well, you rest assured that the man that did this is going to be brought to trial."

Ed Ware, the District Attorney, arranged a grand jury. Ware had encountered the man who'd done the shooting previously, when Ware was campaigning for votes. The man had told Ware he wasn't going to vote for Ware because he'd once overhead some "niggers" say they liked him. Anyway, Ware arranged a grand jury and we all attended. The man got up and said he was just protecting his establishment, that he'd thought the boys had come there to rob him, he was scared of them because they looked like gorillas, and he'd just shot in self-defense. In the course of his testimony, he also said that all his life, he'd hoped not to die before he'd killed him a nigger, and he was very sorry he hadn't killed that one. This is in 1972 now! And it got worse: the grand jury listened to all of that and said "no true bill." No evidence of a crime! And that was the end of that. Some students at Southern wanted to come here and storm the town. And who could blame them? Black people were saying we'd thought we were beyond the turmoil of the sixties and look at this. Absolutely nothing happened to the man. Ed Ware was frank to say that the man was a racist. But the general feeling of too many whites, still today in this parish, is that there's not too much wrong with doing such things because "niggers" usually *are* to be feared.

Larry spent weeks in the hospital with his colon being redirected. The bullet had destroyed a number of areas that had to be removed. Could an incident like that happen today? Oh, yes. In some of the rural parts of Rapides Parish, it's still the 1940s.

It was not long after that incident that Uncle Lester arrived. And within a year of his coming here, I decided to also take in a retarded person. I got the idea from a wonderful local family, the Thomas Parnells, who were having great success with retarded children they took in. They did it for years and managed to train them so well. One of their former charges is now married to another retarded person, holding down a job and managing her home very competently. Since I was pretty housebound anyway, I thought, why not, maybe I can help one of these youngsters.

So I talked to the people at Pinecrest School for Retarded Children. (Now, years before in the mid-sixties, Louis Berry had challenged this school about not being integrated. We'd visited the place and found the black children in a clapboard building, most of them naked and full of feces, and *very* ill-treated. Berry began raising sand about that, told them funding was going to end if they didn't integrate. So they did.)

I asked the authorities at Pinecrest what I could do to help the children. And they said they were always looking for people to take out some of the "upper level" children for weekends or for day trips. "Upper level" meant they were not extremely retarded. They could respond to instruction and were in control of their toilet. But they did need continuous supervision; they couldn't float around unattended.

It was suggested that I come over to meet some of the children. They tried to match people who were comfortable with one another. So they set up an activity, like sewing, and brought together a number of girls they thought I might be compatible with. The attendant would say, "We have a visitor, girls." And I was supposed to just fit in and talk and get to know them. I made several of those visits. And one girl, Pearl, who was very loving, just started calling me "Mama." I didn't so much choose her; she chose me. It's better that way. So many times, they have people who want to help, but they don't want a child who *looks* retarded. They only want someone who looks normal, and then they don't have to explain too much. So the school doesn't let the volunteer make the decision. If you say you want to help a retarded child, and you reject the one that wants you, then they know you're not the person to do this.

"When are you coming back, Mama?" Pearl would ask. And soon she was asking the attendant, "Could you let me go and visit with Mama for a while?" That's how it started. Pearl came to visit me for weekends at first. She and Lester were very comfortable with one another, and she and I got along extremely well. She had adopted me before I adopted her.

Then she came here to stay. I'd take her everywhere, even shopping. She and Plessy got along well, too. Although Plessy's style was quite a bit less gentle than mine, Pearl responded well and was very fond of Plessy. Plessy was always absolutely honest with her friends and she didn't see any reason to change because Pearl was retarded. One time, Pearl announced to us that she was pretty. They'd been telling the children that at the school, trying to bolster them up. And, in comparison to many of the children that had deformities, Pearl was not too bad looking. But "pretty" was stretching it a bit. So when Pearl made this announcement, Plessy said, "Girl, don't fool yourself. You ain't pretty. Now, pretty is somebody who looks like Maggi. And you're not pretty." And Pearl, looking more confused than insulted, asked Plessy, "Are you pretty?" And Plessy said, "No! I'm not pretty. And I had sense enough to know that early 'cause I used to be a pain in the neck. And I found out I'd better start behaving myself. 'Cause if you ain't pretty, you have to be doubly nice to people 'cause you have to compensate for it. So you better act right, child. 'Cause you ain't pretty!" Pearl didn't seem hurt at all. She seemed to take it, as she always took Plessy's honesty, as good practical advice. I didn't really agree with Plessy's philosophy on how to talk to a retarded person, but Plessy was so loving, I think Pearl's worth was validated by Plessy, even when Pearl made what must have been disappointing discoveries, like finding out she wasn't pretty. She just loved Plessy. And, like many retarded people, found it easy to express her love in words and with affection. That was part of the joy of Pearl.

Soon I had a second retarded child. She'd been Pearl's good friend at the school and they'd been missing one another since Pearl left. Pearl first asked if Miriam could come and spend a weekend with us. And when she came and I saw how happy they were together, I asked the people at Pinecrest if she could stay with me, too. Pearl loved her being here. They did their chores together—they'd been taught to make beds, sweep floors, wash dishes, that kind of thing. They didn't always do a good job, and I'd often have to do it over myself, but I encouraged them. They could run the washing machine over at Plessy's launderette, but I had to accompany them or the coins would end up in the cold drink machine rather than the washing machine. They could do a lot for themselves, really. The biggest drain on me was having to take them absolutely everywhere. If I went to a meeting, they had to go with me. If I went to visit Gretchen in Baton Rouge, they'd have to go. Because I didn't think they'd understand all the ritualism of Catholicism, I took them to Bethel Methodist Church. They enrolled in the choir. They both had lovely singing voices and had no trouble remembering the melody and the words to songs.

For exercise, they liked to go into the backyard and pitch a ball back and forth. I bought them bicycles and they'd ride right around here. They learned to swim in the enclosed pool I'd constructed in the backyard. (I'd gotten the lumber for the house that surrounded the pool from Plessy's burnt-down café over on Broadway. And the pool itself was ordered from Montgomery Ward.)

I tried to teach them numbers and letters, but that didn't work too well. One day, they'd be able to identify the numbers from "1" to "4" and the next day, they'd forgotten them. I feel good about their years here, though, because I think they were happy and they did learn many social and practical skills they probably wouldn't have learned at the school. But I must admit, they were no more "literate" when they left than when they arrived.

All the time the girls were with me, I was still attending to Lester. He got along fine with them when he was himself (remember, he was a social worker by training), but sometimes he'd get confused about why these retarded people were here. He'd ask me if I was running a community center, and "Where do you get your funding for this?" But even during those confused periods, he treated the girls well.

About eight months after Pearl and Miriam came, Godmother Ethelle also came to live with me. I hadn't expected that. Frankly, I wouldn't have taken the retarded children if I'd known Godmother Ethelle was coming. But, suddenly here she was, also suffering from Alzheimer's, arriving under rather peculiar circumstances, which it took me and the family a while to figure out.

Some friends of hers I'd never met, a minister and his wife, called me in late 'seventy-four and announced they were bringing her. I didn't know what was going on but I told them fine, she was always welcome in my house. I thought it was for a visit. The minister brought her by Amtrak from Elmsford, New York to LaFayette, then took a bus here. He stayed a few days but told me nothing, really. It took a few weeks and many conversations with her relatives all over the country for me to put together what had happened and to realize she was here to stay.

Godmother Ethelle's only daughter, Theodora, had died about ten months before this. She was deeply bereaved because she was very attached to Teddi, who had lived with Godmother Ethelle at her house in St. Albans. Because of her daughter's death, she couldn't bear to stay in the house and she went to stay with some cousin in Elmsford, New York. In time, she made friends with neighbors, a minister and his family, who persuaded her to turn over her bank accounts and everything to them. They wrote a will and got her to sign it. And after they'd accomplished getting everything away from the old lady, that's when they called me and brought her down here. Now, I'd been encouraging her to come since Teddi's death; I knew how heartbroken she was. Thought a visit might uplift her spirits. So, when they called, I was delighted.

Only when she arrived did I realize how feeble she'd become. But I still thought that when she snapped out of grieving so over the loss of Teddi, she'd be back to herself. Because she'd always been this beautiful, stylish lady, and I thought that was going to come back. So I tried to make her as comfortable as possible. She'd known Lester all her life, and she accepted the two retarded girls easily. I installed her in my bedroom and was convinced that, with love and comfort and good nutrition, I could get her back to her old self.

But it wasn't to be. Mentally, she'd be sharp as a tack one minute and confused the next. And that pattern, as with Lester, became progressively worse. She wasn't strong physically, either. She'd had surgery for a "female problem" a few years earlier and she'd never regained her strength fully. Yet, she always wanted to be doing things. She just didn't have the strength anymore.

Between Lester and Godmother Ethelle and the two retarded girls, I was completely exhausted at the end of every day. I did have some household help with the cleaning and the cooking—Miss Cooper came from early morning until mid-afternoon—but the emotional work was all mine. (No, I wasn't doing better financially. I was still struggling with school bills, the mortgage, Jimmy's taxes, and everything else on just the alimony check. When I realized Godmother Ethelle was here to stay, I had to take a second mortgage on the house to help with her maintenance. I hired Miss Cooper again because I just couldn't handle taking care of the four of them *and* all of the housework.) It was a matter of coping with unpredictable temperaments and dispositions. Now, I don't want to give the impression I was physically spent; I was not as burdened as I would have been if I had to do all the housework and cooking. But it does wear you out coping with an assortment of characters and their idiosyncrasies and all the different things that go to make up each one of us. When you have to cope with your own foolishness and all these other people, it's a drain.

People with Alzheimer's are sometimes miserable to those taking care of them. So there were times when Lester and Godmother Ethelle would be pretty unpleasant to me. But there were hilarious times, too. For example, there was a conversation one morning between the two of them at a point when Lester was quite clear and Godmother Ethelle rather confused. The previous night, as usual, after getting them all bedded down, I had watched a little TV in my bedroom next to the one my godmother was occupying. I did this at the end of the day as a way of unwinding and relaxing. So, the next morning I overhear this conversation at the breakfast table: Godmother

Ethelle says to Uncle Lester, " 'Dette must be doing very nicely with those men in her room every night." And Lester was appalled: "What are you talking about? What are you saying?" "Well," Godmother Ethelle continued, "I suppose she receives some good money from those men who come here every night. They're not Southerners from around here. They're New Yorkers. I can tell by the accents. She must be doing *very* well." By then, Lester was up from the table and totally indignant: "How dare you suggest such a thing about the child!" He always called me a "child" although, by then, I was a hundred years old myself. I was in the next room laughing! This was such a refined, sedate lady that I never thought of her as even knowing anything about that kind of lifestyle. I walked in and said, "Godmother Ethelle, I listen to Johnny Carson late at night after you all have gone to bed." And she looked up at me as if to say, "And what kind of fool do you think I am?"

She clearly didn't buy my story about watching TV, but it really made no difference. By the next day, she'd forgotten the whole conversation. I asked her why she'd said that about the men in my room, and her quizzical response was, "My dear, when did I say such a thing?" Living with two people with Alzheimer's was, to say the least, never dull.

Near the end of his life, Lester was in and out of the hospital. At first, the Veterans Administration Hospital wouldn't take him. They said he didn't have the proper documentation. I'd wanted him put in the section for army officers; it was a kind of old folks home for old officers. But, at that time, only white officers were in there. They were mainly old men who'd been in World War I (and there weren't many black officers in that war). The area for enlisted men was desegregated, but not the section for officers. So I wrote to Nelson Rockefeller, who'd been on the Urban League's Board of Directors when Lester was Executive Director and who was then running for Vice President. He immediately wrote the hospital, and Lester was accepted. Once there, he was treated very well. Weekends, we'd bring him home. The black employees at the hospital—from the orderlies and kitchen folks to the very few professionals—gave him special attention all the time he was there. They were proud to have him there, proud to be taking care of a black officer, and such an important and charming black man, at that. I think he was comfortable for that period. Lester died in his sleep in 1976.

By then, Godmother Ethelle was in and out of the hospital, too. She started having seizures, something related to epileptic seizures, although she'd never had epilepsy. And my ex-husband, who was her doctor, kept urging me to put her in a nursing home. I kept saying she was not ready for that, but he insisted, "She *is* ready for it. You're the one who's not ready for it. You're going to injure her more than help her. You have no training in the catheter business. No nurse's training." And she did need all that.

So I finally put her in the Heritage Manor Nursing Home. It was a difficult, wrenching decision for me. I visited her daily. She'd be sitting there making the motions of making hats. She'd been a designer of hats all her life, and, apparently, was still seeing them. I'd say, "What'cha up to?" "Well," she'd answer, "I don't think this is going to be quite suitable to her face. What do you think?" And I'd answer, "Gee, you know better than I do." It was so sad having to watch both of these intelligent, charming people deteriorate. Somehow, their mental deterioration was more painful for me than the physical deterioration. Because, if you don't have your mind, do you have your *self*? They had both been so wonderful to me and there seemed to be so little I could do for them at the end of their lives. Never, never enough to repay them.

Godmother Ethelle died in the nursing home in late 'seventy-seven. And, by then, I realized I was facing burnout with all this caregiving stuff. The state had recently opened up a school in Rustin for retarded people of Pearl and Miriam's level. I made inquiries and both of them were accepted there. We were all unhappy at their leaving, but, because they could stay together and this new facility was so much more pleasant than Pinecrest, Pearl and Miriam seemed to adjust surprisingly well. And I knew, I really knew, that after the turmoil of the sixties, the immense responsibility of running Headstart, and all the caretaking I'd done in the seventies, I needed time to heal. Time to take care of Odette.

One of the things that helped me understand how important this was was the new literature on adult children of alcoholics I stumbled upon around that time. I learned that we tend to overdo the caretaking of others because of our having had to take care of our alcoholic parent so young. Now, understand that I have *no* regrets about what I did; I still believe we are our brother's keeper. But, our first responsibility, I came to realize, is to ourselves. And I hadn't been taking as good care of myself as I had of others. In recent years, though, I have.

Since traveling is something I've always loved, I've done a *lot* of that since the late seventies. My trips have really been the highlights of my life.

My first trip was to Haiti, the Virgin Islands, Puerto Rico, and the Dominican Republic. I'd been to Haiti before with Godmother Mattie, but I was only twelve then and the trip was really wasted on me. I couldn't see what in the world we had to climb up the Citadel for; it was just a crummy, old castle. But, this time, I went with a real appreciation of Christophe and L'Ouverture and the remarkable feat of these enslaved Haitians being able to defeat Napoleon's army and gain their independence. This was the only independent black-run country in the entire Western hemisphere in the nineteenth century. As a black person, I have to feel pride in what the Haitians accomplished. But I feel pain too: the poverty in Haiti is just awful to see. And the contrasting wealth was awful to see, too. There are people there who go to Paris to shop as easily as I go to the supermarket. They have opulent homes with lots of servants. And the poor are anxious to become servants because that, at least, insures food. But there are hovels everywhere. We went by horse to the Citadel and saw all these shacks that were maybe four by six feet in space—just large enough for people to go in when it rained and be sheltered. But all of the household operations took place out of doors. They cooked out of doors; they ate food out of doors; they washed clothes out of doors. They were not well-fed people. And not clean at all. The land was impoverished, making it impossible for them to grow enough to eat.

Haiti has been hurt from the outside, from the policies of the United States and others, and it's been hurt from the inside. By the greediness of the ruling class. My heart goes out to the Haitian people. Perhaps I feel especially close to them because the maternal grandfather I loved so much, Peter DesVerney, was of Haitian descent. I don't know. But going to Haiti was a wonderful and terrible experience.

Two years later, I went to Europe with a group of people from Baton Rouge, New York, Ohio, and Pennsylvania. We went to Spain and Portugal. In Spain, I was pleasantly surprised by the extensive influence of the Moors that's so evident. These mixed-race North Africans occupied Spain for four hundred years, and their presence in the culture and the genes of the people is far greater than most Europeans want to admit. In Lisbon, Portugal, we went to castles and palaces and what had been the Jewish ghetto. Some of the houses in the ghetto were fascinating because the outside would be so underwhelming while the interiors were very impressive. These were the homes of merchants who had achieved some wealth. But they had to hide it because of the resentment of Spanish gentiles. This ghetto was from the time of the Inquisition, when the Spanish king was trying to force everyone to accept the

Catholic faith.

I went to Morocco another year. And Mexico the next. I had a chance to compare the Mayan pyramids to the Egyptian pyramids I'd seen on one of my excursions during the war. My traveling companions were shocked at seeing the altar where human sacrifices were done. I remember their saying that this was awful, these people were pagans. And I said, "Aren't we all? What in the world is the communion ritual but symbolic consumption of human flesh and blood?" Many of them felt very superior to this ancient religion, but all I can see is one religion repeated with different rituals all over the world.

Japan, the following year, was a big disappointment because all I saw was Tokyo. They had Americanized themselves beyond being Japanese. One evening, we went to a Japanese nightclub, and the show was "A Night on Broadway," all the same songs that you'd hear in the States. The only thing that was the least bit different was that they served us hot saki. I thought, all this Americanization is so awful! But, then, we went to a Shinto temple, and that was quite nice and very Japanese. The gardens were beautiful and I was relieved to find the Japanese had maintained bits of their own culture in at least some corners of their city.

The following year, 1984, was the most wonderful of all the trips I've made: I went to mainland China. I'd always wanted to go to China. Remember, I'd asked to go when I was in the Red Cross? It intrigued me because it was so far away, and I'd always had the memory of that distant cousin who'd married a Chinese man and was obliged by custom to send her first-born son back to China. It seemed like it was really another planet.

I don't know what impressed me more—the China of antiquity or the China of today. There was the wonderful feeling of a people who have survived so much and have changed so much, have moved fully into the twentieth century, while retaining their own culture. Not like what I'd seen in Japan at all. But, then, I only saw Tokyo.

The people of China were very hard-working, very clean. They maintained their family orientation and never, never put old people "out to pasture." Older people are kept in the home and remain an integral part of the family, taking care of the children. One day, I wandered out of my hotel alone and met a young woman who wanted to practice her English. She invited me to her home to meet her grandmother. This family was still occupying one of those back-alley places that are really little more than huts. China has made every effort to provide everyone with good housing, but, because of limited money and time, some of it is ugly because it was thrown together quickly. This family was waiting for completion of a high-rise, where they would live in a better apartment. But their one-room hut was clean and had flooring and the bare essentials of furniture. As humble as it was, it was far more livable than many shacks I've seen here in Rapides Parish. Everyone in the alley spoke freely about their lives. They didn't seem to be monitored at all. And everything they had to say about their country and their condition was positive and optimistic. They knew how far China had come since the days it was run by Europeans and Americans. The Chinese people had been on the bottom in their own country, and poverty and literal starvation was rampant. The people in the alley lived humbly, but because they knew how terrible things had been before the 1949 Revolution, they believed in their country today.

This upbeat attitude was even more obvious when we visited a kindergarten. These were the happiest little kids I think I've ever seen! And I don't believe you can force happiness on children. You can't say, "Act happy and loving." These children were singing and speaking English well—English is taught at every kindergarten in the country because it's the commercial language—and their joy at being alive was entirely real.

Since the China trip, I've been back to Japan, to Paris, and to the Caribbean again. That's what I think of first when I think of the 'eighties. I think of the wonderful trips; they were my indulgence. They nourished me. It's like I was preparing myself, without knowing it, for what was to come: *the* most devastating event of my entire life.

It happened in February of 1989. I was alone in my house in Alexandria. It was night and I was asleep. What awakened me was the cold metal of a knife against my throat and, simultaneously, a man's voice announcing in the worst street language that I was going to be raped and killed.

And it began. I was kicked and cursed and dragged by the hair from room to room. Every orifice in my body was penetrated by him. It went on for almost three hours. He was absolutely crazy—drunk and on drugs. And that's what kept him from carrying out his plan to kill me. He finally just passed out, fell into a stupor. And I crawled into a closet in the next room with one of those portable phones clutched in my hand. I got 911 and whispered that I needed help, terrified that my voice might revive him and he'd kill me. But I did give the operator my address. I remember her telling me to open the front door for the police, and I said, no, I wasn't leaving the closet. How did I know he wouldn't wake up? I couldn't take that chance. And she said OK, if he got in, the police could get in. And they did. So fast. In maybe three or four minutes. Five of them came into the house. That's when I came out of the closet, when I heard them in the house. That monster was in such a stupor, he didn't wake up even when they were standing right over him. But they were still cautious in putting the handcuffs on him before they roused him.

The police, two of them black and the others white, could not have been gentler or kinder if I'd been their own mother or grandmother. I remember a slim blond fellow putting cold compresses on my swollen face and finding a coat to cover my torn garment. They called an ambulance, which came quickly too. I remember the attendants being very gentle as they put me on the gurney and then lifted me into the ambulance. But I was hysterical. Sobbing, incoherent. They could see all the bruises, though, so they were very gentle.

At Cabrini Hospital, there was the examination. Oh, it's so awful. After being raped, you have to undergo this humiliating inspection of every part of your body. When you don't even want to be touched by anyone. And the questions! The pressure to give details, to *relive* the rape. Believe me, the horror of the event doesn't stop at the end of the rape. When they were finished with the questioning, they gave me a sedative to help me sleep. But that was ridiculous. It had no effect at all. No drug could have calmed me enough to sleep after what I'd been through.

I stayed in the hospital overnight. Then my son Jimmy, a physician, took me to his home in Baton Rouge to recuperate. No bones had been broken; there was no serious damage to my body. But my soul! It had been so beaten, it didn't seem to exist anymore. And this body I was in, it might not be damaged, but it had been so violated. Shame. That's what the overwhelming feeling was: shame. It was dirty. Dirty beyond filth. And I kept trying to wash away the dirtiness. I'd take a bath every time I got a chance and I'd scrub my skin to the point of rawness. I'd only let my children see me take one bath a day (I knew how to act normal), but the minute they'd go out, I'd sneak back into the bathroom and take another bath and another bath and brush my teeth over and over again.

My children all came to be with me. Gretchen took time off from her job as a clinical psychologist in Iwakini, Japan. Maggi took a leave from her administrative position at UCLA. And Terry, who's always been such a tender person, I remember him just sitting beside my bed and trying to hold my hand. But I couldn't. I cringed at anyone's touch, especially the touch of those I loved most dearly. I felt so unworthy. So dirty.

Those feelings, the repeated bathing, brushing my teeth ten and twelve times a day, all of that lasted a long time. And the nightmares have never stopped. They're much less frequent now, but I can never tell when I'm going to relive the rape again, again in my dreams.

What's helped the most is the group therapy I got into. Right here in Alexandria. The groups were for rape survivors, and they were so valuable to me. Most of the time, I was the only elderly woman in the group. The other women were quite young, many of them teenagers. All of them dazed and bitter. With all that shame I knew so well. And guilt. When they would recount what happened to them, their eyes and their voices would lower. And so did mine.

From all the talk during therapy—and we did a heap of talking 'cause that's the only remedy—from all of that, I came to realize that we were all saying the way we survived was to leave the body being violated. You mentally exit and become a spectator to the assault, as though it was happening to someone else. And your mind focuses on how to outwit your murderous assailant. The therapist urged the young women to let their sweet spirits reenter their battered bodies. Sometimes they protested, "But you don't understand," because they knew the therapist had never been raped. But she was right. Only when you can accept this reunion of your mind and your body, and when you can believe again that your soul does exist, can you begin to heal.

My heart went out to those tormented young women. It was so unfair for them to be robbed of their "selves" so early in life. My own healing really got underway when I began to worry more about their losses than about my own. When I began to think about how I, an old woman, might be able to help them find their way back into their lovely young bodies. To stop them from feeling too unworthy to make that return. (As in the past, I was finding myself getting through my own pain by becoming concerned with others.)

From my therapy groups, I struck up friendships with some of the girls. We'd sometimes have these little twosome lunches—and just gab. We could convince ourselves that we had won. We were alive. We did nothing to cause what happened to us. And, slowly, we knew, we really *knew*, we had nothing to be ashamed of. Instead of being numb, we could be angry. That was healthier. And I saw lipstick go back onto their young lips. And I saw a glow of confidence return to some eyes. I could gloat to them that I'd personally arranged the capture of the monster who'd hurt me. I told them all about the closet and the whispered phone call. And I told them about his getting a thirty-year sentence. Some of the girls mustered the courage to testify in court about their cases. And when they saw justice done, that strengthened them tremendously. We were not losers, we told one another. (And, by then, I believed it!) We were victors.

Now, I know talking about the experience of being raped is still taboo. It makes people uncomfortable when I bring it up. But why shouldn't I talk about it? I did nothing wrong, and yet this horrendous thing happened to me. And if it could happen to me, at this time in my life, it could happen to anyone, couldn't it? Some good things did come out of it. I got the opportunity to help some young women who seemed to be willing to listen to this old lady. And it made me cherish living even more. I have to talk about it. It was the most devastating event of my life, and looms larger for me than the War, civil rights, politics, births, murder trials, the divorce—everything!

And I can still say I've had a good life. After all of that, even the divorce and the rape, I really feel it's been a good life. In my later years, I've learned how important it is to take care of yourself. But that doesn't mean I was all that altruistic before. No. For the most part, as I said, I was doing what gave me pleasure. I'm not Miss Goody-Two-Shoes, or whatever that expression is. But I did sometimes sacrifice myself too much; I was very much the sacrificial wife. I grew up thinking you're always supposed to be nice to people, even at your own inconvenience. But being sacrificing and subservient is *not* what we're supposed to do. Yes, we are our brother's keeper. But looking out for others should give you pleasure, and if it doesn't, don't do it. Taking care of Uncle Lester and Godmother Ethelle and the retarded girls gave me pleasure. Tutoring kids today does too. If I encounter a child who doesn't like math and all of a sudden I can help him fall in love with some numbers, to me, that's fun. What might look like altruism to others is enjoyment to me. And if I'm not going to enjoy these kids coming in here for tutoring, keeping my candy jar full of candy for them, then they shouldn't come in here.

That doesn't mean you'll always be able to feel joy. No, pain is a part of living. If you don't have enough pain, you don't have any way of measuring your joy, I think. So, I've had enough pain. I can't actually think of anything else that the gods can dish out. What else can there be?

I guess some people get worn down by pain; they don't exercise their right to get on top of it and put it aside. If you start letting all that stuff pile up, then you can destroy yourself. You'd better let go. And it's necessary to find that out fairly early because I think you can get into the habit of holding on. That's not to say you can throw pain off immediately. But I think if you can find some work to do or somebody else with something that you can worry about with them, it can diminish what you're worrying about for yourself. This is how I healed from the rape. This is how I've healed from all the painful things I've gone through. The pain will go away slowly because your interest gets to be on something that is very much in the present, and you find some pleasure in what is the present. And you don't have enough room for both feelings.

The point is that human beings have the power to replace one kind of feeling with another, to replace one mindset with another. They have that choice. And when we don't do it, we do our own self a disservice because nobody's suffering but you. And there're more choices. You can think, "Oh, my God, how can I live with this?" or you can say, "God did it; he's got to help me live with this and get rid of it." And then go do something that is absorbing and you find pleasure in that. So you have less and less room for the pain.

My only sadness today is not about any of the events of my life. I don't even feel a profound sadness about the rape. No, I've let it go. What does bother me deeply, though, is the state of our communities and the state of the world. Those of us who lived through the radicalism of the thirties, the optimism after World War II, and then the Civil Rights Movement, and wanted to see changes made, I think we saw the changes happen and then the roadblocks immediately follow. It seems to me that, in many ways, America is traveling back, not just to 1954 but to 1854. In race relations, I mean, in the increasing polarization of the races. This is a great sadness.

By polarization, though, I don't mean cultural distinctiveness. No, I think that trend is good. For most of our history, there's been pressure for everybody to become a pseudo-Anglo-American. Today, people who are not "Anglo" have demanded that that stop, that they be allowed to hold onto and showcase their own cultures. I think that's as it should be. Each nationality should be allowed to be a visible, meaning respected, member of this country.

It's the hostility and disrespect between groups that troubles me. Especially that of whites toward others, although there's certainly distrust between some other groups, too. But whites still have the most power to keep others down. And whites are the most afraid, I think, afraid of losing a country they think is theirs. I've been fighting that, it seems, all my life. In the mid-sixties, we seemed to be making some progress. But as demands for equity increased and as immigration of darker people increased, the more fear, the more backlash. My dream would be that all these different groups be recognized and re-spected and have the same opportunities. That we all enjoy this wonderful cul-tural smorgasbord that is America. But I don't see that happening. No, I see something very different.

The backlash since the sixties and the upside-down priorities of a govern-ment that doesn't put people first, all of that has us in pretty bad shape. And the drugs. I just feel so awful about the drugs and the extent of the crime.

Yes, there is in me a great sadness about the state of the world. I wish I was smart enough to make some contribution to changing it. In all those years that I was thinking I was making a little contribution, I found a lot of happiness in that. Then, when you realize that the changes you worked so hard for haven't gone to the extent that you'd expected them to, you're deeply dismayed by that.

But I'm not sorry I did any of it. It did give me pleasure. I may have been too sacrificing as a wife, but what I did for my children, for our community, the taking care of people here, that was right, that was me being the best me and enjoying myself. No, it wasn't altruism at all. It should never be. Self-sac-rifice is not part of doing what you should do. If you are a part of the Creation, you ought not to be doing things to destroy yourself. If you have respect for yourself—other people would phrase it, if you are a child of God—then you are real important. And what else can you be but a part of something that cre-ated all this? Don't tear it down.

In so many ways, I've been very fortunate. I have wonderful children and grandchildren. Besides my own four children, there are a number of young people who seem to have adopted me as an extra mama. They call me "MaDette," a combination of the Louisiana term "MaDear"—for "Mother Dear"—and my name. I love having friendships as close as family with peo-ple of all ages. That's part of what keeps me so involved in life. That and my oil painting. I even get paid for doing portraits of folks around here. And there's my volunteer community work. Yes, I'm still meddling; I still enjoy that. But, I must say, my greatest pleasure does come from watching all these "children" of mine grow and achieve—from my backyard "mess," from Headstart, the civil rights workers, all of them. What pleasure I get from being a part of their lives!

Of all the people that I lived with in that house in Fordham, there are only two left besides myself: Wilbur, the middle one of my three boy cousins, and my brother's widow, Dessie Walker Harper. My dear brother, Jack, just died. That's a big hole in my heart—that all of those people aren't here anymore. But the "family" I've created since coming to Louisiana is huge and wonderful. They are my foundation. Absolutely, the most important part of my life.

I've been so fortunate. I've seen many of the people of this century who were making contributions and talked to them face to face, some right here in this house. Yes, it's been a good life. Anybody else might think, "now, that was a bit of a mess," but to me, it wasn't. The good times were wonderful and I haven't let myself be destroyed by the difficult times. You have that choice. All of us have things come along that can really throw you. And you can fold up and decide not to get up in the morning and let the rest of your life go by. Or you can say, well, that's that and I'm me and I'm not going to let that conquer me. You have to keep on. You can't let yourself be stopped. If you're alive, *live*.

Notes

PREFACE

1. Kristina Minister, "A Feminist Frame for the Oral History Interview," in *Women's Words: The Feminist Practice of Oral History*, edited by Sherna Berger Gluck and Daphne Patai (New York: Routledge, 1991).

2. C. Wright Mills, *The Sociological Imagination* (New York: Oxford University Press, 1959).

3. A number of writers discuss this pattern in the narratives of black women. See, for example, Regina Blackburn, "In Search of the Black Female Self: African–American Women's Autobiographies and Ethnicity," in *Women's Autobiography*, edited by Estelle C. Jelinek (Bloomington: Indiana University Press, 1980), pp. 133–148; and Bernice Johnson Reagon, "My Black Mothers and Sisters or On Beginning a Cultural Autobiography," *Feminist Studies* 8 (Spring 1982): 81–95. Susan Stanford Friedman explores the positive function for individuals in subordinate groups of strong identification with their communities. See Friedman, "Women's Autobiographical Selves: Theory and Practice," in *The Private Self*, edited by Shari Benstock (Chapel Hill: University of North Carolina Press, 1988).

CHAPTER I

1. The full names of Odette Hines' godmothers were Martha Frazier Wiggins, Hattie Frazier Walker, and Ethelle Rhone Jackson.

CHAPTER II

1. Edwin Durock Turpin was related to Thomas Jefferson in the following way: his father, William Turpin, was the son of Thomas Turpin and Mary Jefferson Turpin. Mary was the sister of Peter Jefferson, the husband of Jane Randolph Jefferson and father of Thomas Jefferson. Thus, because they had parents who were siblings, Edwin Durock's father was Thomas Jefferson's first cousin. See Augustus Turpin Granger, "Edwin Turpin of Goochland County, Virginia," *Goochland County Historical Society Magazine* 25 (1993): 21–36. Also, Fawn Brodie makes reference to Thomas Turpin as one of the executors of Peter Jefferson's estate in *Thomas Jefferson: An Intimate History* (New York: W. W. Norton, 1974), p. 38.

2. Will DesVerney did indeed play a role in Randolph's choice. Two biographers of A. Philip Randolph state that "W. H. DesVerney," at a meeting held at his home on 139th Street in Harlem, was one of the three or four (the two accounts vary) porters who first invited Randolph to consider organizing sleeping car porters. See Daniel S. Davis, *Mr. Black Labor: The Story of A. Philip Randolph, Father of the Civil Rights Movement* (New York: E. P. Dutton, 1972), pp. 45–47; and Jervis Anderson, *A. Philip Randolph: A Biographical Portrait* (Berkeley: University of California Press, 1986), pp. 155 and 168.

3. In 1904, Mary McLeod Bethune (1875–1955) founded the school that was to become Bethune-Cookman College. She also founded (1935) and was first president of the National Council of Negro Women. Influential in Franklin Roosevelt's administration after she was appointed director of the Negro Division of the National Youth Administration (NYA) in 1934, Bethune was able to help Odette Harper Hines get the job at the NYA (discussed in Chapter III). See *Black Women in America: An Historical Encyclopedia* s.v. "Bethune, Mary McLeod" by Elaine M. Smith (Brooklyn, NY: Carlson, 1993), pp. 113–127.

4. Maggie Lena Walker (1867–1934) became the first woman bank president in the United States in 1903. The home on Leigh Street described by Odette Hines is now a national historic site under the National Park Services. See *Black Women in America: An Historical Encyclopedia*, s.v. "Walker, Maggie Lena" by Gertrude W. Marlowe (Brooklyn, NY: Carlson, 1993), pp. 1214–1219.

CHAPTER III

1. For more information on Angelo Patri, see Patri, *A Schoolmaster of the Great City* (New York: Macmillan, 1917) and *The Questioning Child and Other Essays* (New York: D. Appleton, 1926).

2. For a discussion of the acting career and political activities of John Garfield, see Robert Sklar, *City Boys: Cagney, Bogart, Garfield* (Princeton, NJ: Princeton University Press, 1992).

3. Jamaican-born black nationalist Marcus Garvey (1887–1940) was founder and leader of the Universal Negro Improvement Association, the largest organization of African–Americans in the 1920s and arguably the largest that has ever existed in the United States. For a compilation of his speeches and writings, see Amy Jacques Garvey, ed., *Philosophy and Opinions of Marcus Garvey*, (New York: Arno Press, 1968–69); and Robert A. Hill, ed., *The Marcus Garvey and Universal Negro Improvement Association Papers*, (Berkeley: University of California Press, 1983). There are numerous studies of Garvey and his movement, including John Henrik Clarke, *Marcus Garvey and the Vision of Africa* (New York: Random House, 1974); and Tony Martin, *Race First* (Dover: Majority Press, 1986; first published Westport, MA: Greenwood Press, 1976).

CHAPTER IV

1. Walter White (1893–1955) was the Executive Secretary of the NAACP from 1931 to 1955. In addition, he was an advisor to both Franklin Roosevelt and Harry Truman, played a key role in the formation of the Committee on Fair Employment Practices during World War II, and was a consultant to the U. S. delegation to the United Nations in 1945 and 1948. See his autobiography, *A Man Called White* (New York: Viking Press, 1948); and *Dictionary of American Negro Biography*, s.v. "White, Walter (Francis)" by August Meier and Elliott Rudwick (New York: W. W. Norton, 1982), pp. 646–650.

2. Claude McKay (1889–1948) was a Jamaican-born poet and novelist prominent during the Harlem Renaissance. His best known novel, *Home to Harlem*, was published in 1928. More highly regarded today as a poet, McKay's volumes of poetry are *Spring in New Hampshire* (1920), *Harlem Shadows* (1922), and *Selected Poems* (1953). See *Black Literature Criticism*, edited by James P. Draper, s.v. "Claude McKay" (Detroit: Gale Research, 1992) Vol. III, pp. 1375–1401; and *Dictionary of American Negro Biography*, s.v. "McKay, Claude" by Arthur P. Davis (New York: W. W. Norton, 1982), pp. 418–420.

3. Joel (J. A.) Rogers (1883–1965) was a Jamaican-born, self-educated journalist and historian. He became the first African–American war correspondent when he covered the Italian–Ethiopian War in 1935 for the Pittsburgh *Courier*. His publications include *100 Facts About the Negro* (1934), *Sex and Race* (1940), and *World's Greatest Men of Color* (two volumes, 1946 and 1947). See *Dictionary of American Negro Biography*, s.v. "Rogers, Joel (J. A.)" by Rayford W. Logan (New York: W. W. Norton, 1982), pp. 531–532.

4. Ralph Ellison (1914–1994) is best known for *Invisible Man* (1952), a work that has been called the most important American novel of the twentieth century. For a dis-

cussion of his writings and list of biographical and critical sources, see *Black Literature Criticism*, edited by James P. Draper, s.v. "Ralph Ellison" (Detroit: Gale Research, 1991), Vol. I, pp. 673–706; and *Black Writers*, s.v. "Ellison, Ralph (Waldo)" by Judy R. Smith (Detroit: Gale Research, 1989), pp. 176–183.

5. Carlton Moss (1910–) is one of the first African–American documentary film makers. After his success as a writer for radio, he became prominent in Hollywood as the writer of and actor in *The Negro Soldier*, a film used by the army for training troops in 1944 and 1945. See Thomas Cripps, *Slow Fade to Black: The Negro in American Film, 1900–1942* (New York: Oxford University Press, 1993), pp. 379–380. Since then, Moss has been a college professor and a producer of numerous documentaries on various aspects of African-American life and history. In 1993, he retired from his faculty position in the University of California Irvine's Program in Comparative Culture.

6. The results of Ella Baker's investigation were published in "The Bronx Slave Market," by Ella Baker and Marvel Cooke in *The Crisis* 42, no. 11 (Nov. 1935): 330–31 and 340. For more information about Ella Baker, see Chapter V, note no. 2.

7. Klaus Mann was a prolific writer in his own right. See Peter T. Hoffer, *Klaus Mann* (Boston: Twayne Publishers, 1978).

8. Richard Wright (1908–1960) is best known for *Native Son* (1940), the first novel by a black author to become a Book-of-the-Month Club selection. This novel, *The Outsider* (1953), and the short story "The Man Who Lived Underground" (in *Eight Men*, 1961) are considered his best fiction. For a discussion of his work and a compilation of critical sources on Wright, see *Black Literature Criticism*, edited by James P. Draper, s.v. "Richard Wright" (Detroit: Gale Research, 1992) Vol. III, pp. 1994–2021; and *Dictionary of American Negro Biography*, s.v. "Wright, Richard" by Michael Fabre, translated by Melvin Dixon (New York: W. W. Norton, 1982), pp. 671–673.

CHAPTER V

1. Odette Harper Hines' article on Pigfoot Mary is discussed (with a citation to "Odette Harper") in David Levering Lewis, *When Harlem was in Vogue* (New York: Alfred A. Knopf, 1981), pp. 109–110 and 328.

2. Roy Wilkins (1901–1980) was a journalist hired by the NAACP in 1931 as Assistant Executive Secretary to Walter White. After White's death in 1955, Wilkins served as Executive Secretary of the organization until he retired in 1977. See Roy Wilkins, *Standing Fast: The Autobiography of Roy Wilkins* (New York: Viking Press, 1982).

George Schuyler (1895–1977) was a journalist best known for the satirical novel *Black No More: Being an Account of the Strange and Wonderful Workings of Science in the Land of the Free* (1931) and for his conservative political views. See *Black and Conservative: The Autobiography of George S. Schuyler* (New Rochelle, New York: Arlington House, 1966); and *Black Writers*, s.v. "Schuyler, George" (Detroit: Gale Research, 1989), pp. 506–507.

Thurgood Marshall (1908–1993) joined the legal staff of the NAACP in 1936, serving as chief legal counsel from 1938 until his appointment to the federal bench in 1961. Nominated for the Supreme Court by Lyndon Johnson, Marshall was confirmed in 1967, the first African–American to become a justice of the Supreme Court. See Carl Rowan, *Dream Makers, Dream Breakers: The World of Justice Thurgood Marshall* (Boston: Little, Brown, 1993).

3. Ella Baker (1903–1986) was an activist from the 1930s until her death. Before going to the NAACP in 1940, Ms. Baker had been involved with consumer education and cooperatives, both in the Young Negroes Cooperative League and the WPA. At the NAACP, Ms. Baker was a field secretary and, later, director of branches. In 1957, she became the Executive Director of the newly formed Southern Christian Leadership Conference (SCLC) in Atlanta. In 1960, having called the first conference of students who had been sitting-in all over the South, she became advisor to the Student Nonviolent Coordinating Committee (SNCC), which developed out of that conference. For more information on her extraordinary life and contributions, see Ellen Cantarow, *Moving the Mountain: Women Working for Social Change* (Old Westbury, NY: The Feminist Press, 1980), pp. 52–93. See also *Black Women in America: An Historical Encyclopedia*, s.v. "Baker, Ella" by Barbara Ransby, pp. 70–74.

4. Lester Granger had become executive director of the National Urban League in 1941 and would remain in that position until 1961, when he was succeeded by Whitney Young. In addition to this and his other accomplishments discussed by Ms. Hines in Chapter XII, Lester Granger also "served as chairman of the Federal Advisory Council on Employment Security, as special advisor to Secretary of the Navy James Forrestal during World War II, and as the architect of the policy established by the U. S. Navy for ending racial segregation." *Encyclopedia of Black America*, s.v. "Granger Lester" by Arthur P. Davis (New York: McGraw-Hill, 1981), pp. 418–420. For a discussion of his work at the Urban League, see Jesse Thomas Moore, Jr., *A Search for Equality: The National Urban League, 1910–1961* (University Park, PA: Pennsylvania State University Press, 1981).

5. In his autobiography, White discusses in detail the events Ms. Hines refers to: the attack on his family during the 1906 Atlanta "race riots" (Chapter I), his father's death (Chapter XVII), and his own near-escape in the South (Chapter VI, wryly titled "I Decline to be Lynched"). See White, *A Man Called White, op. cit.*

6. Newspaper accounts of this event state that the two boys were arrested for "attempting to rape" the girl, taken to the Clarke County Jail, and, late that night, taken out of the jail by a crowd of fifty and hanged. No mention is made of the mutilations in these accounts. See, for example, the New York *Daily News*, Oct. 13, 1942, p. 3. How-

ever, a Nov. 7, 1942 report I located in the NAACP Archives, written by Madison S. Jones, Jr. (Youth Director for the NAACP), who travelled to Quitman and interviewed three "associates" and one cousin of the murdered boys, supports Odette Harper Hines' version of the story. The report states that the boys were killed immediately at the scene; it does not mention an arrest. Jones' description of the mutilations is also quite similar to Ms. Hines'. (See NAACP Archives, Library of Congress, Group II, Series A, Container 411.) When I mentioned the discrepancy in the accounts to Ms. Hines, she stated that white newspapers in that period often printed stories in a way that made injustices to blacks seem less outrageous.

CHAPTER VII

1. According to the 1950 census, the city of Alexandria had a population of 34,913, of which 41.5% were black. The parish of Rapides, of which Alexandria is the seat, had a population of 90,648, of which 33.2% were black.

The occupational profile reflects the parish's reliance on agriculture and lumber, black men's concentration in the low-paid jobs in those industries, and black women's concentration in service work, especially domestic service. The main occupations for black men were "laborers, except farm and mine" (1,915), "operatives" (1,113), "service, except private household work" (606), and "farm laborers and farm foremen" (559). Black women were in "private household work" (1,615), in "service, except private household work" (741), "operatives" (257), and "farm laborers and farm foremen" (183). Clearly, the overt racial discrimination of the period, supported by poor education (the median school years completed for blacks was 4.5 years in 1950), kept most African–Americans in Rapides Parish locked into low-wage occupations. See U. S. Department of Commerce, Bureau of the Census, Census of the Population, 1950: Number of Inhabitants, Vol. I (Washington, D.C.: U. S. Government Printing Office, 1952), p. 18–11; Census of the Population, 1950: Characteristics of the Population, Vol. II, Part 18 Louisiana (Washington, D.C.: U.S. Government Printing Office, 1952), pp. 18–23, 18–25 and 18–92.

2. This slight difference in various parishes' attitudes toward black registration might be partially explained by the varying sizes of the black population. The 1940 census indicates that 36.7% of the population of Rapides Parish was "Negro," whereas there were seven Louisiana parishes where blacks accounted for over 50% of the population. Not coincidentally, the parish Ms. Hines mentions as allowing no black voters, West Feliciana, was the parish with the highest proportion of blacks in the state: 76.4%. U.S. Department of Commerce, Bureau of the Census, Sixteenth Census of the United States, 1940: Characteristics of the Population, Vol. II, Part 3, Kansas–Michigan (Washington, D.C.: U.S. Government Printing Office, 1943), p. 364.

3. For more information on Jesse Owens' career, see his autobiography, *The Jesse Owens Story* (New York: Putman, 1970); and William Baker, *Jesse Owens: An American Life* (New York: The Free Press, 1986).

CHAPTER X

1. For James Farmer's account of this incident, see Farmer, *Lay Bare the Heart: An Autobiography of the Civil Rights Movement* (New York: New American Library, 1985), pp. 246–254.

2. In 1957, the integration of nine black students into Central High School in Little Rock had elicited white mob violence, the resistance of Governor Orval Faubus (who used the Arkansas National Guard to block the students from entering the school), and the bombing of the home of Daisy Bates, president of the NAACP. President Eisenhower had to federalize the Arkansas National Guard and send in 1,000 paratroopers from the 101st Airborne Division to quell the violence. In 1960, efforts to integrate New Orleans public schools also elicited white mob violence and the closing of two schools. In that situation, President Eisenhower and the Justice Department remained inactive.

3. Nicholas Katzenbach was the U.S. Attorney General and John Doar was the Assistant Attorney General, Civil Rights Division of the Justice Department.

CHAPTER XI

1. Executive Order 8802, issued on June 25, 1941, focused on both the desegregation of war industries and the establishment of the Committee on Fair Employment Practices. The Order stated, in part:

1. All departments and agencies of the Government of the United States concerned with vocational and training programs for defense production shall take special measures appropriate to assure that such programs are administered without discrimination because of race, creed, color, or national origin;

2. All contracting agencies of the Government of the United States shall include in all defense contracts hereafter negotiated by them a provision obligating the contractor not to discriminate against any worker because of race, creed, color, or national origin;

3. There is established in the Office of Production Management a Committee on Fair Employment Practice, which shall consist of a chairman and four other members to be appointed by the President. . . . The Committee shall receive and investigate complaints of discrimination in violation of the provisions of this order and shall take appropriate steps to redress grievances which it finds

to be valid. The Committee shall also recommend to the several departments and agencies of the Government of the United States and to the President all measures which may be deemed by it necessary or proper to effectuate the provisions of this order.

For the complete Executive Order and A. Philip Randolph's statement at the time of its issuance, see Randolph, "The March on Washington Movement, 1941" in Thomas R. Frazier, ed., *Afro-American History: Primary Sources* (New York: Harcourt, Brace & World, 1970), pp. 334–341.

Index